Taro Ashihara

Taro Ashihara

Program and Style

Preface by
Masao Noguchi
Introduction by
Taro Ashihara

l'ARCAEDIZIONI

Editorial Director USA
Pierantonio Giacoppo

Chief Editor of Collection
Maurizio Vitta

Publishing Coordinator
Franca Rottola

Graphic design
Studio CREA, Milano

Photographs
Akira Inoue, Harunori Noda (Gankosha),
Hattori Studio, Isao Inbe, Katsuaki Furudate,
Kouji Horiuchi, Nikkei Architecture, Seihan Sato,
SS Tokyo, Shigeru Kaneko, Shinkenchiku Co. Ltd.

Editing
Martyn J. Anderson

Colour separation
Litofilms Italia, Bergamo

Printing
Poligrafiche Bolis, Bergamo

First published October 1997

Copyright 1997
by l'Arca Edizioni
All rights reserved
Printed in Italy

ISBN 88-7838-037-7

Contents

6   Architect as a Cultural Profession. The Works of Taro Ashihara
by Masao Noguchi

8   Program and Style
by Taro Ashihara

11   Works

12   M-House

16   G-House

22   S-House

30   Ichikudo Building

34   Kasama Nichido Museum of Art

46   Australian Embassy, Tokyo

54   Villa-N

60   Sirocco

66   Yamanashi Prefectural Nursing Junior College

76   Tokyo Metropolitan Office, Niijima Branch

82   F-House

90   Shiroishi N°2 Primary School

102   Hinomaru Driving School

114   Johnson Products Kakegawa New Factory

124   Mizushima Salon

139   List of Works

Architect as a Cultural Profession
The Works of Taro Ashihara
by Masao Noguchi

We have had four generations of architects since World War II. The first was the Kenzo Tange generation that emerged in the 1960's. The second generation followed in the 60's and 70's, represented by three architects, Kisho Kurokawa, Fumihiko Maki and Arata Isozaki. The third generation of architects, from the 70's to the 80's, is represented by Tadao Ando and Toyo Ito. There is now a fourth generation that emerged in the mid 80's. The character of this generation is based on two aspects that were never experienced by the former three generations. One is the fact that they spent their youth in becoming architects, amid the rapid growth of Japanese economic power. Though very young, they have the advantage of contact with wealthy clients, and can realize their own works, which is quite different from the unbuilt situation in most European cities. Tokyo is forever changing, especially in the fourth generation. Another aspect which characterises this generation is the fact that there are no more masters to follow.

The last three generations are valid references for the fourth generation, but they are not in any way disciples of these three generations. They realise their own buildings by themselves, free from the disciplines and style of the last three generations.

The works of Taro Ashihara, who belongs to the fourth generation, reflect the context of the 1990's in Japan. During the 1980's, post-modern architecture became virtually indistinguishable from commercial architecture. In contrast, a number of architects still focus on the human subject in their works, transforming the overt language of Japanese urbanism - through the flow of time, light and air - into an invisible language system, generating spaces that relate to human emotions and aspirations. Ashihara's early works, for example, Villa-N, S-House, F-House and M-House, represent this tendency. However, if the human subject is to be found in these four representative works, the very methods for creating architecture in the midst of cities and communities are to be found in larger office buildings and public constructions. Contemporary Japanese cities, Tokyo in particular, may appear to be a jumble of widely diverse elements, but there exists a hidden order. Ashihara insists that this is an urban phenomena that has appeared as result of mediation, in an attempt to combine diverse terms at a high level. Looking at the buildings in the towns created by Ashihara, we realise that he is not initially trying to create forms. This is because he believes form to be the result of mediation in the community. It is no easy matter to try to create the Tokyo landscape against the backdrop of society's severe conditions of investment, business and economic efficiency.

In the same way, the form of his architectural works that are surrounded by nature, such as the Kasama Nichido Museum of Art and Villa-N, originate from mediation between the natural environment, topography and the structure itself. This concept is poles apart from the postmodernist trend, which starts with forms and their structures.

By combining the languages of forms to create an architectural structure as a composition, Ashihara's concern is to give birth to architecture whose natural form contrasts effortlessly with the site.

This is what we may describe as the invisible form creation system that exists within the hidden order mentioned earlier. This common theme runs throughout all of his works, and his is sincere architecture that results from mediation with the surrounding context. This architecture yields text, and is composed within a new context.

Besides the mediation with cities and with nature that we have spoken of till now, Ashihara has recently displayed a concern with mediation with people. This is clearly evident in the primary school at Shiroishi City, completed this year. This school is a stark criticism of schools built according to preconceived plans. It is an unprecedented work, borne of a revolution in the process of creating spatial structure and form. The city mayor, educators, children and parents all participated in this process from its earliest stages, with the aim of creating a new kind of school space. This is the task that Ashihara has chosen, that of mediating all the various dreams and hopes of those who will use his buildings, and giving form to that harmony.

It is said that he learned this in his youth at a workshop held in Japan by Lawrence Halprin. Such works, the results of human mediation, present forms and space that involve an astonishingly original system. Thus, among the many different architects of the fourth generation, if we were to try to place Ashihara simply, it would have to be as an architect who fulfills a role as a contributive individual within the social network. This stance is quite distinct from the outmoded aesthetic authorial view of architecture as an art form, and may be seen in terms of an actual physical struggle with society itself.

He occasionally alludes to three keywords, network, commercialism and originality. These terms are helpful in understanding Ashihara's profession. The idea of network comes from placing importance on international communication (which means there are offices where collaboration is possible), and is expressed in the desire to foster effective links with people in all kinds of fields in Japanese society. Commercialism does not refer to the commercialist notion of chasing profits, but states that attention must also be paid to society and the mood of the times, and to architecture that can be materialised as business. No matter how artistic a work one tries to create within the Tokyo context, it will eventually be deemed worthless and torn down, if its individuality alienates it from society and commerce. Tokyo is full of such examples. In order to create a work that will survive Tokyo, it is essential to be able to study and forecast the vicissitudes of a turbulent society. It is safe to say that these conditions are practically non existent in Europe. The two keywords we have mentioned above are used to describe Ashihara as a social architect, but the final element that describes him is originality. While he himself rejects self - satisfied authorism, he does state that in his completed works there must be nature and his own originality. Within the process of creating architecture, he constantly keeps these three focal points in mind, and tries to bring forth meaningful text in various contexts. This fourth generation will be the one that leads the vanguard into the 21st century, and of this generation it is Ashihara's work that has the best sense of balance, and gives us the feeling of a new trend in sociality. In the future, Japanese cities will undergo changes at even more dizzy speeds, and there will be dramatic changes in the form and shape of society and activity. In the midst of all this fluctuation, the new profession of cultural architect brings forth new architectural and spatial creations, with modernism as their foundation, which return the impact to the cities, society and to the age, and it is Taro Ashihara who continues to respond to the challenge.

Program and Style
by Taro Ashihara

The present age has reached a deadlock in modernism. In the post-industrial society, modernism has presented programs that emphasize functions, efficiency and comfort from the logic of production in the building of cities and architecture. Also, the aesthetic principle of modernism - that says what is functional is beautiful - even led to the development of an international style of its own. Today's society, however, is undergoing dramatic changes in various aspects: for instance, moves away from the industrial society, harmonization of east-west ideological confrontation, decentralization of power, shift in focus from production to consumption, and the emerging era of individualism. I have wondered why the so-called post-modern architecture, which had made its grand debut against this backdrop, has been increasingly viewed in recent years as an unwanted fallout of the bubble economy. This may be attributed to the fact that post-modernism has been regarded as nothing more than an antithesis to the style-focused aesthetics of modernism.
It is true that post-modernism has made significant contributions in opening up the freedom of expression from the clogged state of modernistic architecture, but it has failed to assemble the power and strength to go beyond modernism.
If there is an element that has the strength to overcome modernism today, it must be totally new programs that are adapted to changes in society. At present, I do not know what aesthetic principles and styles these programs may present us, but it is clear that society needs programs that will enable us to finally leave modernism behind.

Recovery of Individuality, Multiplicity of Meaning and Reciprocity
The philosopher Yujiro Nakamura defines modern science by three principles: 'universality', 'singularity of meaning' and 'objectivity', and notes that their opposites: 'individuality', 'multiplicity of meaning' and 'reciprocity' have been lost over the years.
For the contemporary city and architecture, the key to surpassing modernism may lie in the recovery of the three long-lost features. Prior to these Industrial Revolution, people lived in the Gemeinschaft community, or a group with an intimate relationship based on kinship, fellowship or common traditions. In the modern era, that has transformed itself into the purpose-oriented Gesellschaft society. The future society will need to incorporate urban and architectural programs that help harmonize the Gemeinschaft elements in them.

Architect - from maestro to mediator
Architecture - from a work of art to body of motion. The ideal architect in the world of modernism is the maestro.
He has socially-backed programs, comprehends people in terms of models and is a genius at producing rationally accountable, original forms one after another. He has crystallized and culminated architecture into works of art and sent them out to the society. Today, however, such geniuses have no place in our society - the recipient - although they may be present in the minds of an architect - the creator - in the form of self-complacency. The current complicated society rejects inflexible programs, and individuals do not like to be bundled together as models.
The contemporary architect is a mediator who creates various relationships by mixing with people, getting into and working with all sorts of social environment to develop something concrete in the form of architecture. Architecture here may be seen not as works of an individual but a body of motion that involves the real society and numerous people. A step toward the recovery of 'individuality', 'multiplicity of meaning' and 'reciprocity' would be to regard the architect as a body of motion that formulates architecture and cities.

As an antithesis to modernistic approaches to urban design and architecture, Charles Jencks called for respect of individuality in his book *The Language of Post-Modern Architecture*, while Robert Venturi emphasized the need to respect 'multiplicity of meaning' in his *Complexity and Contradiction in Architecture*. I would like to propose that we respect 'reciprocity', the remaining element, in today's cities and architecture. In Japan, many rural towns and villages are launching various campaigns to promote their locality. If we seek to go beyond modernism, a very important point in the process would be to foster indigenous elements in each locality, tolerate multiplicity of meaning and develop a campaign that leaves room for participation and responsive action. It seems to me that a path towards the creation of new social values may lie beyond this horizon.

Figure of Architecture and the Sense of Connectedness
Architecture that may be viewed as a 'body of motion' also offers a totally different aspect: that of an externalized figure. Regardless of the intent of the architect, those on the receiving end can choose to have an internalized world in their consciousness as a figurative projection of the externalized architecture. Also, they can share that inner world with other people. Today, the universal, single-meaning 'isms' and 'styles' of modernism do not provide us the fulfillment of an inner world even if they carry strong messages. In this modern Gesellschaft society, the alienated population is seeking an inner world full of life, of being true to oneself and being human - a sense of being connected with his or her own self, with others, society and nature. The important key words in this 'connectedness' may include social participation, public nature and ecology. The architectural figure can serve as a device that helps people internalize this sense of connectedness in their consciousness. To this end, architecture must tolerate 'individuality' 'multiplicity of meaning' and 'reciprocity', and at the same time, be open to the nature, city and people.

Open Architecture
The architecture I visualize today has the following systems:
1. Structural system open to the environment. The structural system of architecture should be open to the natural environment and man-made urban environment. Various attempts are being made on the basis of this perspective, for instance, ecological design that seeks harmonious coexistence with the global environment, architecture open to the city and architecture that embodies the city. Regarding parts that have become the subject in the concept of 'holon', considerations should be made so that they are open to the holon of higher and lower order, and they are positioned in the context.
2. Spatial system open to functions. Architecture should have a spatial system that flexibly responds to the functions required by the society. The spatial system not only responds passively but also plays a role as an element that allows the formulation of new functions in that society.
3. Process system open to society. Architecture should have an open system in all its processes from the planning stage to construction, completion and demolition. It is important to design a continuing, flexible system that incorporates the participation of people in society.
The open-system architecture may be termed the life-principle architecture that assumes a place in our society and cities, one that continues to grow. Life is nothing but a set of functions of voluntary cells - that comprise the parts - to get together and produce some kind of order. Our societies and cities are called on to breathe life into architecture.

Works

M-House

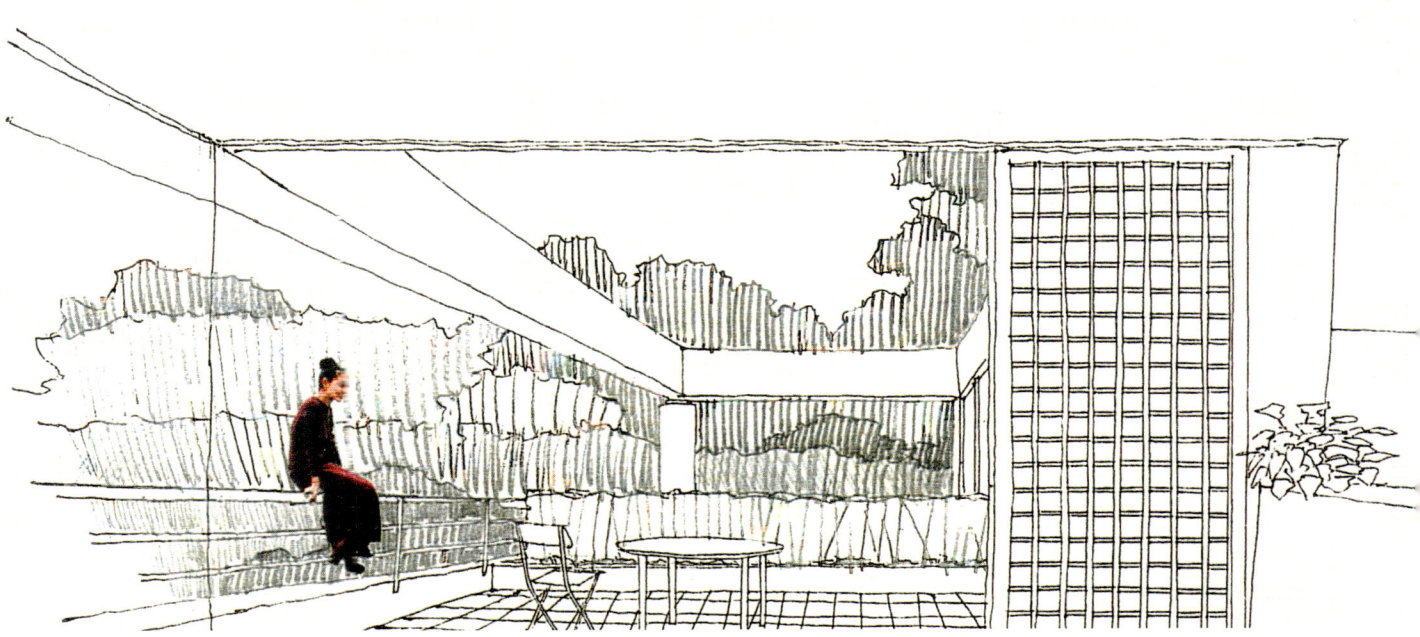

Before beginning work on the plans, I considered how best to work scenery, wind and sunlight into a simple cubic structure. The walls of the stairwell leading up to the favoured second floor were done entirely as a glass lattice, inviting the outer environment to become part of the interior decor. The basement floor serves as a multi-purpose hall.

This was the first building that I designed after establishing my own firm. Placing myself in the midst of a bountiful natural environment, I chose only agreeable things, and rejected anything undesirable to me as an architect. I feel that that was an extremely basic task in creating architecture.

Site plan.

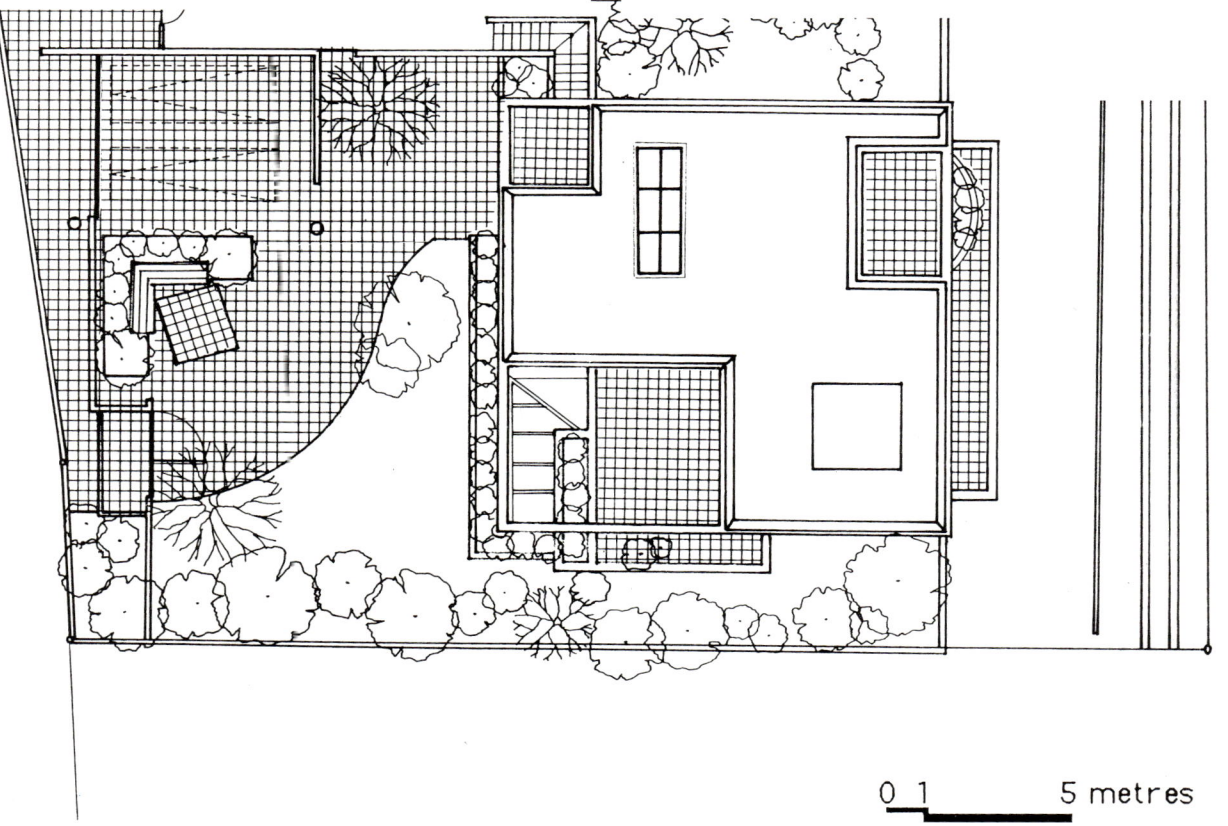

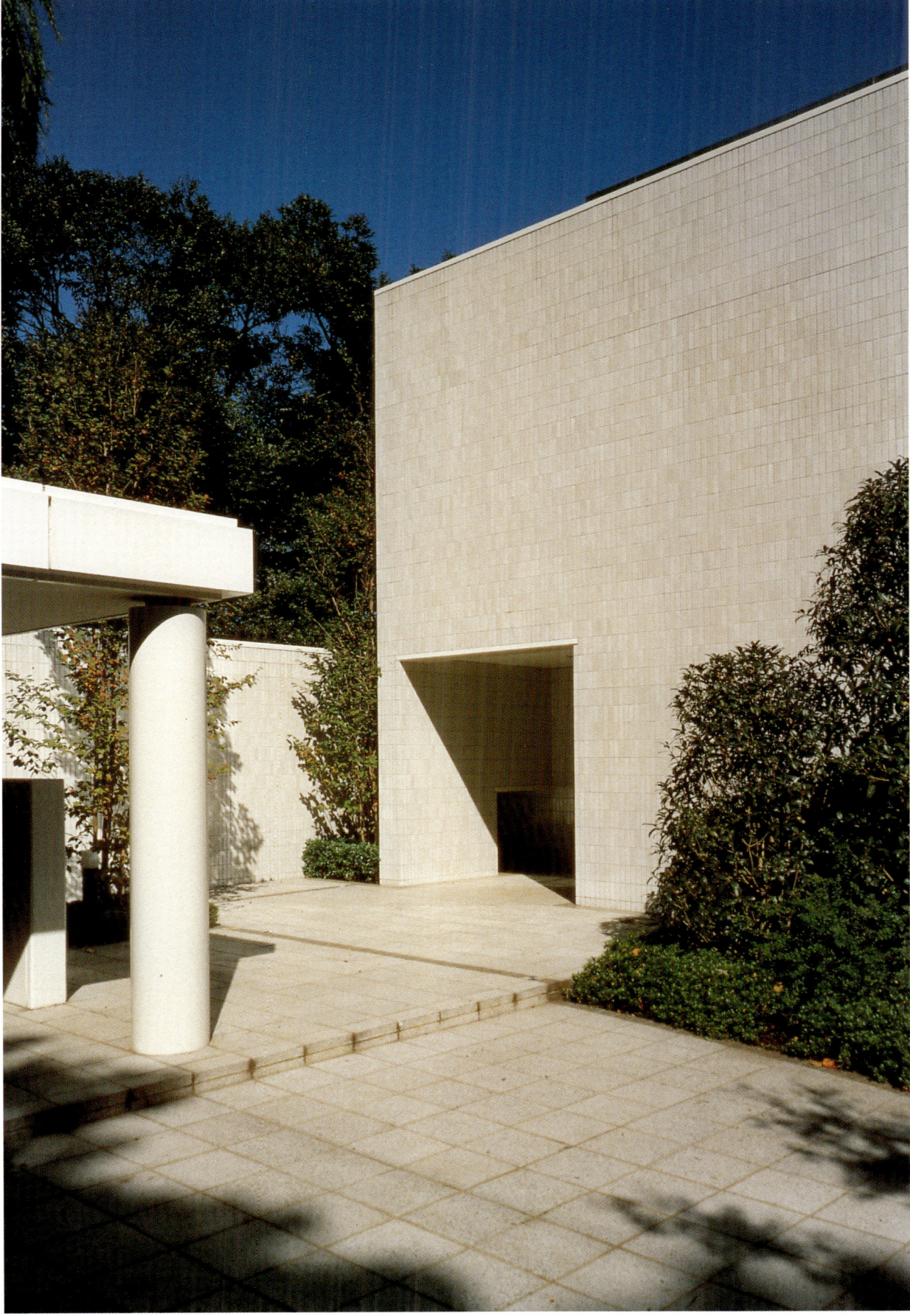

The main entrance to the house. The structure of this single-family house built in Denenchofu, an exclusive residential area of Tokyo, is a concrete box which opens onto the surrounding environment.

The south-east facade of the house seen from the detached parking lot.

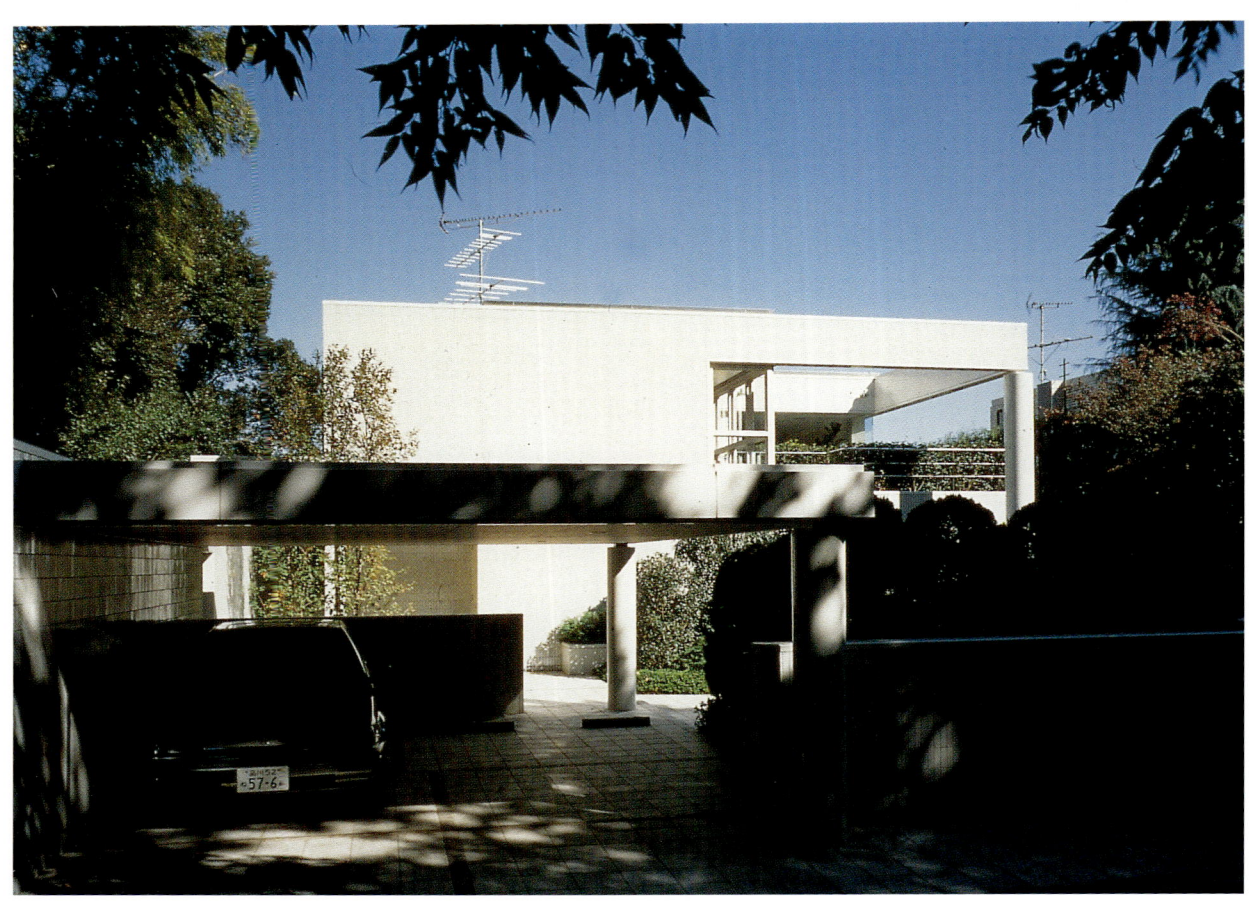

Right, first floor plan and, left, second floor plan.

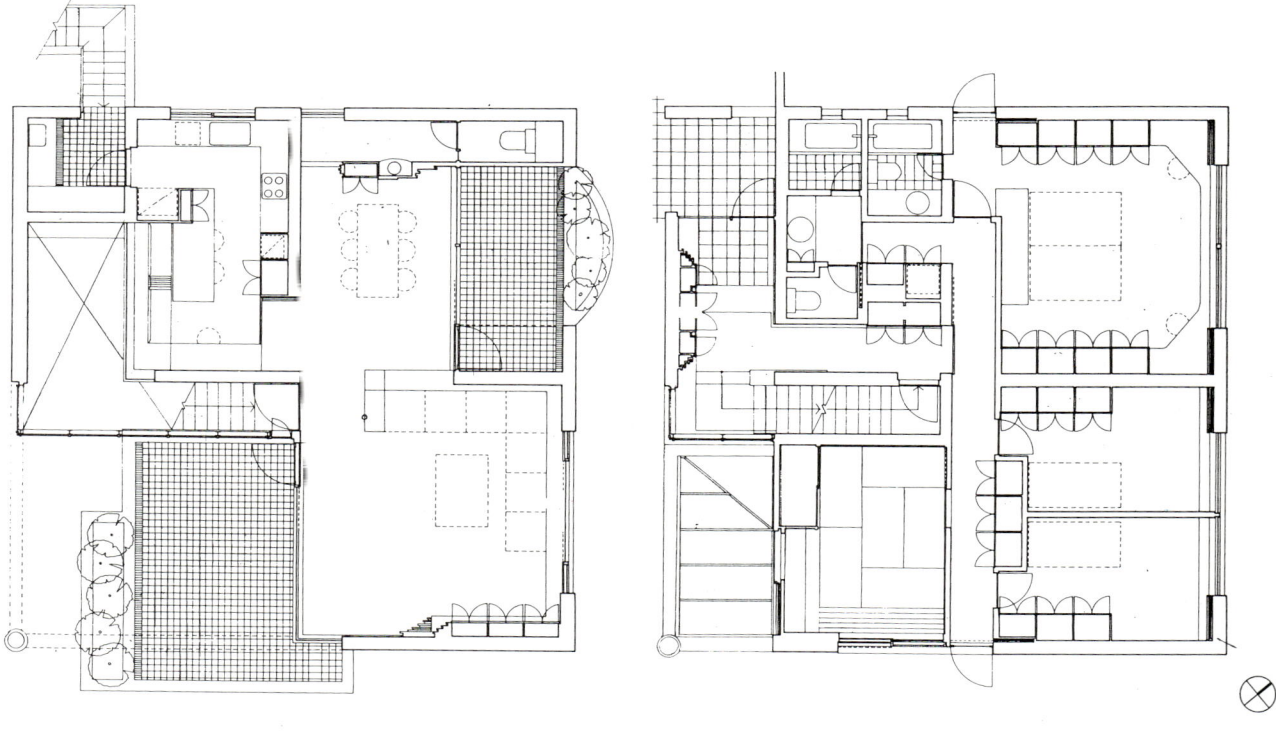

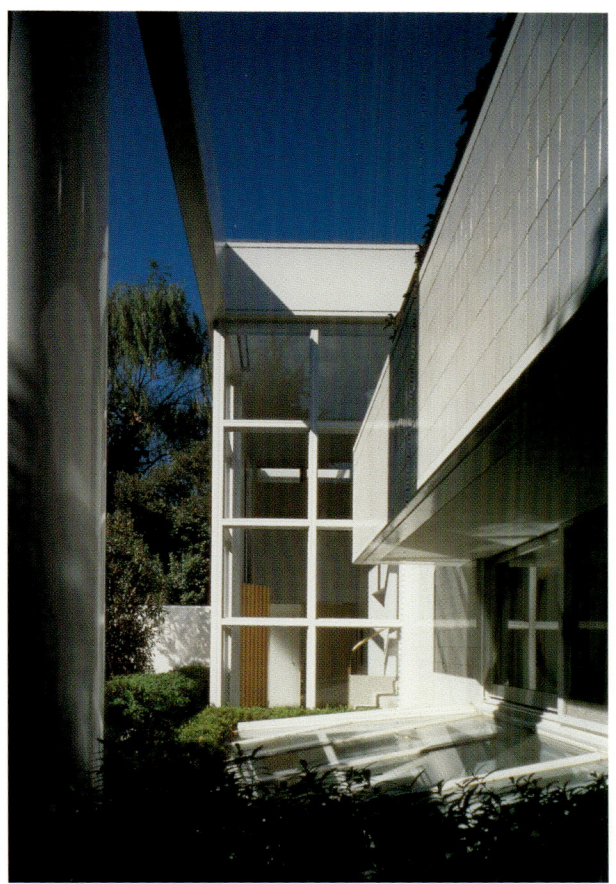
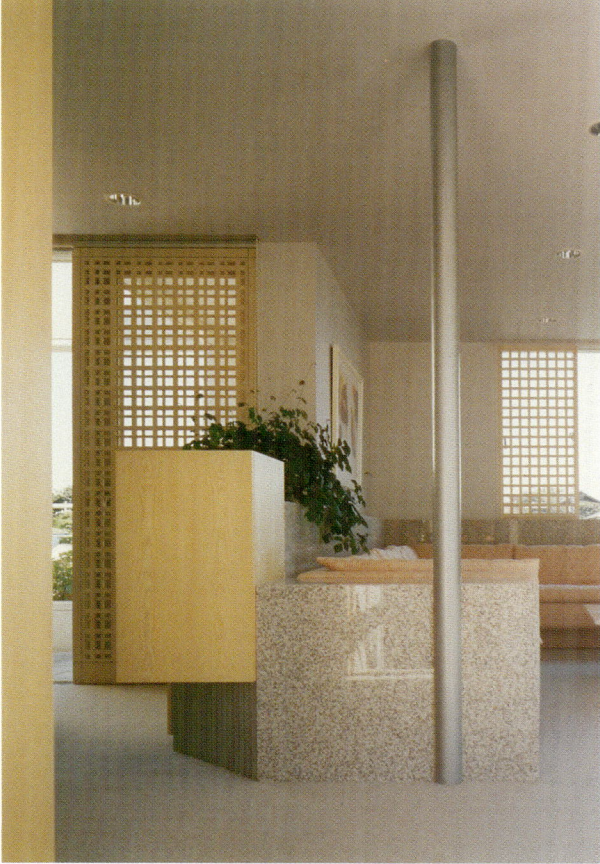

External view of the double-height glazed hall, and partial view of second floor living room.

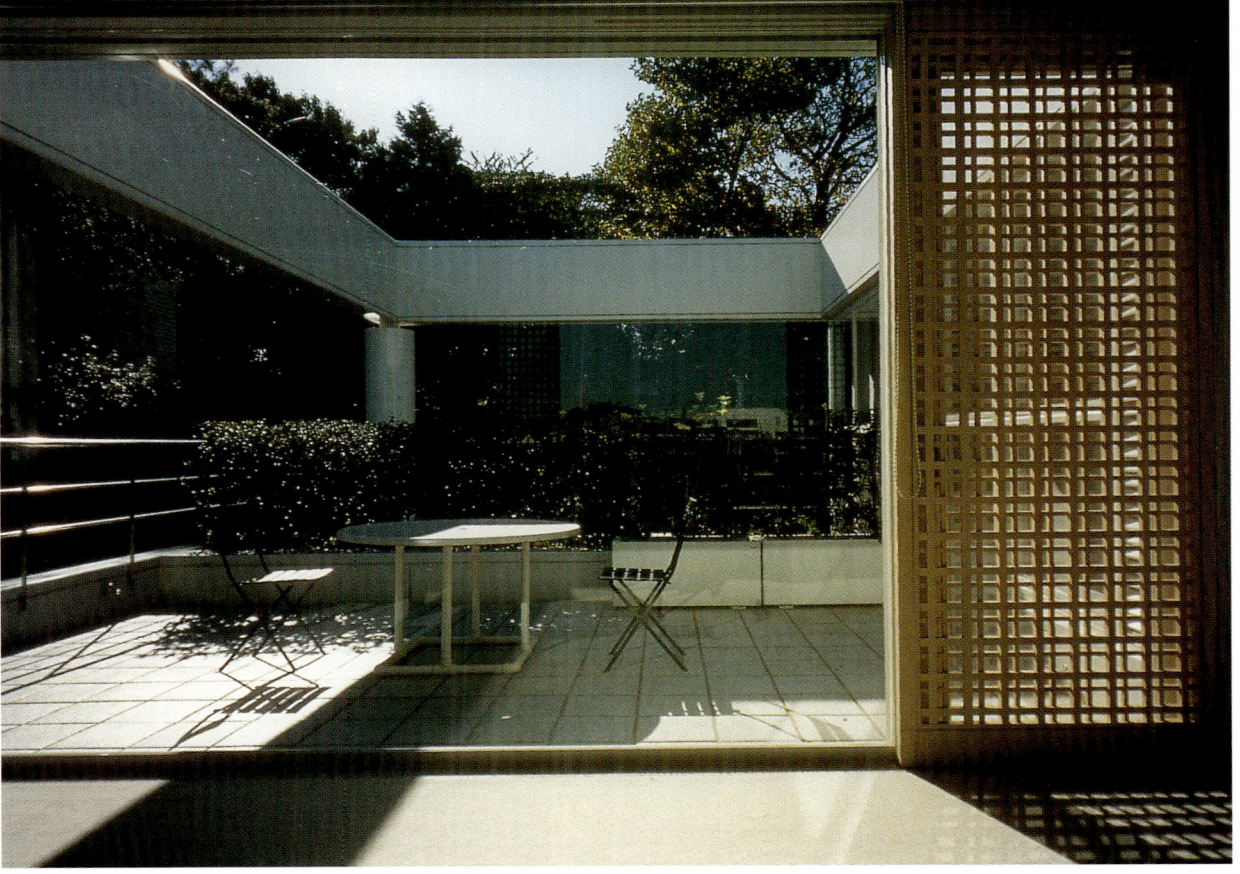

Second floor main terrace.

G-House

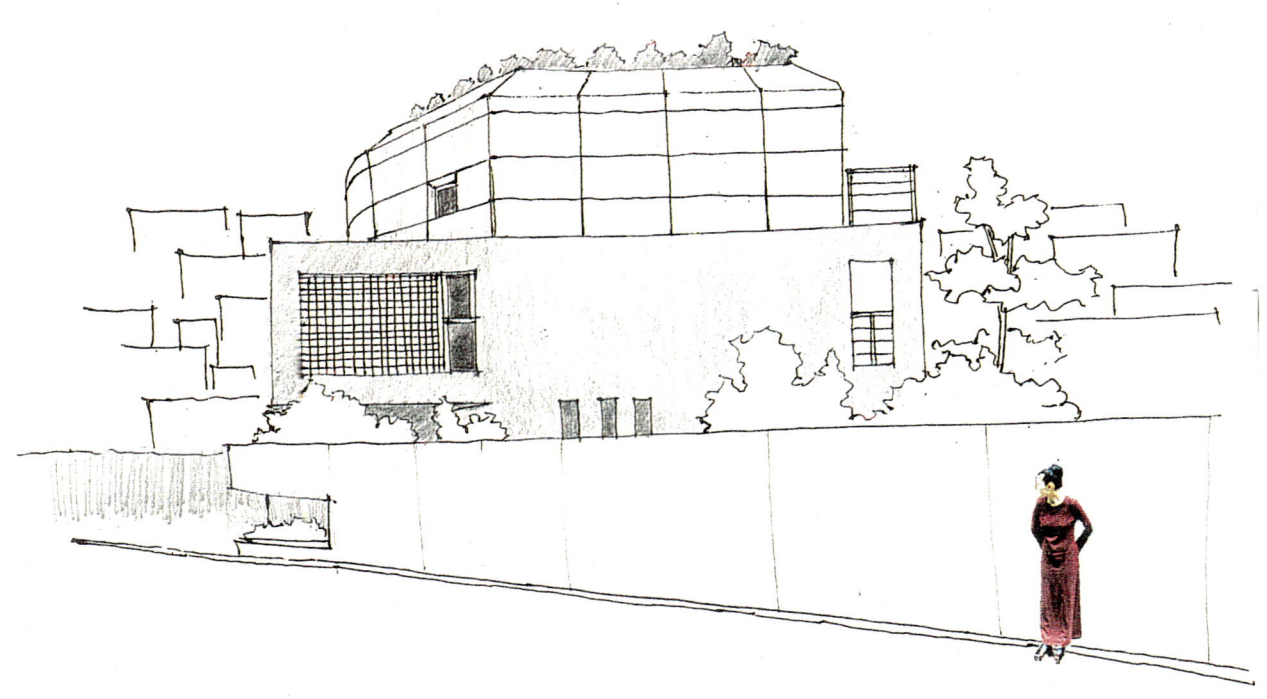

The area has long been a popular location for many large houses, and in recent years there has been a rapid development of houses for foreign residents. The dramatic increase in land prices, and changing generations, have resulted in many conventional houses being demolished and replaced by semi-high rise dwellings. From economical reasons, I was asked to obtain maximum capacity, within the legally permitted range. The building is five stories, with the fourth and fifth stories serving as the owner's residence, and the first to third stories used as apartments for rental to foreigners. The basement was designed as a parking space with direct approach from the street, at a low level. Sunshine hours regulations necessitated a set back format, and I worked hard to complete the structure by dint of interior and exterior decoration. Articulation of the shape was achieved by the use of different materials. For the exterior, aluminium panels were used on the fourth and fifth floor roofs which, together with the exposed concrete finish of the third floor section, form the upper section of the main body. A blue glass mosaic embosses the rigid frame structure. This articulation was aimed at reducing the overpowering mood of the structure's mass, in order to create a light and contemporary image.

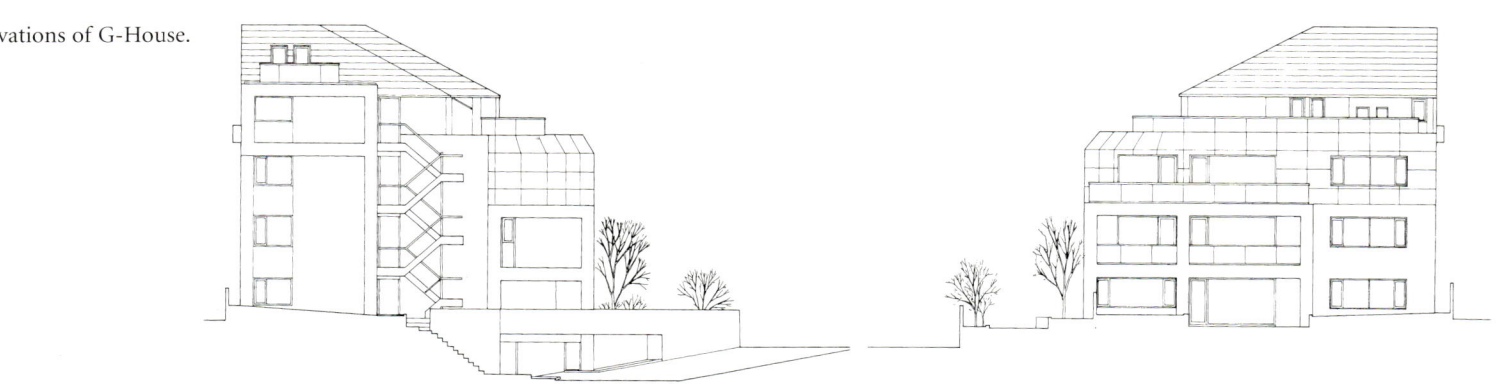

Side elevations of G-House.

For the exterior, aluminium panels were used on the fourth and fifth floor roofs which, together with the exposed concrete finish of the third floor section, form the upper section of the main body.

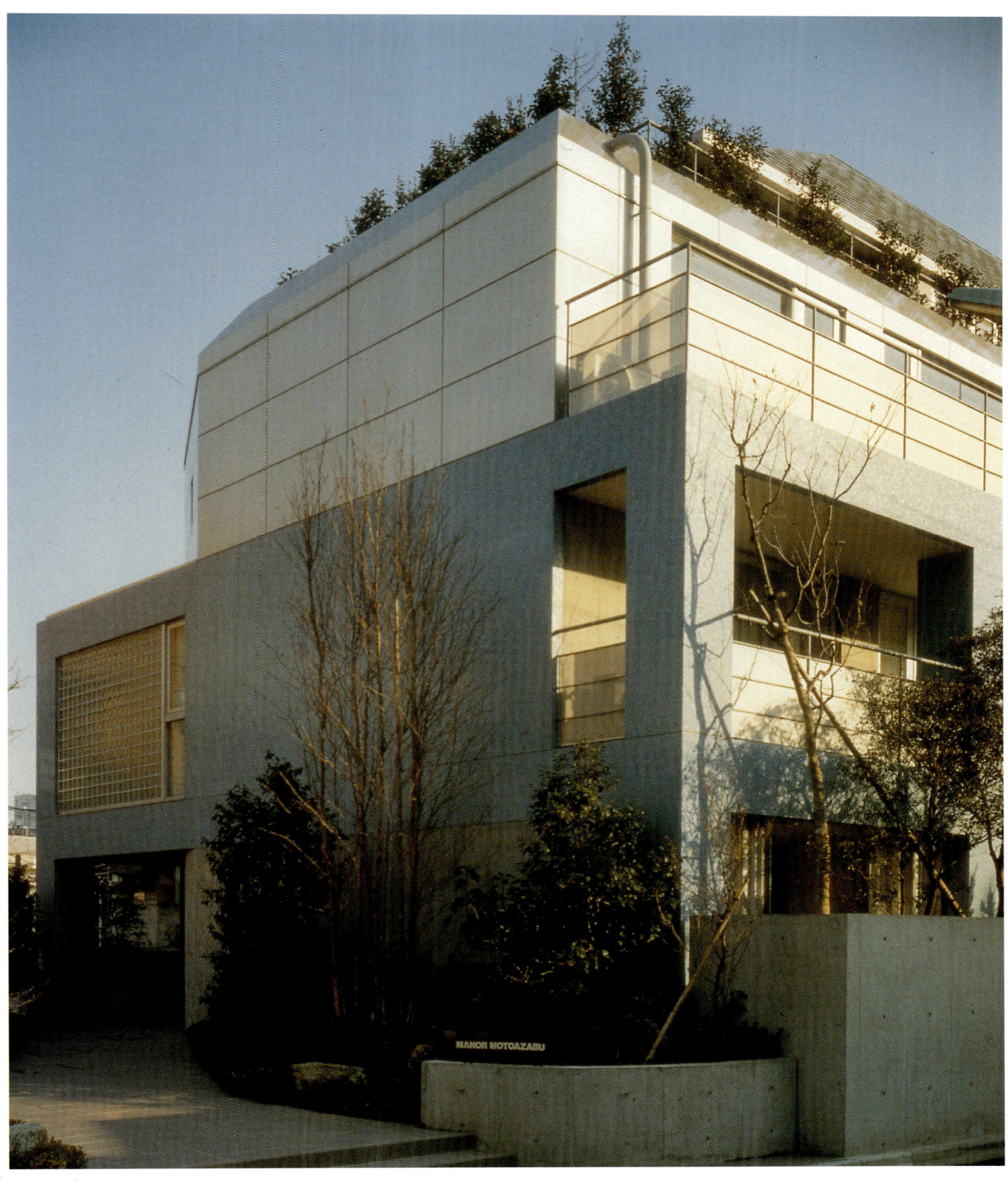

Natural light flows into the entrance corridor through the wide glass facade giving onto the garden.

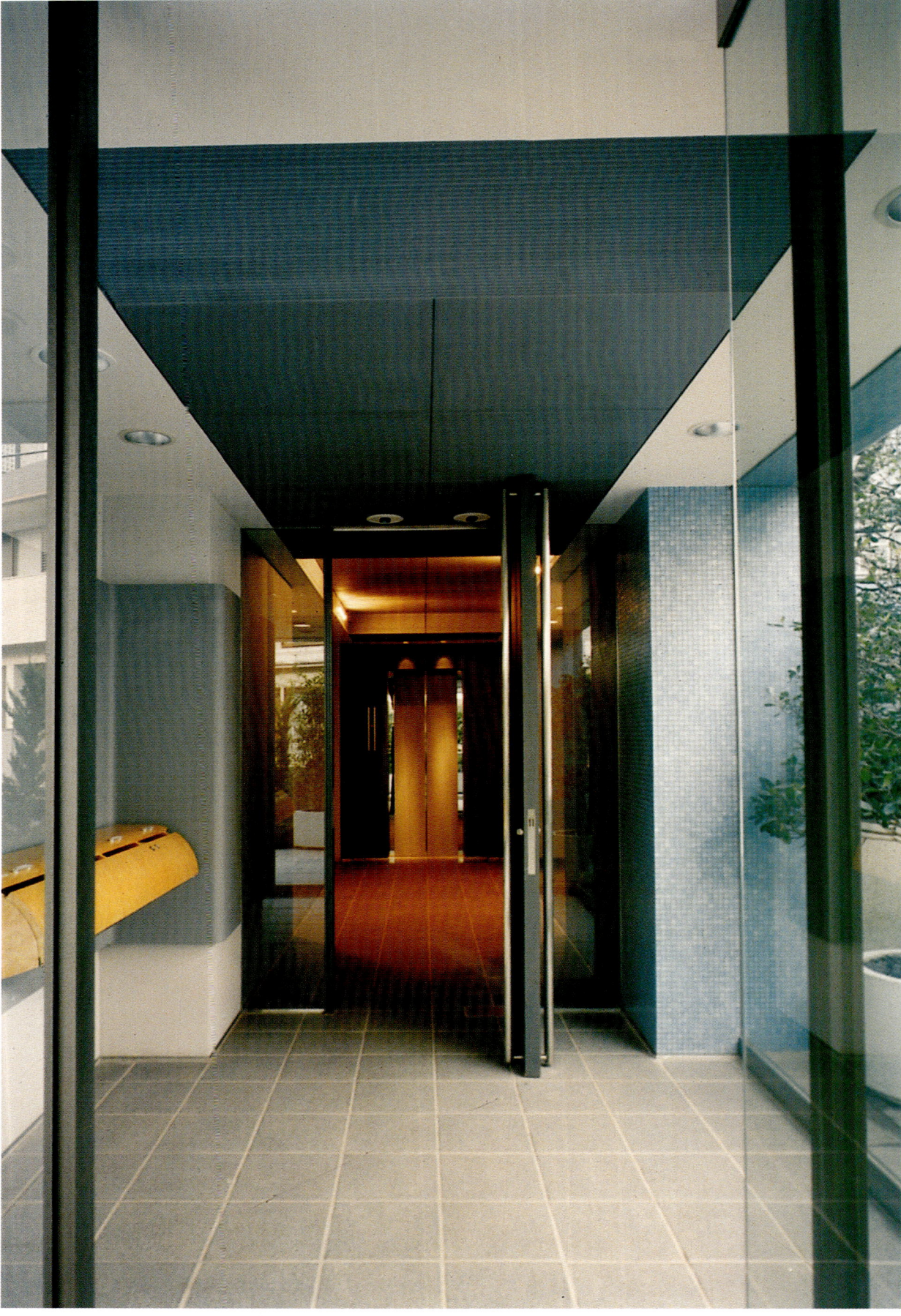

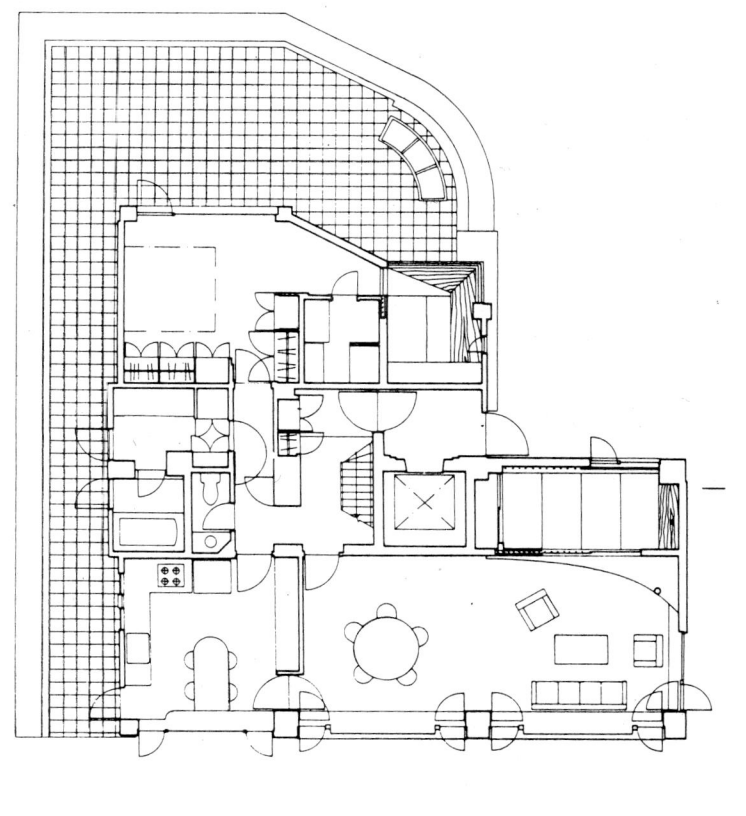

From top of page down, plans of the first, second, and fourth floors.

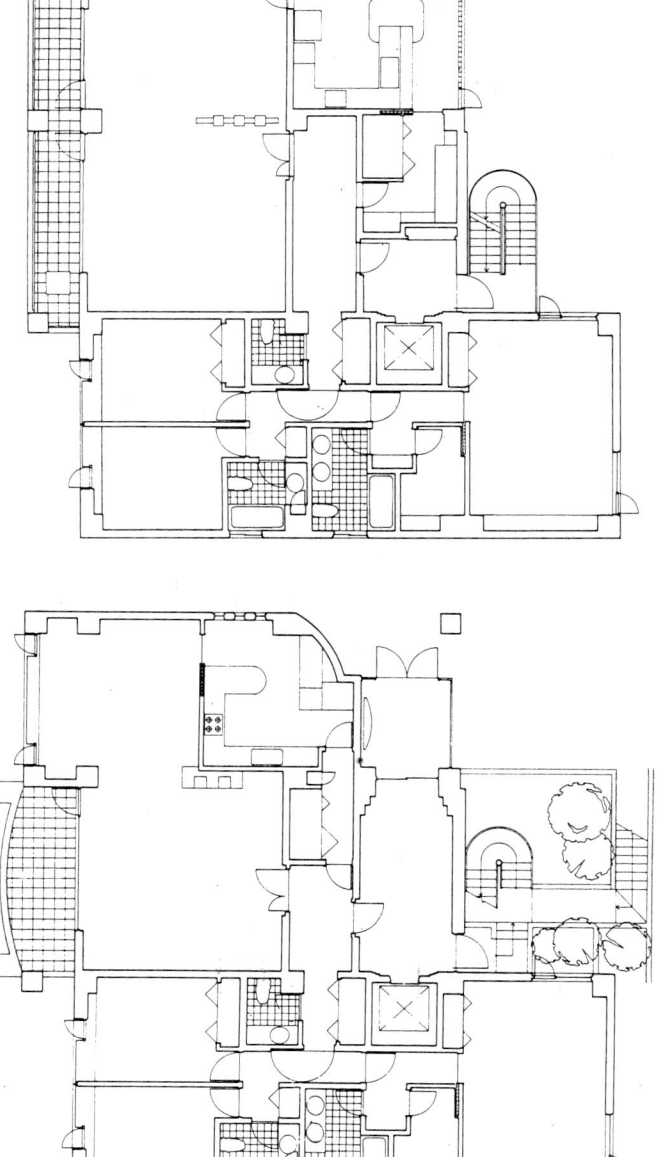

One of the corridors in the sleeping quarters.

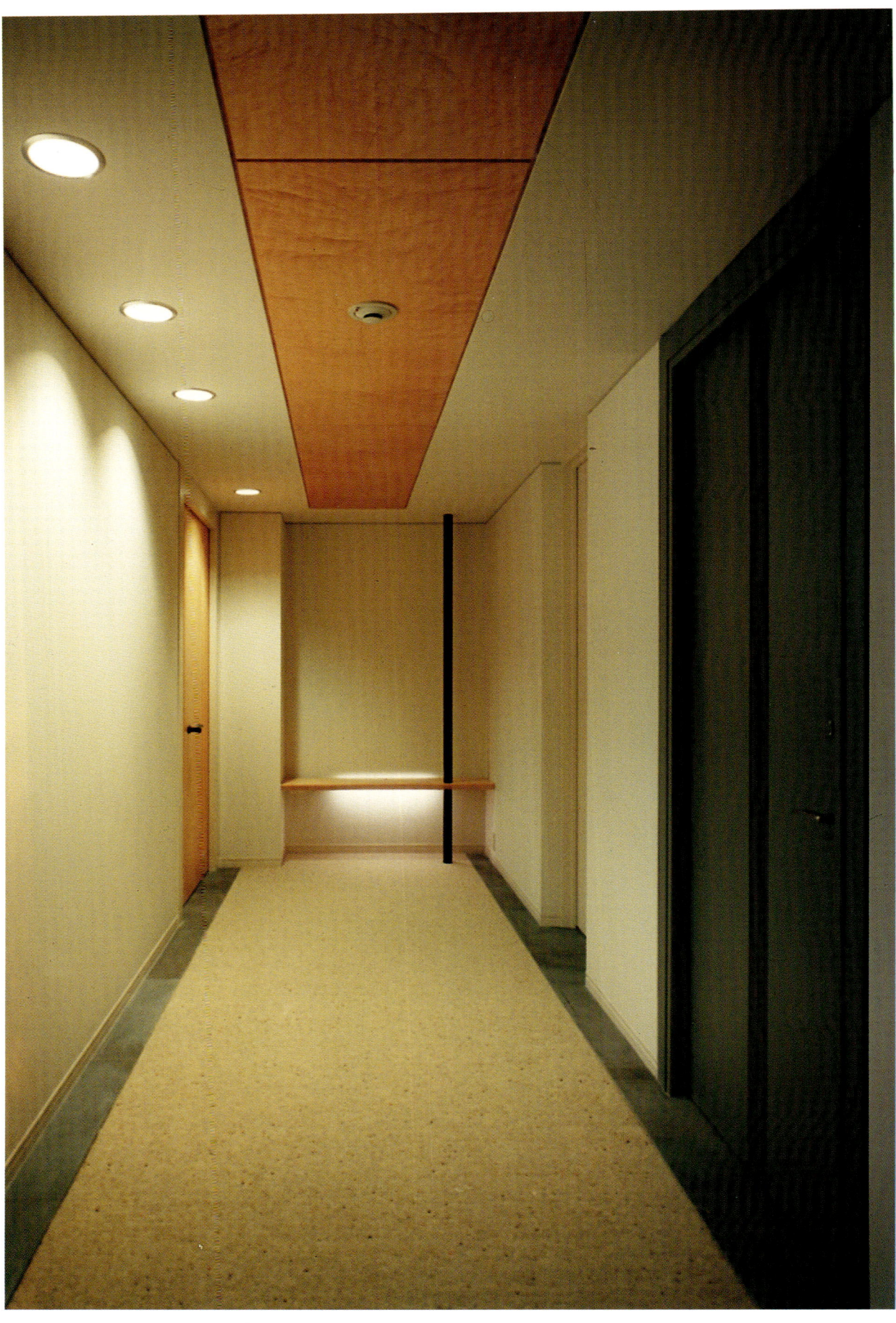

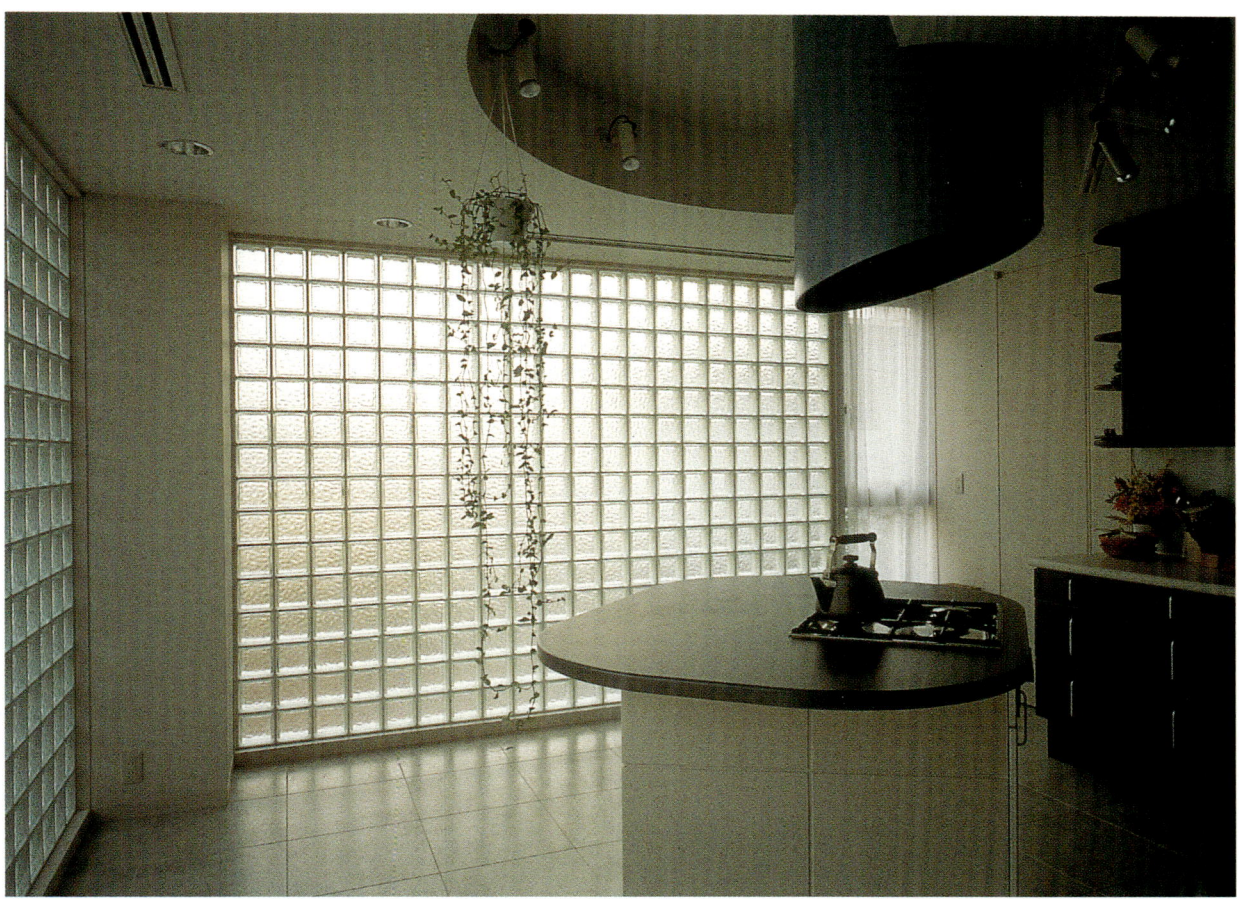

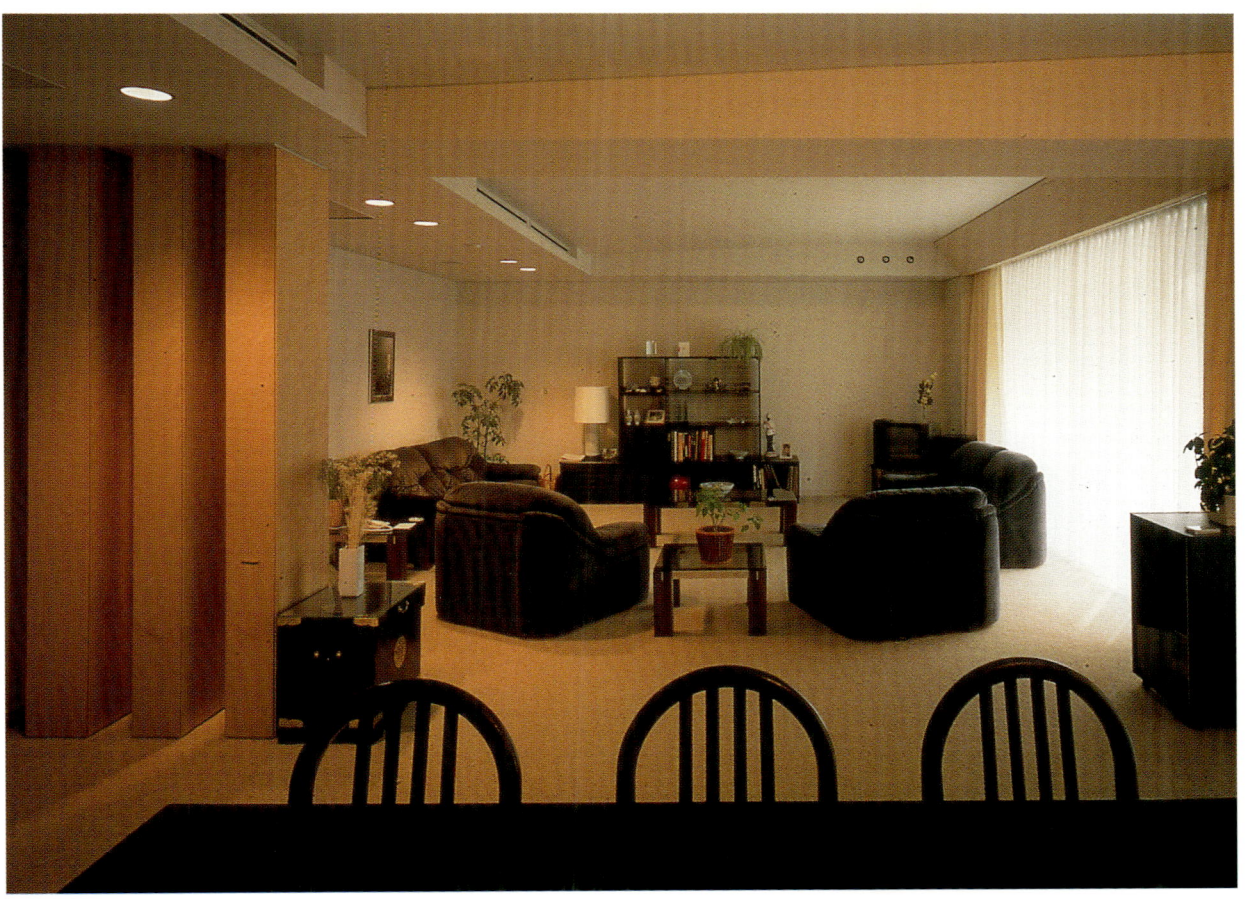

The kitchen and, below, living quarters.

S-House

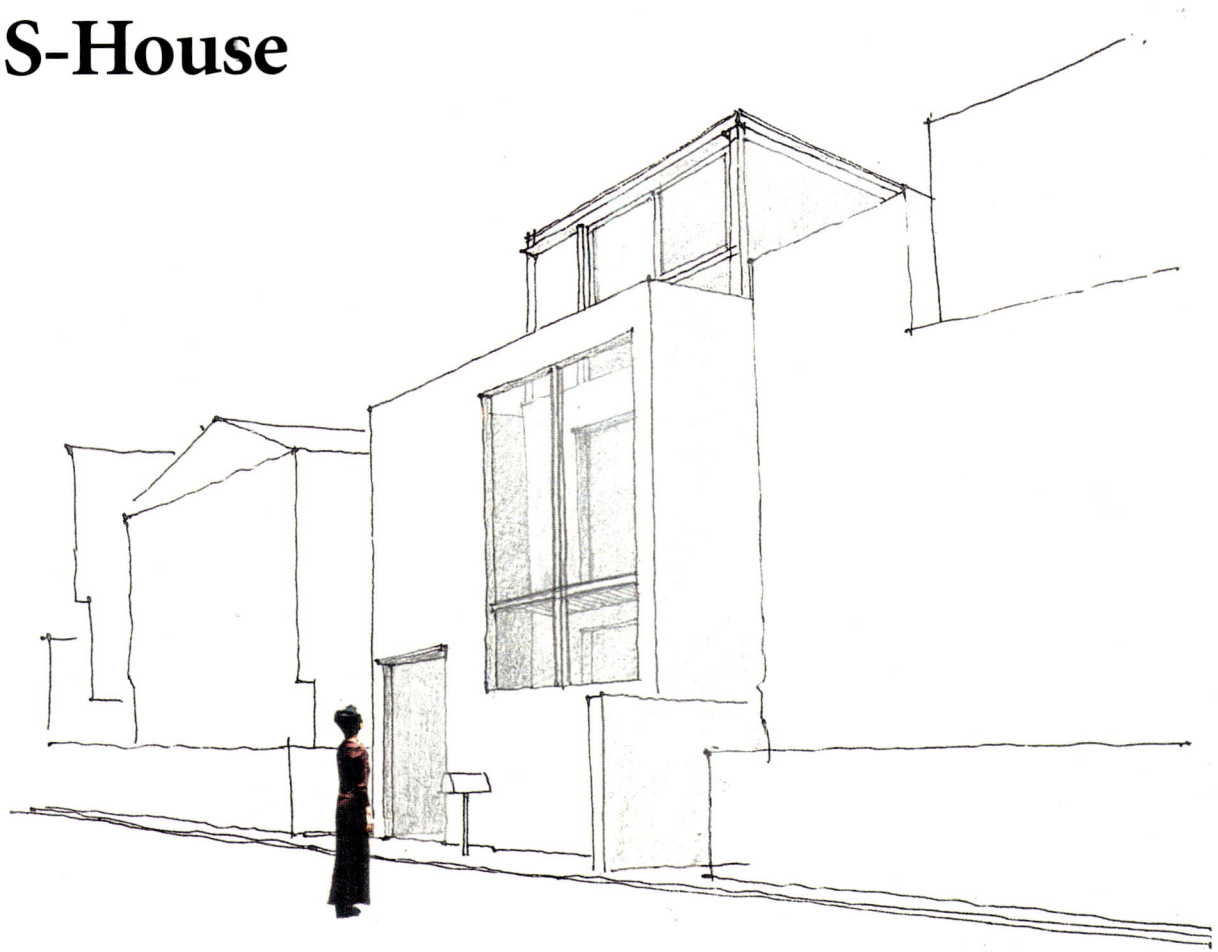

A wooden two-storey structure, built as part of a mini development, was torn down in order to make way for a new residence to be designed for the 52.8 F. The property faces a narrow winding alley that eventually turns into a cul-de-sac that proves too narrow for cars, and is surrounded by ready built houses.

The plan started with the idea of inserting a three-storey concrete box that would stand in isolation from its surroundings, and to create a richness within, like a retreat in the city.

Entering the box from the road, one passes through an open entrance court and reaches the second floor entrance via an external stairway. There is a living room, and stairs which connect the rooms on the first and third floors. Open stairways and sky lights are used in the structure of external and inner spaces, in order to avoid a feeling of cramped space.

The building is currently being leased to a computer software company with a very young staff. Even when used as office space, the particular features of this building are unchanged.

I believe that cities are further energised by the intricate interweaving of human consciousness and a building like this.

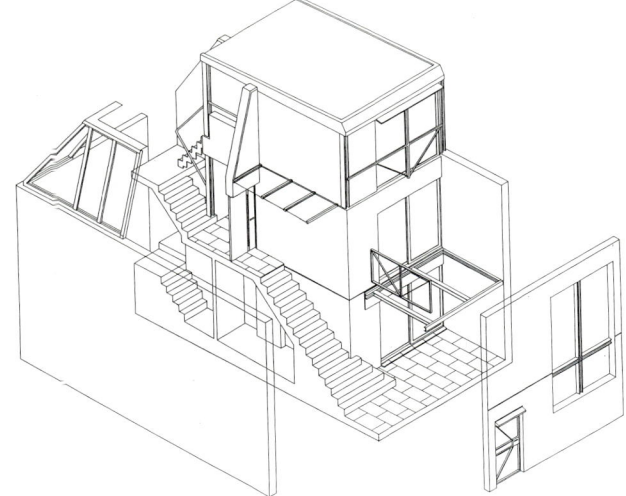

Axonometric drawing of the three-storey house, built on a 80 sq.m. lot.

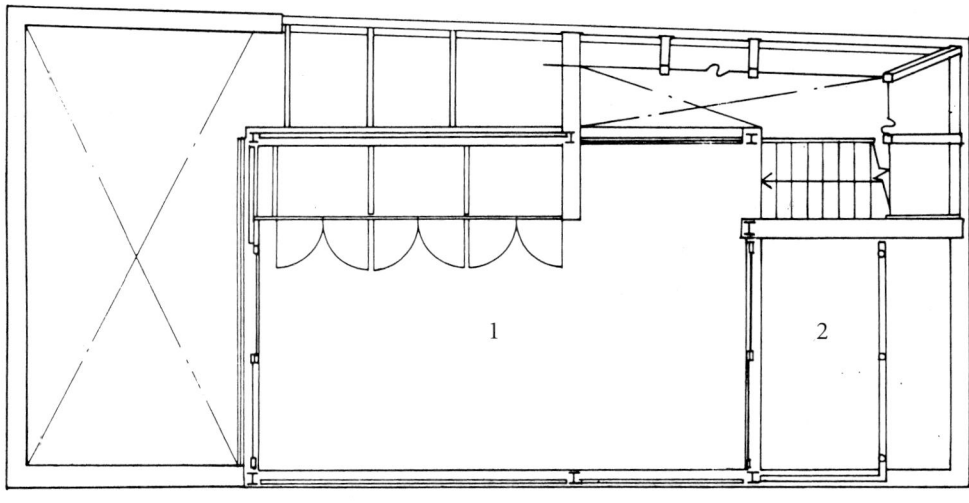

From bottom up, plans of first, second and third floors.

1. Bedroom
2. Terrace

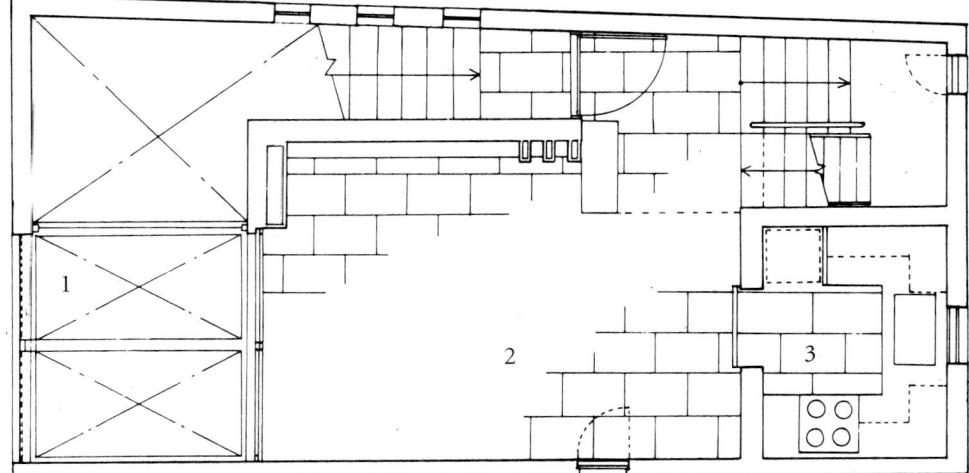

1. Terrace
2. Living Room
3. Kitchen

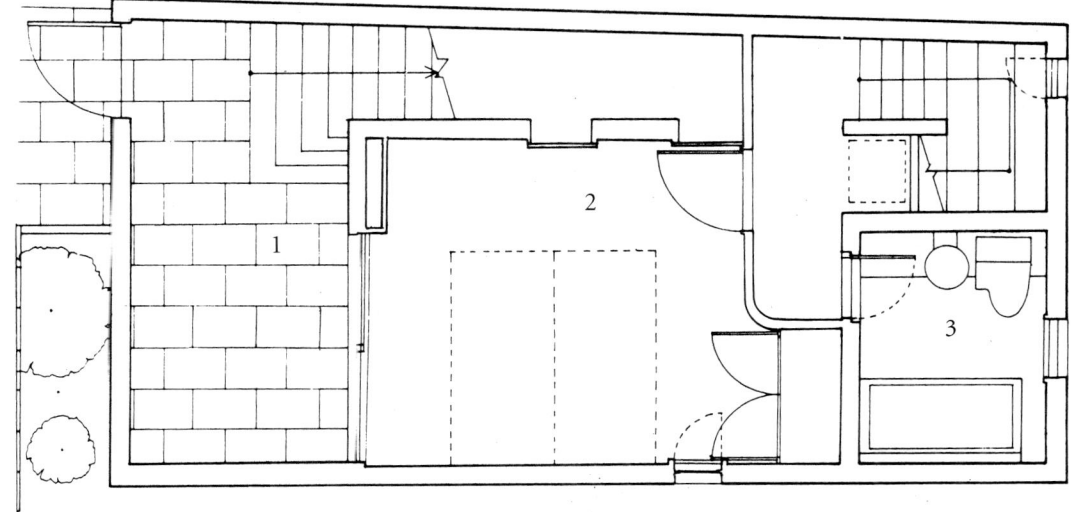

1. Entrance
2. Bedroom
3. Bathroom

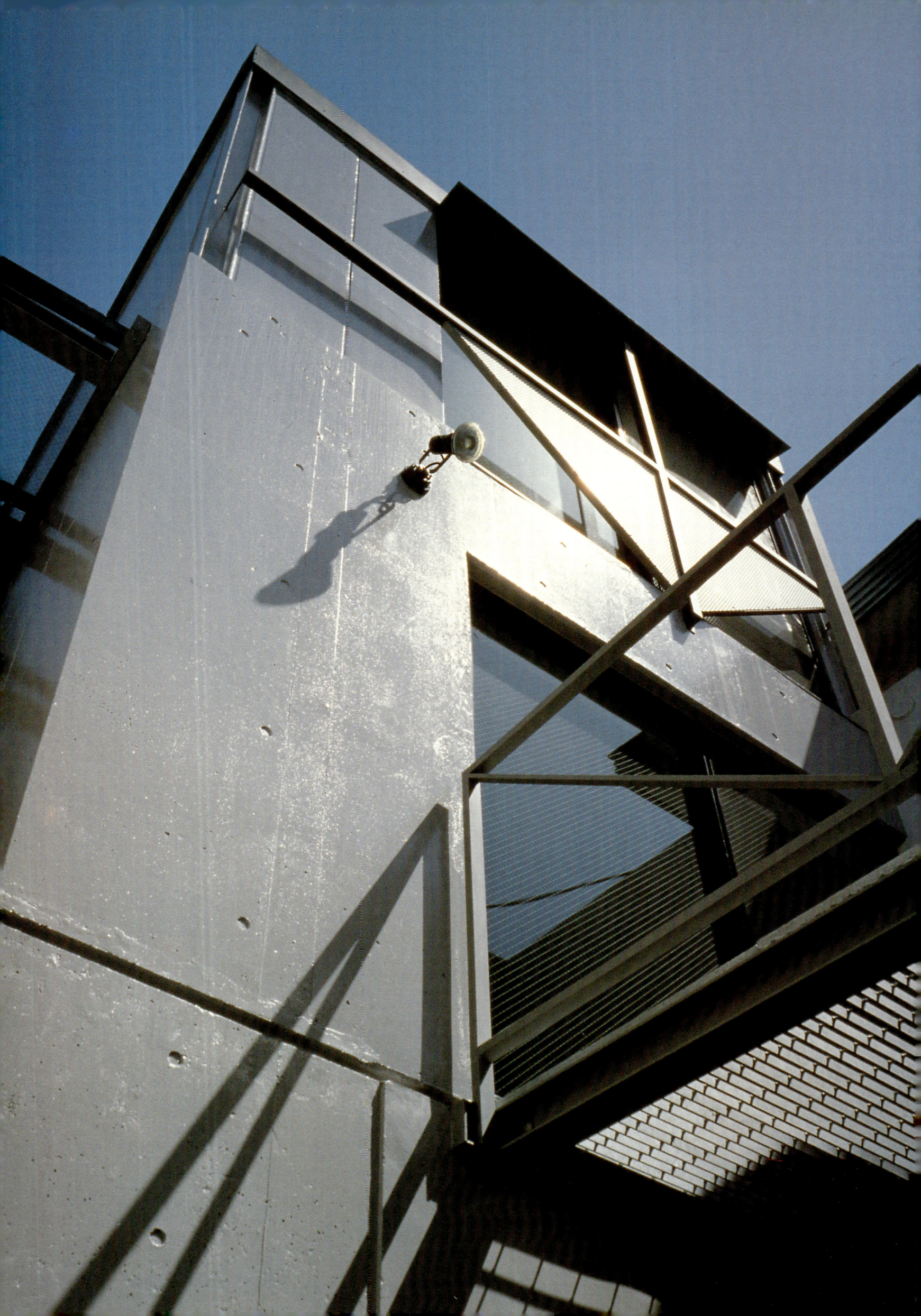

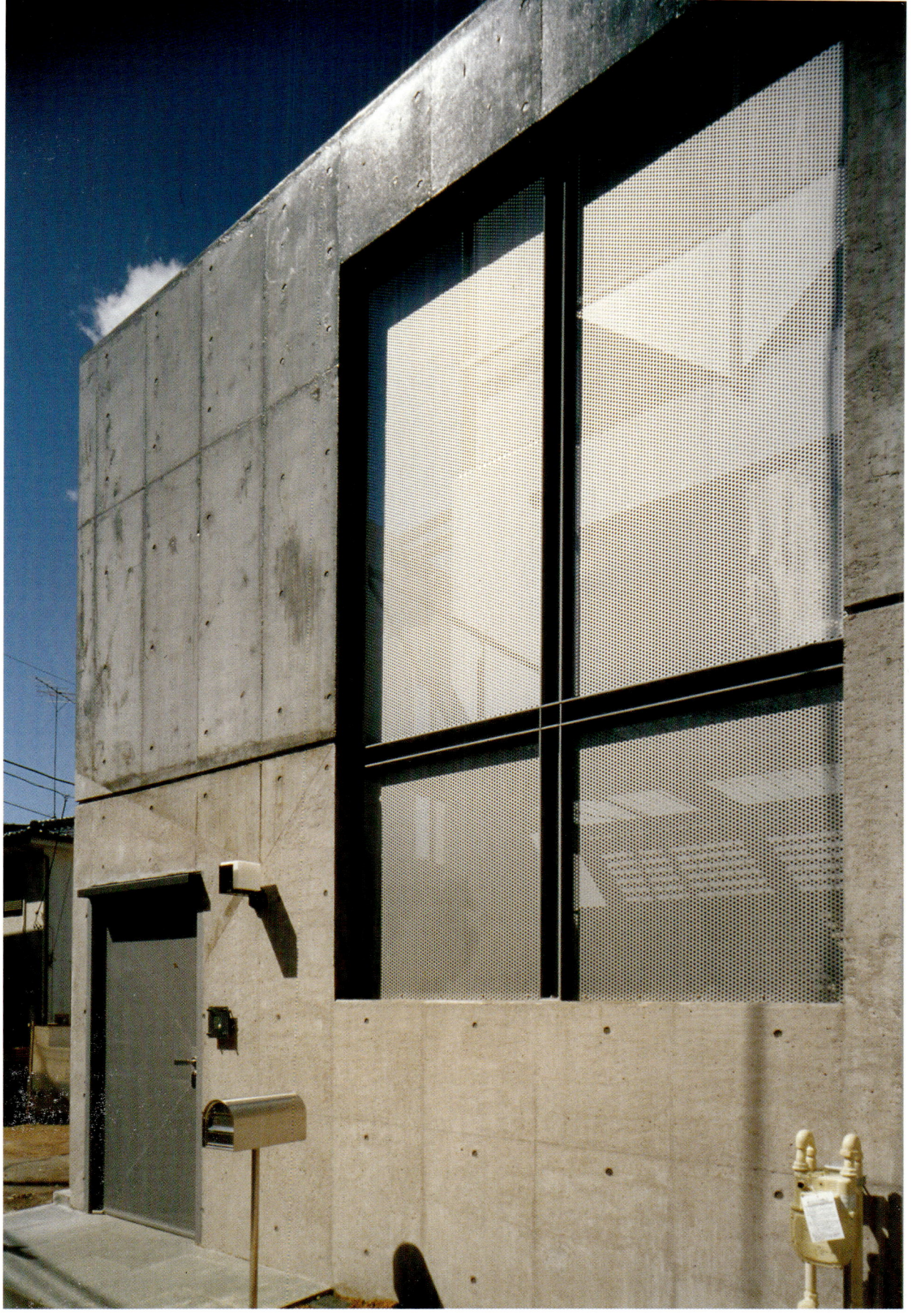

Main facade of the building, a concrete box open to the sky. Previous page, detail of the terrace at second floor.

25

Entrance court with the external staircase which leads to second floor. The court is sheltered by punched aluminium panels which allow natural light to flood in.
Opposite page, the transparent door of the court seen from the second floor entrance.

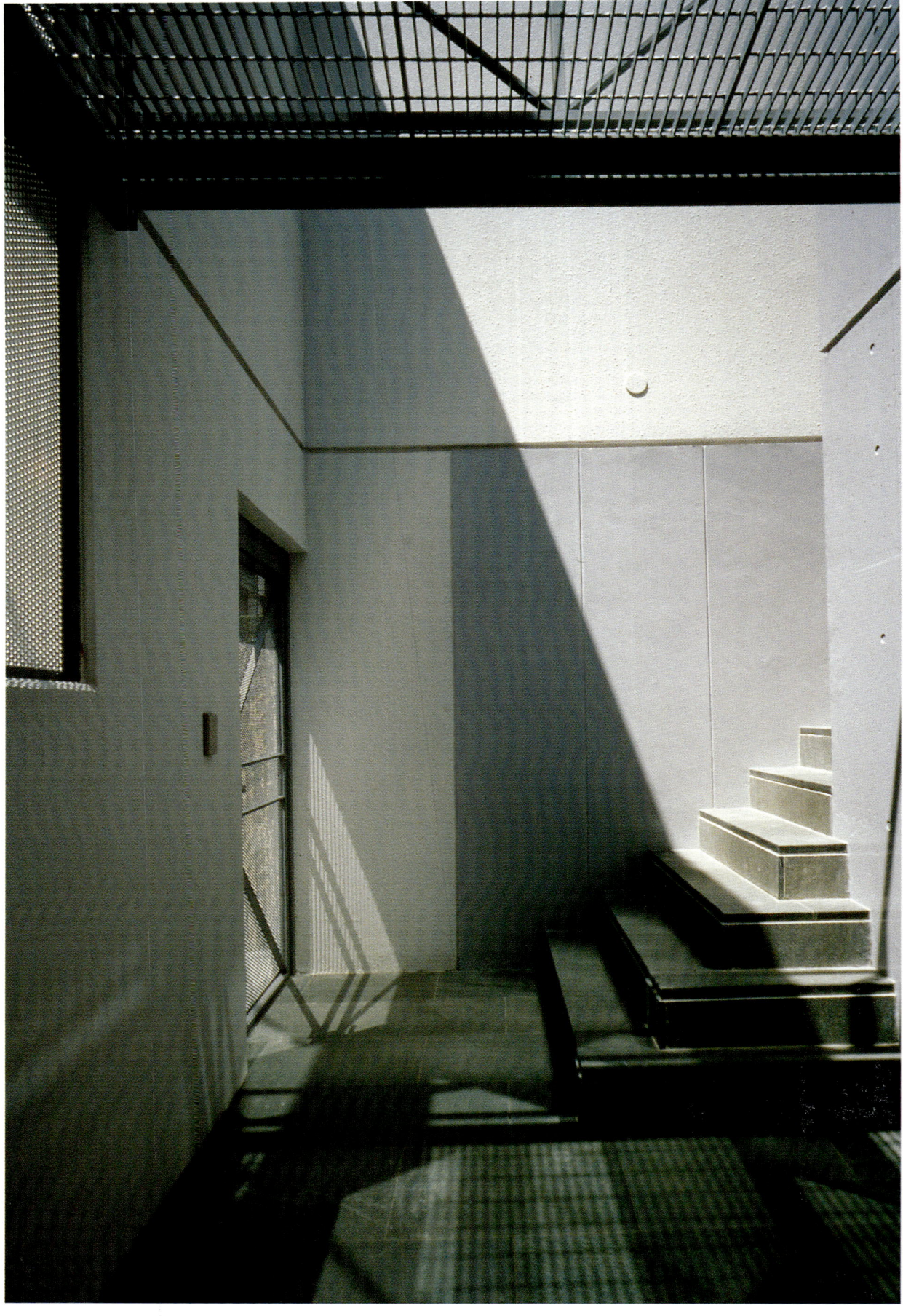

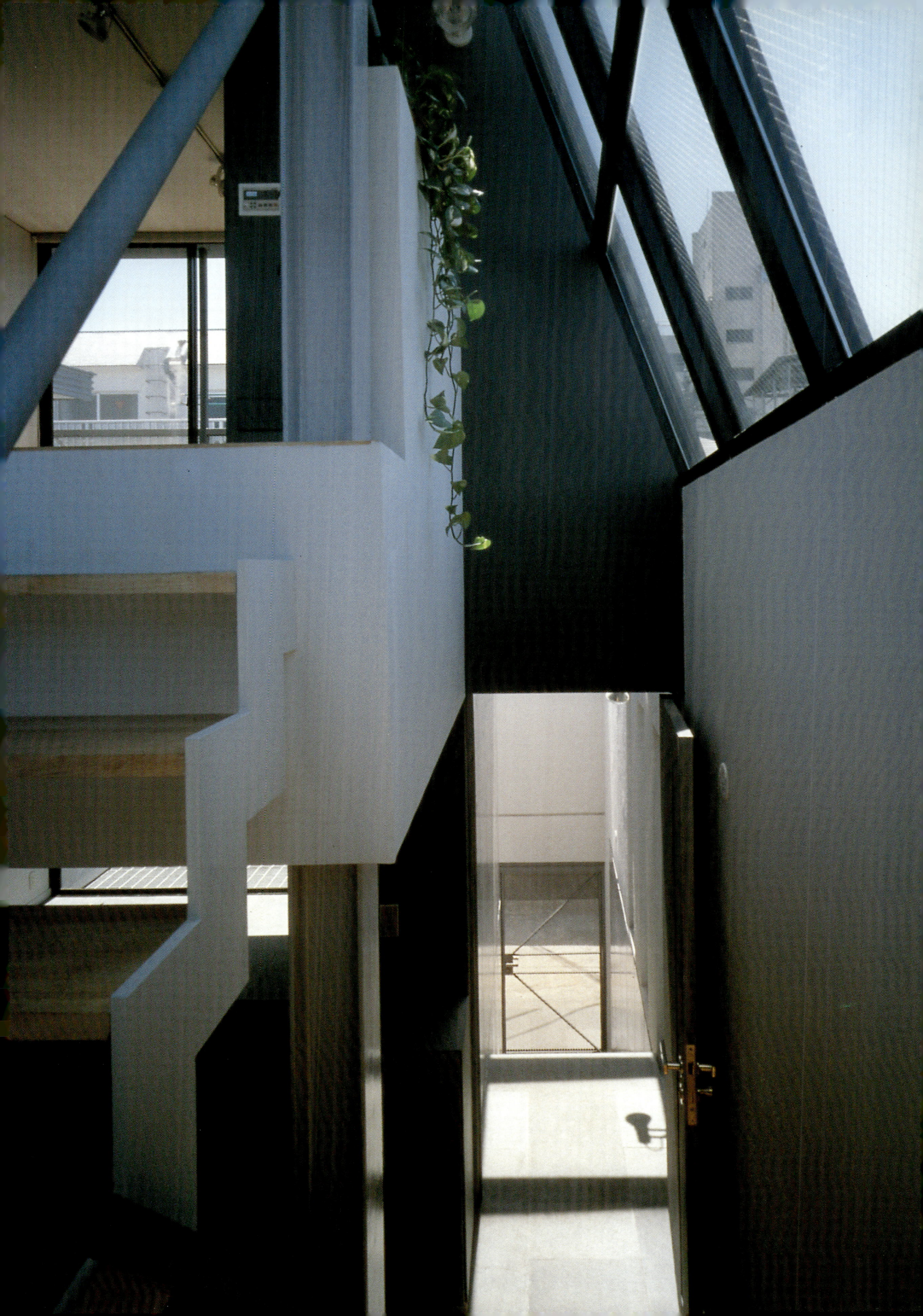

One of the outside staircases connecting the two separate levels of the house.

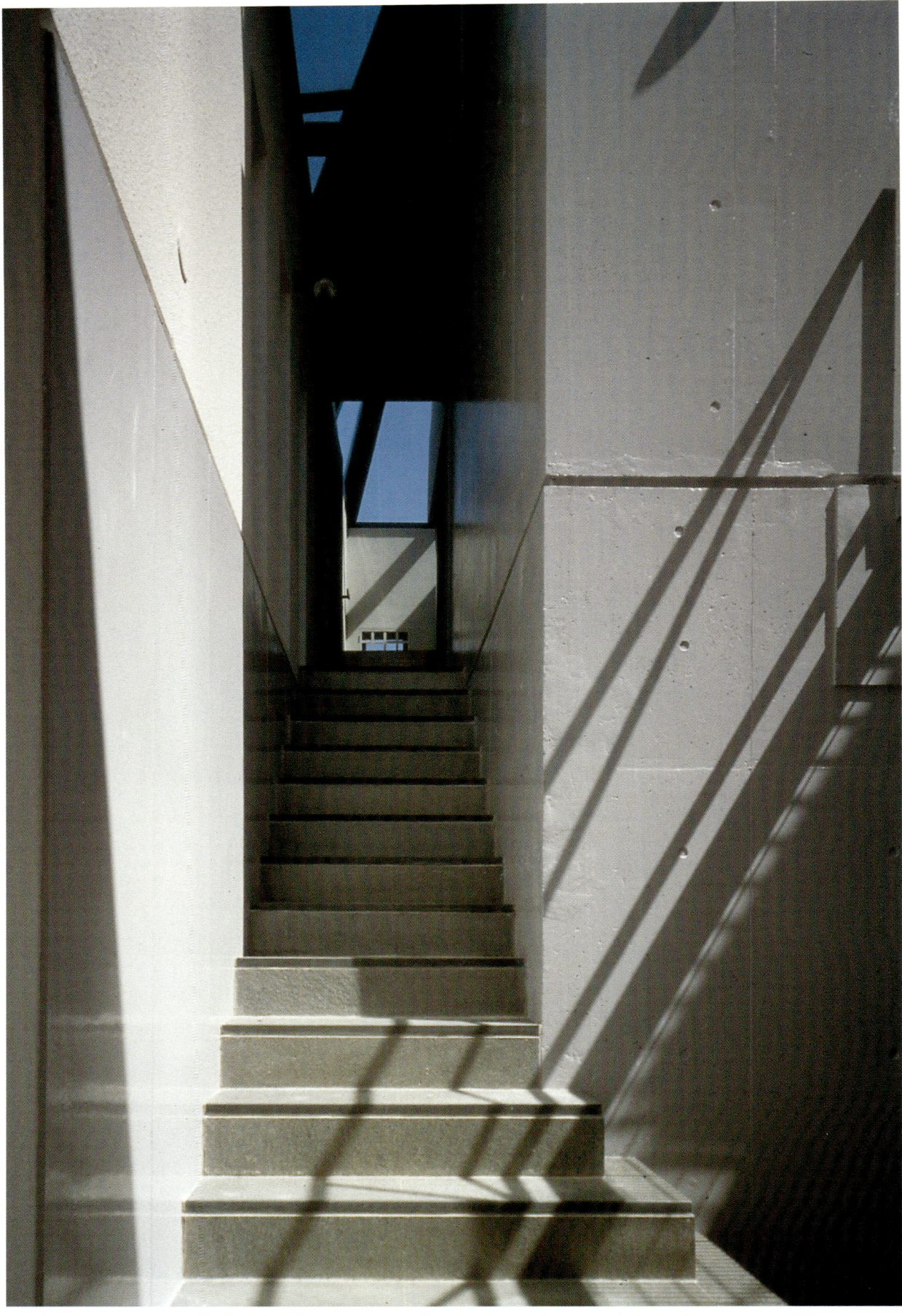

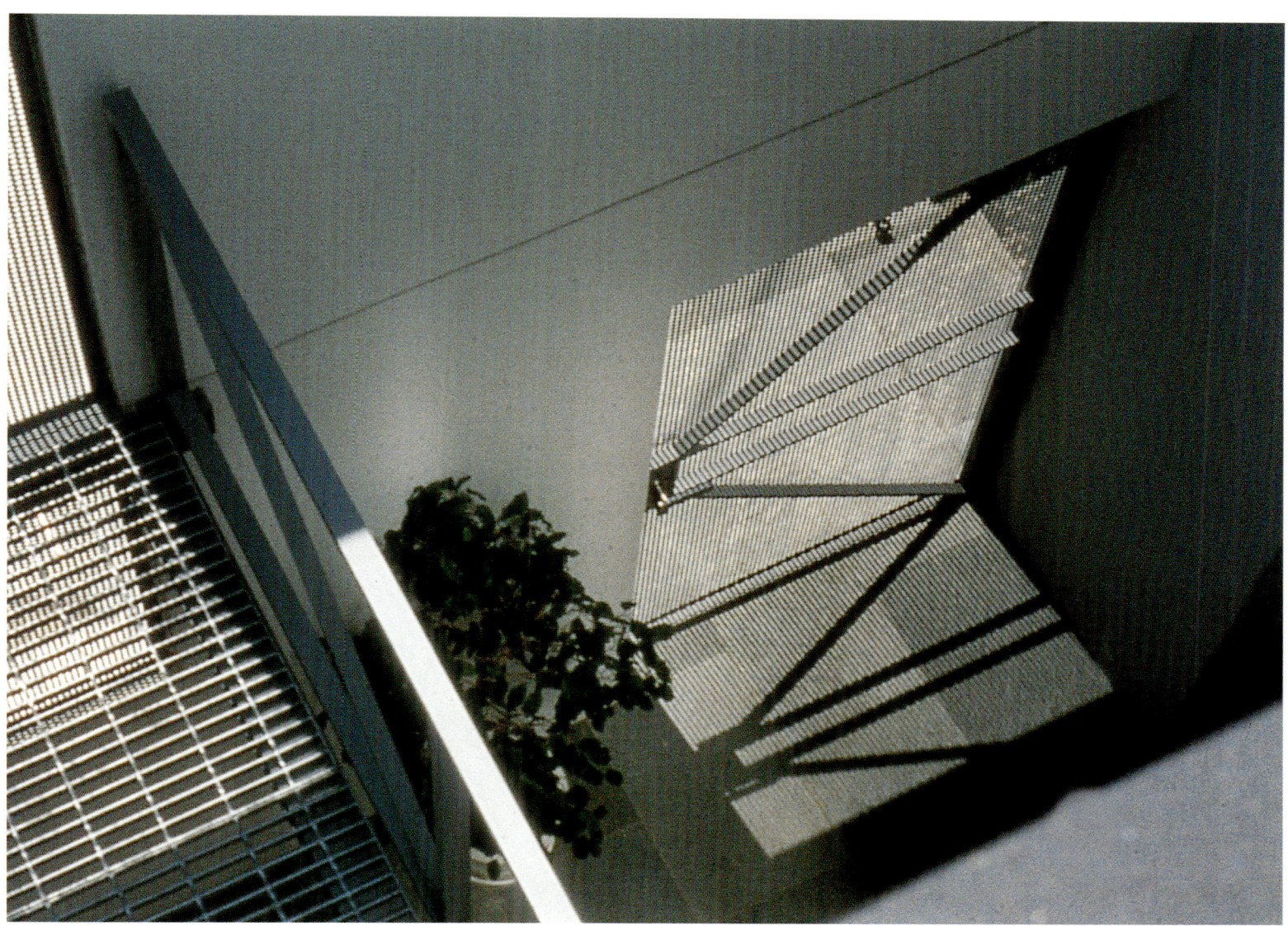

View from the entrance, that opens onto an internal courtyard, of the outside gallery on the second floor.

Ichikudo Building

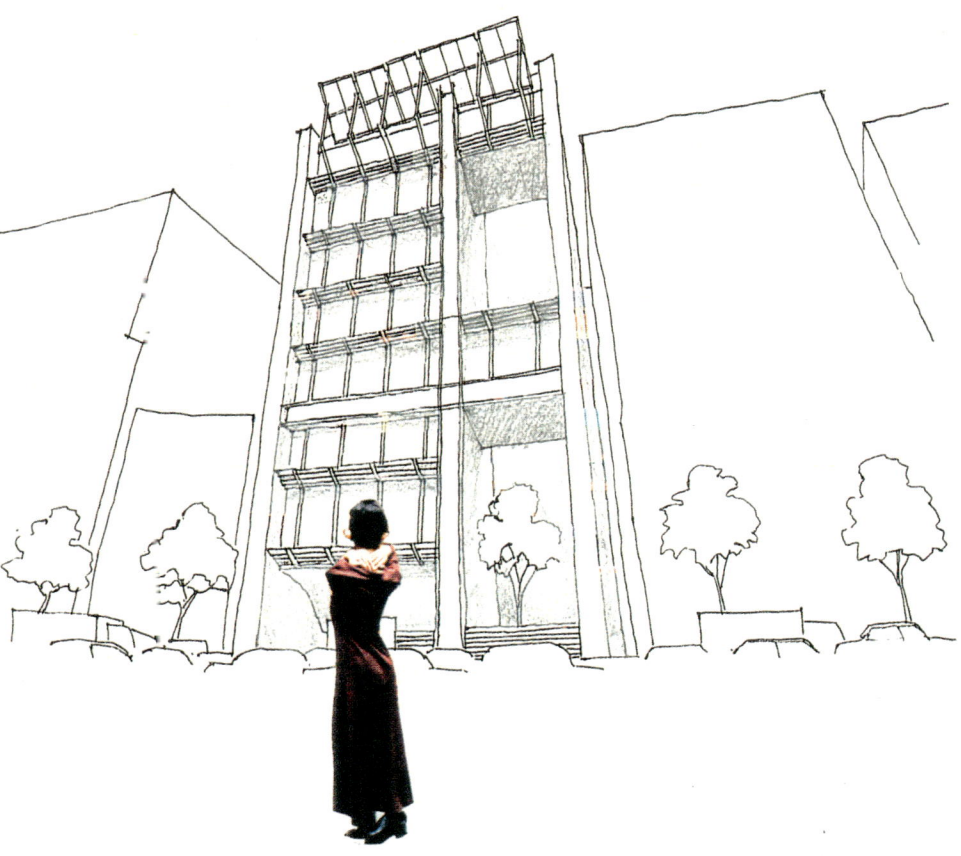

The Ichikudo Building is situated in Tokyo's Tsukiji. As the waterfront proceeds with development, the environs are also undergoing transformation.
The property is owned by a printing company that has been doing business on this site for many years. With the factory function taken care of elsewhere, the plan was to tear down the existing building, and to use the space as the company headquarters and president's residence, with the remaining space utilised efficiently as tenant offices.
During the design stage, my intention was to create an image of the company as a custodian of local culture, and to create an architectural space that would fulfill the needs of an area transforming itself in preparation for the coming age, and those of an OA functioning building, and at the same time give a sense of richness. The top floor was to be used as a residence, with all floors from first to eighth linked by an open well. This open well serves as a kind of *tokonoma*, an alcove giving a sense of depth to the facade, and provides the working area with a leisurely space to relax the eyes. There is also an external stairway that links each floor, and can function as a place of activity.
The facade avoids using a curtain wall to give a surface layer design, but involves a huge corten steel cross, metallic ribs, a fence, etc. Office buildings need to have an identity, not only as component elements of the neighbourhood, but also for the people involved in administration work. Consideration also needs to be given to well-rounded comfort in office spaces as areas of human activity.

Bottom of page, sketch of the facade. Following page, view of the finished facade.

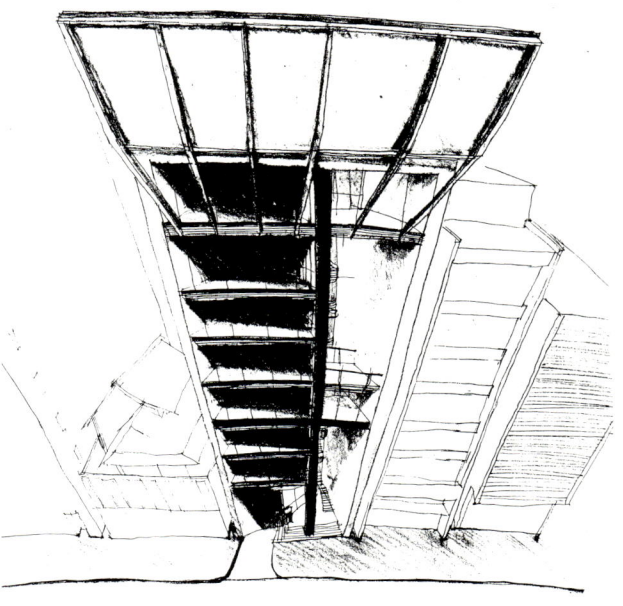

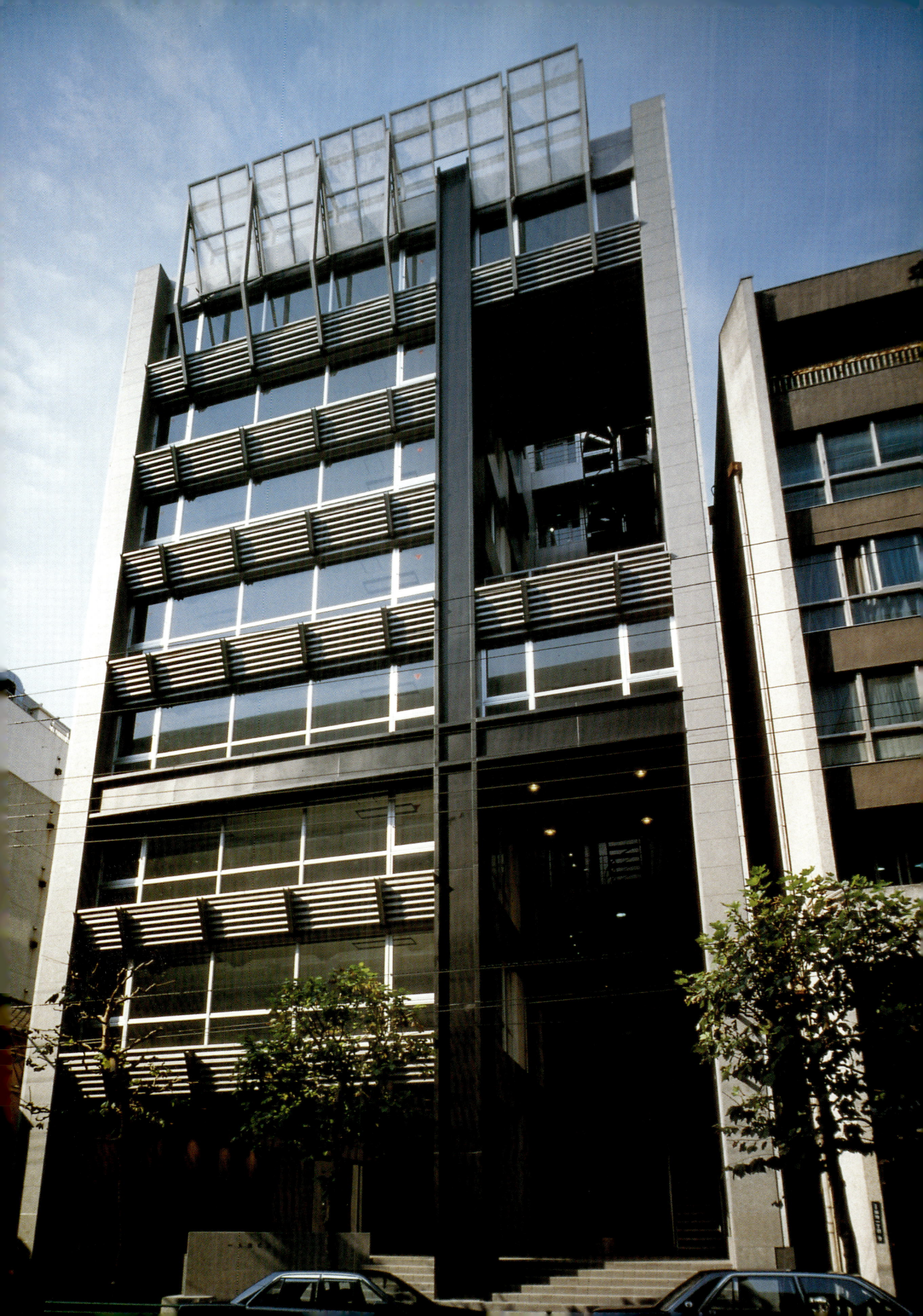

Plan of first floor and standard plan.
Opposite page, view of the interior space used as offices.

Key 1 (left)
1. Entrance porch
2. Entrance Hall
3. Elevator Hall
4. Janitor's Room
5. Office
6. Slope

Key 2 (right)
1. Meeting Room
2. Office
3. Meeting Room

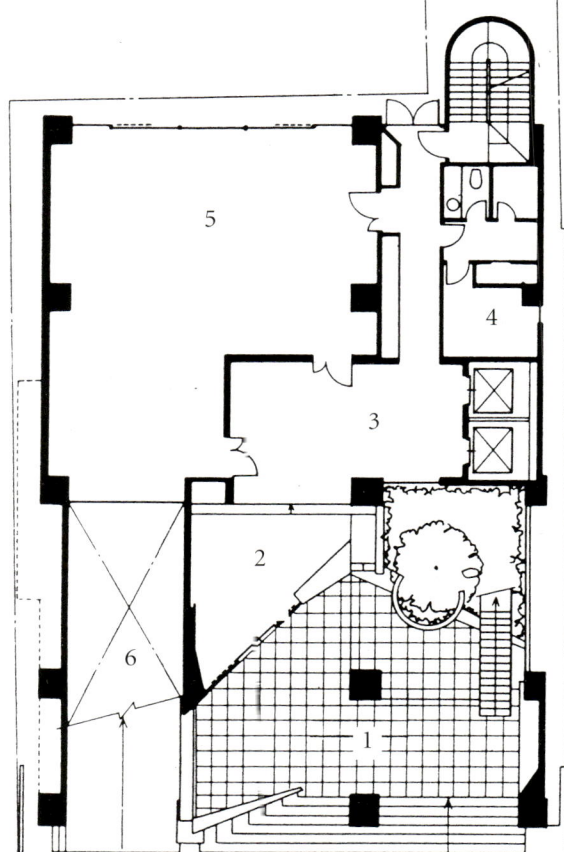
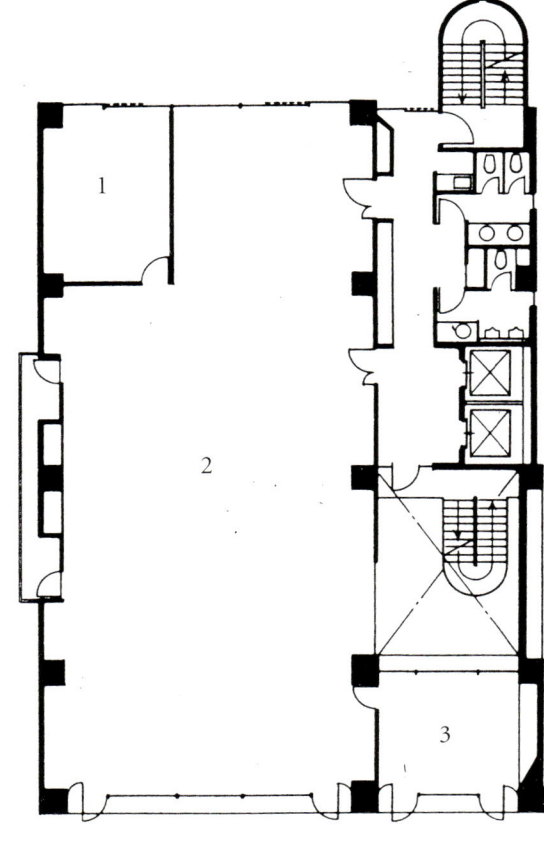

Axonometry, and detail of the open well.

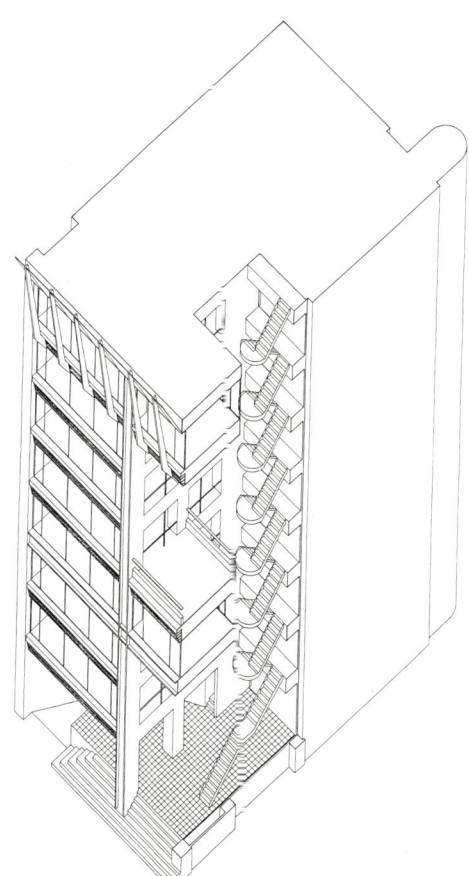
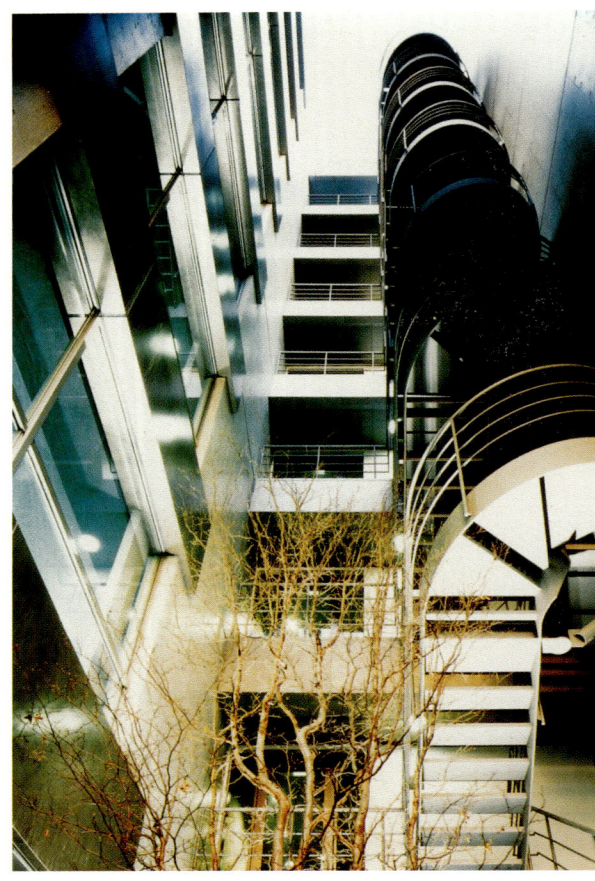

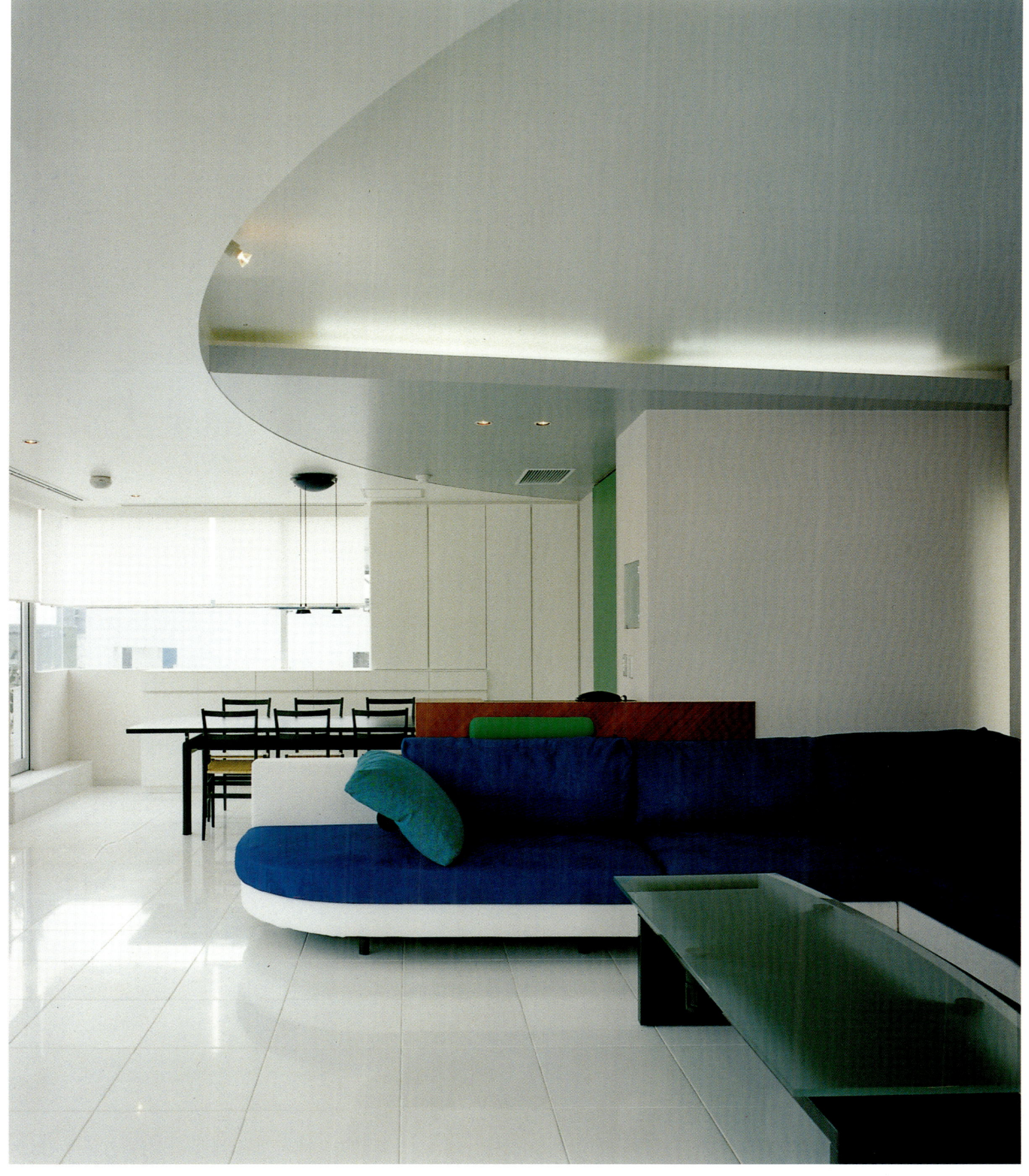

Kasama Nichido Museum of Art

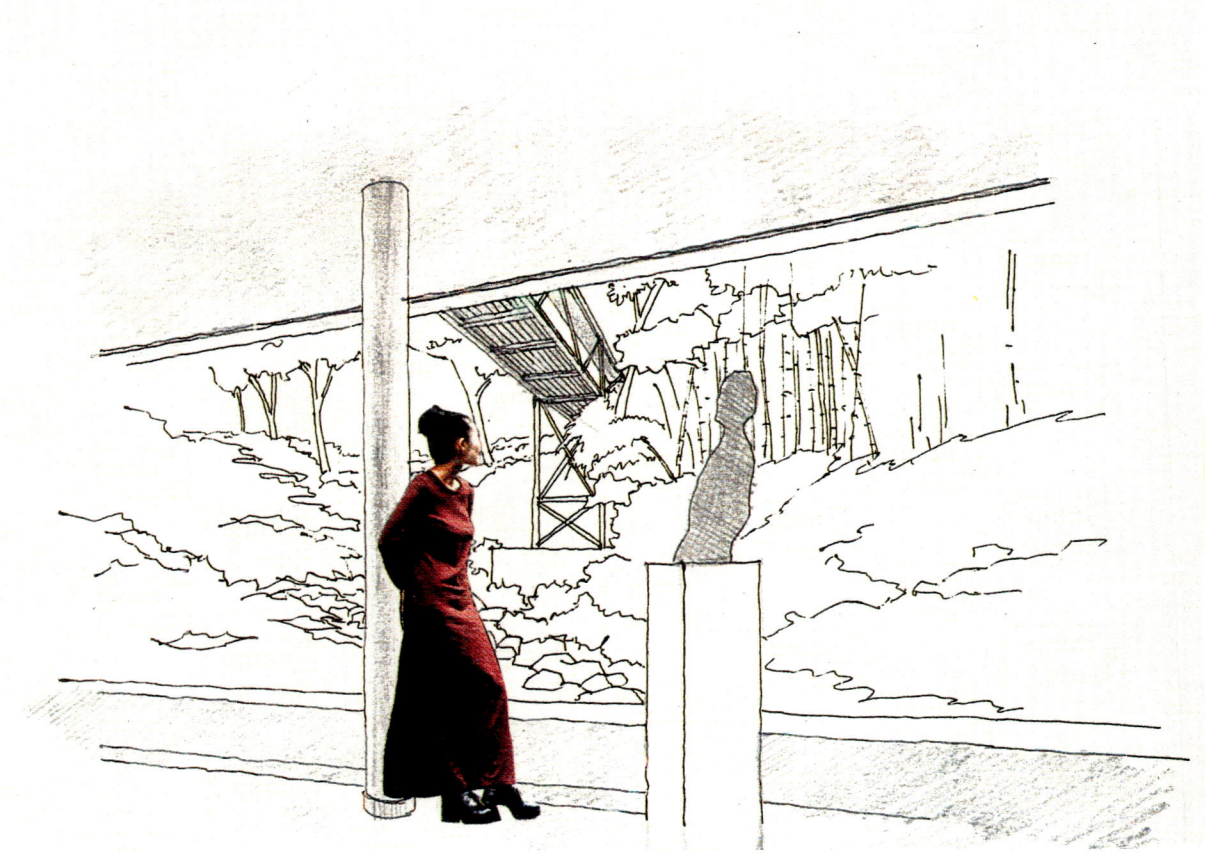

Kasama Nichido Museum of Art was opened in 1972, and the West Wing was opened in 1985. The new museum is the East Wing, and was planned as an addition to the existing facility, to complement exhibition and storage space.

About the design, my first thought was to utilise the conical topography of the foot of Mt.Shiroyama, with its trees and bamboo groves, to connect the new wing cleverly with the existing art museum, to create an artistic space by a link between nature and art. The space connected to the existing museum is distinctly separated from the entrance connected to the town by a huge mural on the side of the exhibition wing. The administration wing on the entrance side is deliberately scaled down, so as to brings its size closer to that of the town, while the other side is simple and grand, confronting the natural scenery. From the rooftop, there is a bridge that seems to interpenetrate the bamboo grove from the air, and connects to the sculpture garden of the existing museum.

In contrast to the organic elements of nature, the form of the building is extremely geometrical, composed of simple shapes, articulated one after another, in an attempt to position the museum as the 'figure' against the 'ground' of the lifestyle and history of the town.

The value of architecture can be found in its relationship to the cultural context. The creation of architecture that has a true significance to its existence requires the examination of the significance of that architectural structure through its continuous and discontinuous relationships to time and space.

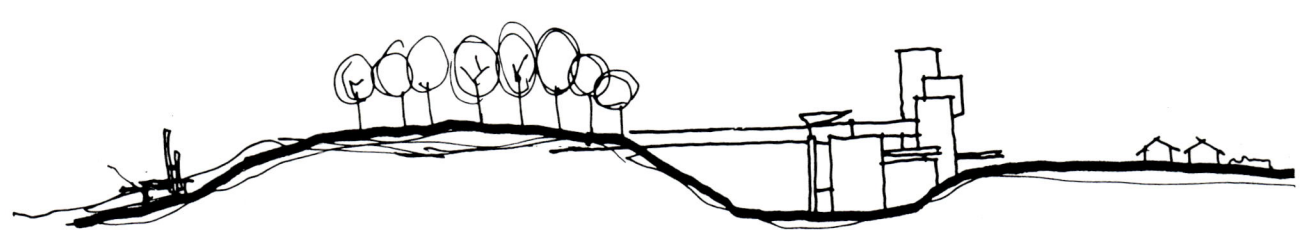

Plans of the first floor, second floor, and roof. Bottom of page, perspective sketch of the building. Following pages, view of the building from the entrance side.

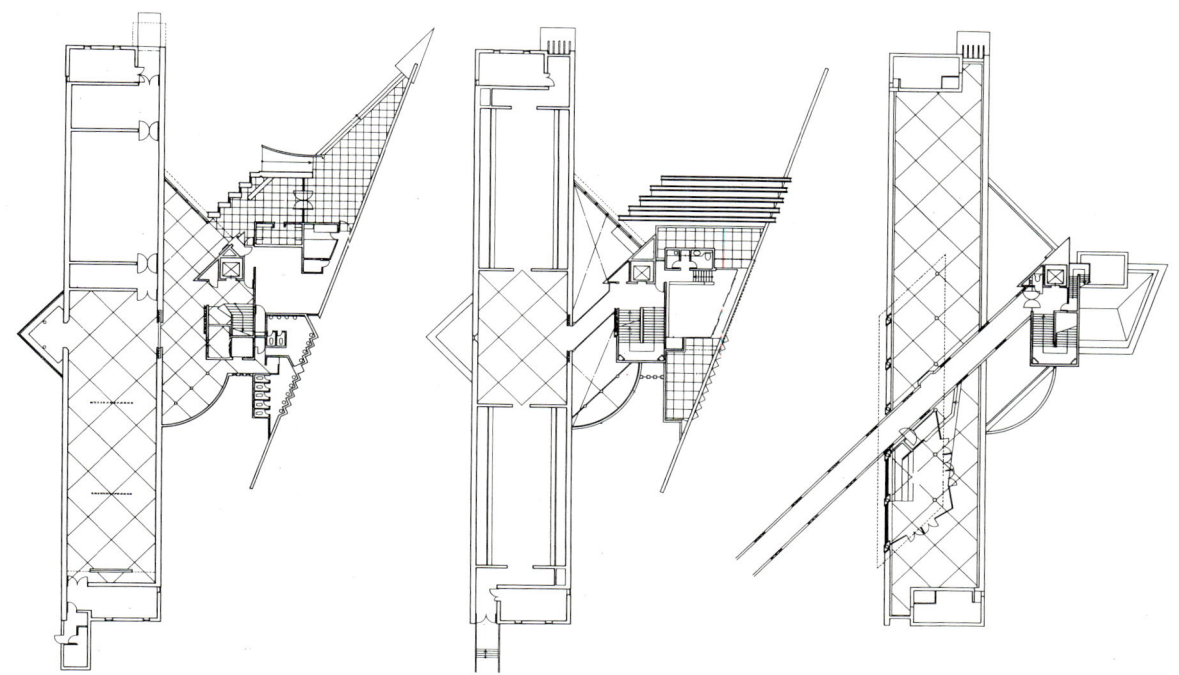

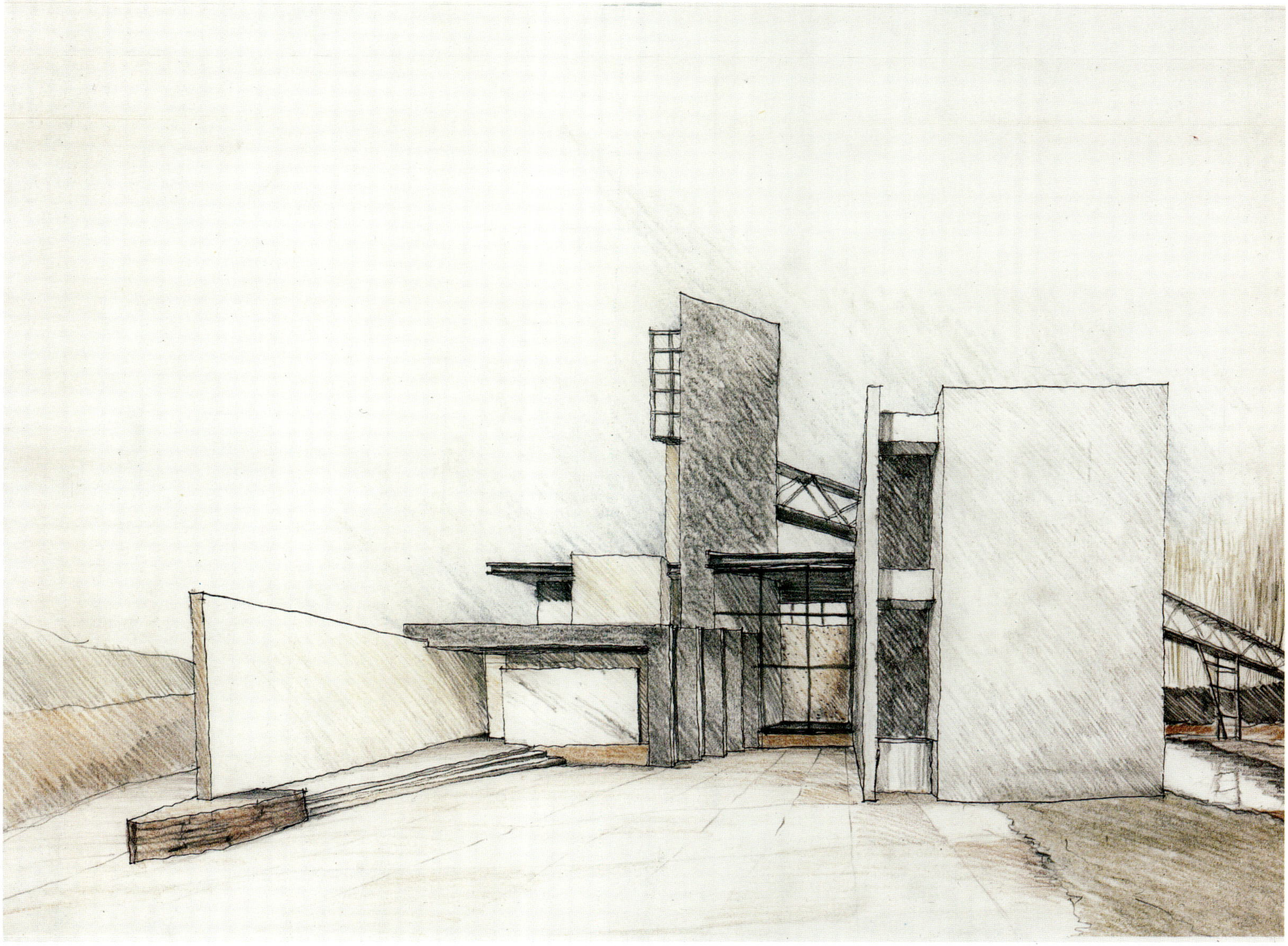

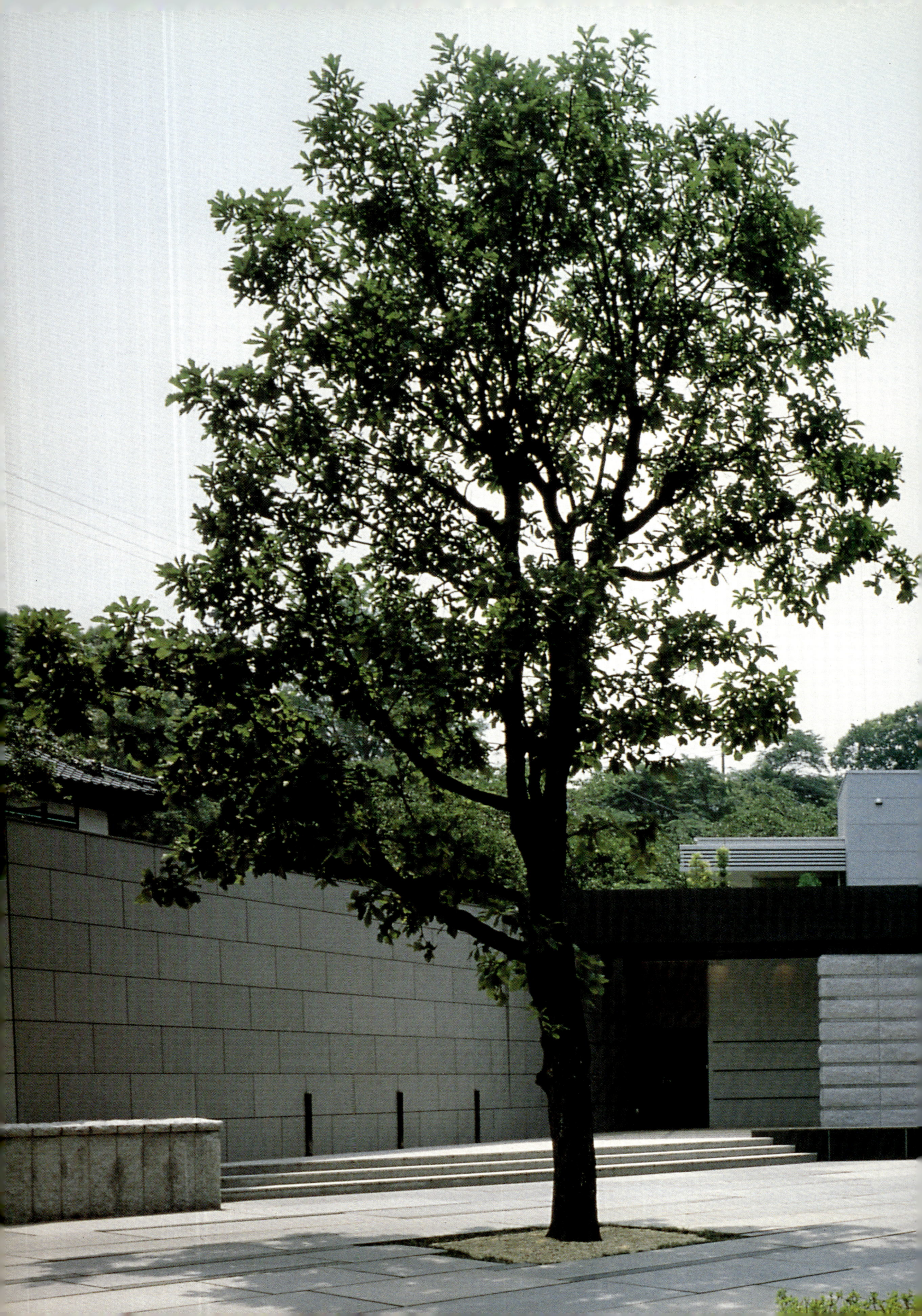

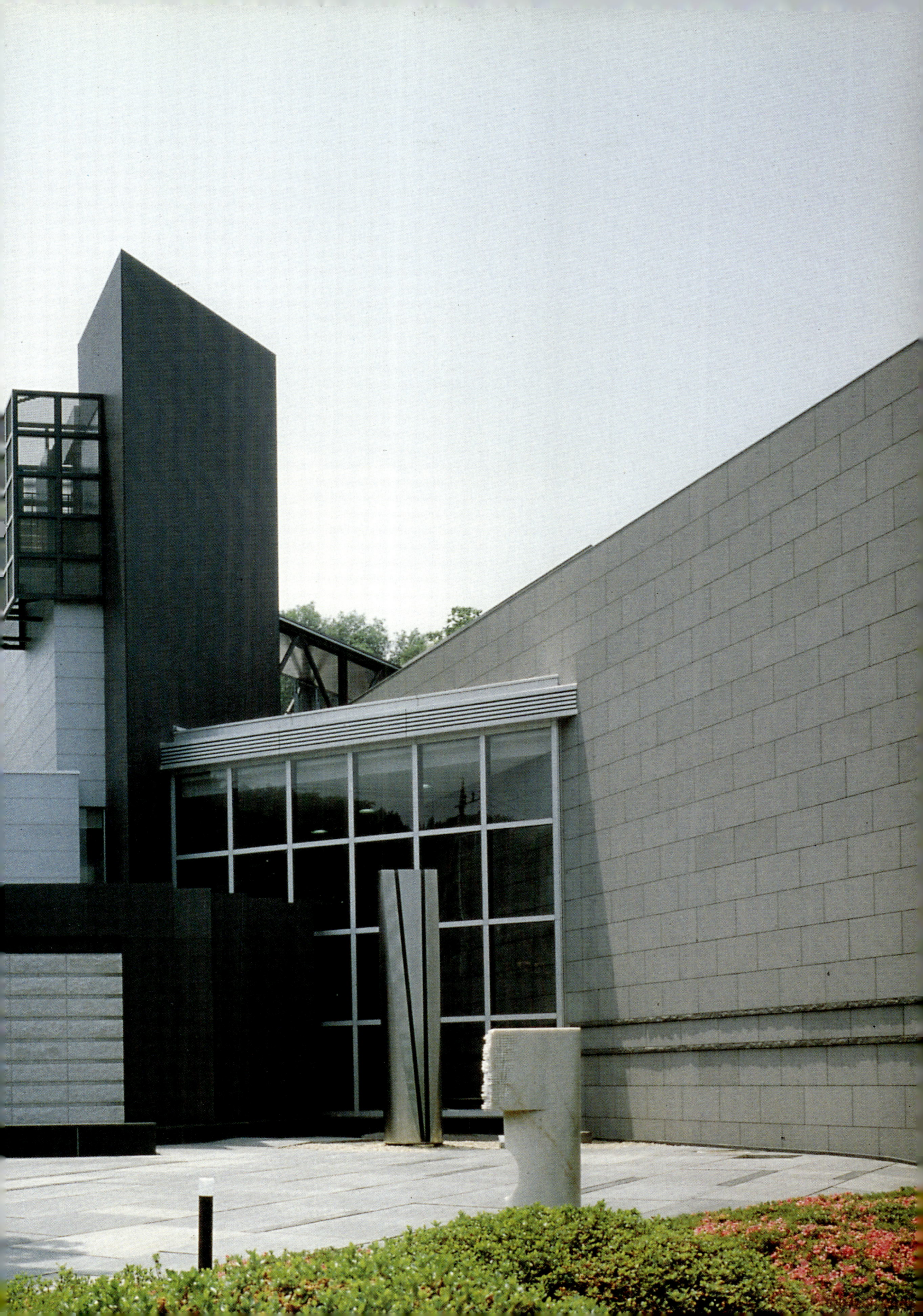

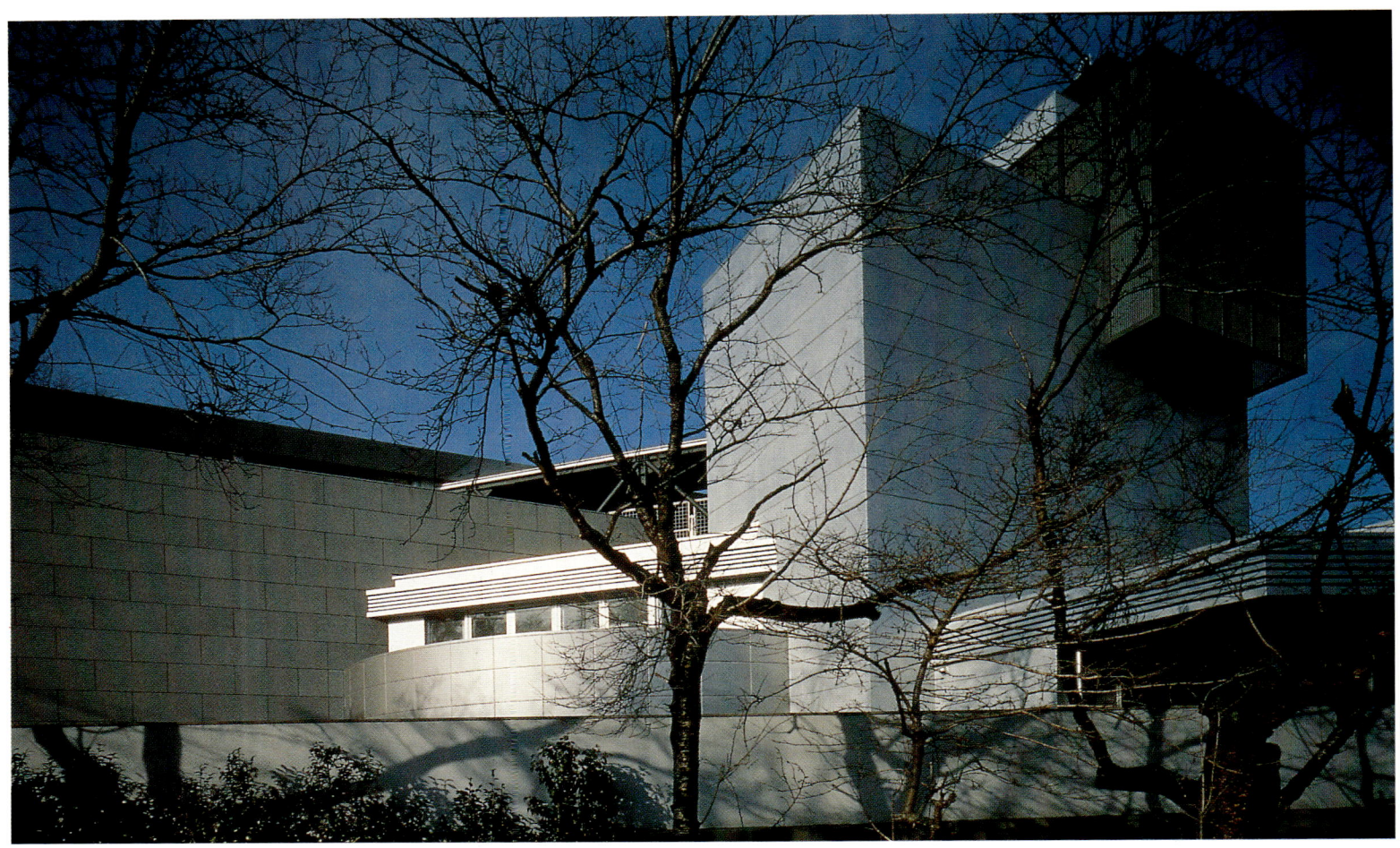

The building seen from the west side and, bottom of page, view of the bridge connecting the complex to the facing hill.

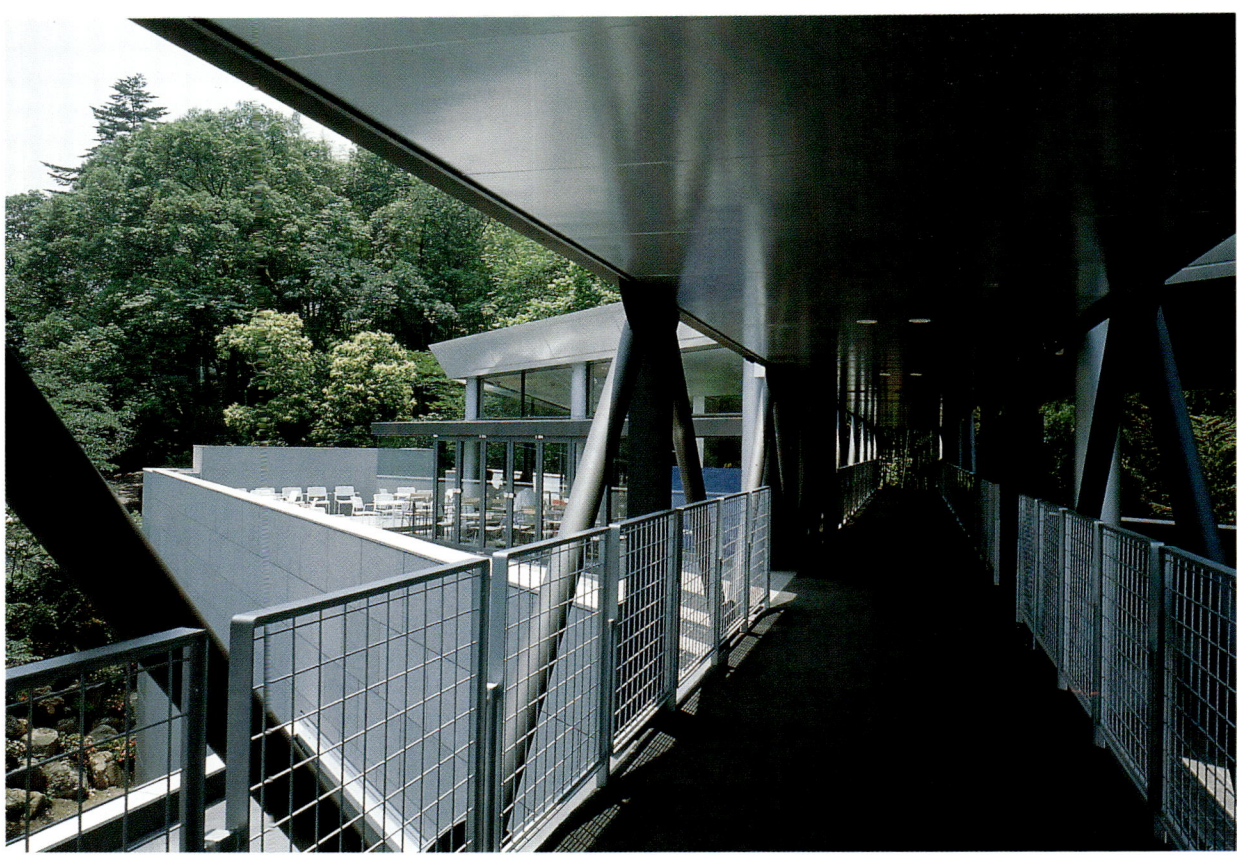

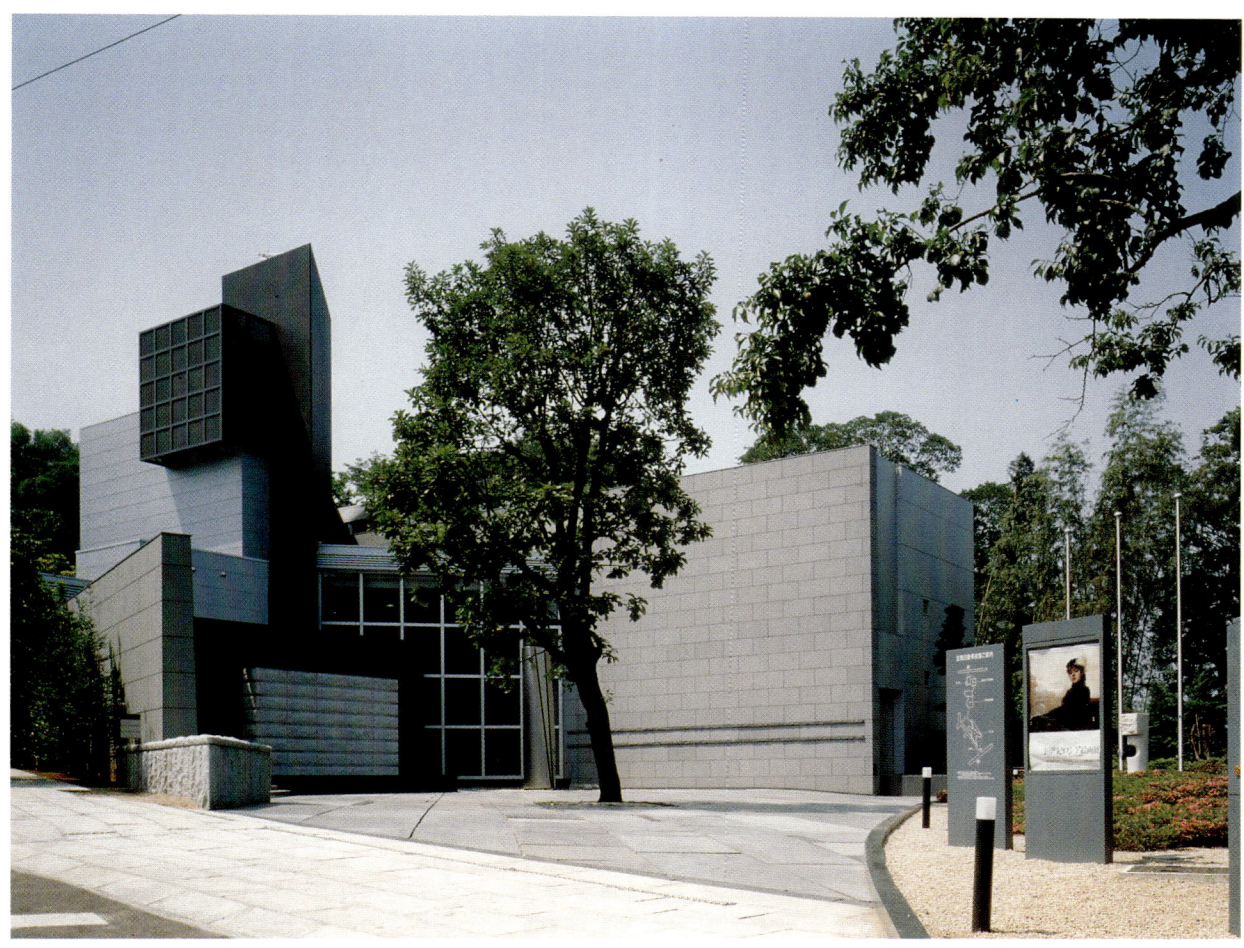

Detail of the terrace and, bottom of page, another view of the bridge. Following pages outside views of the complex.

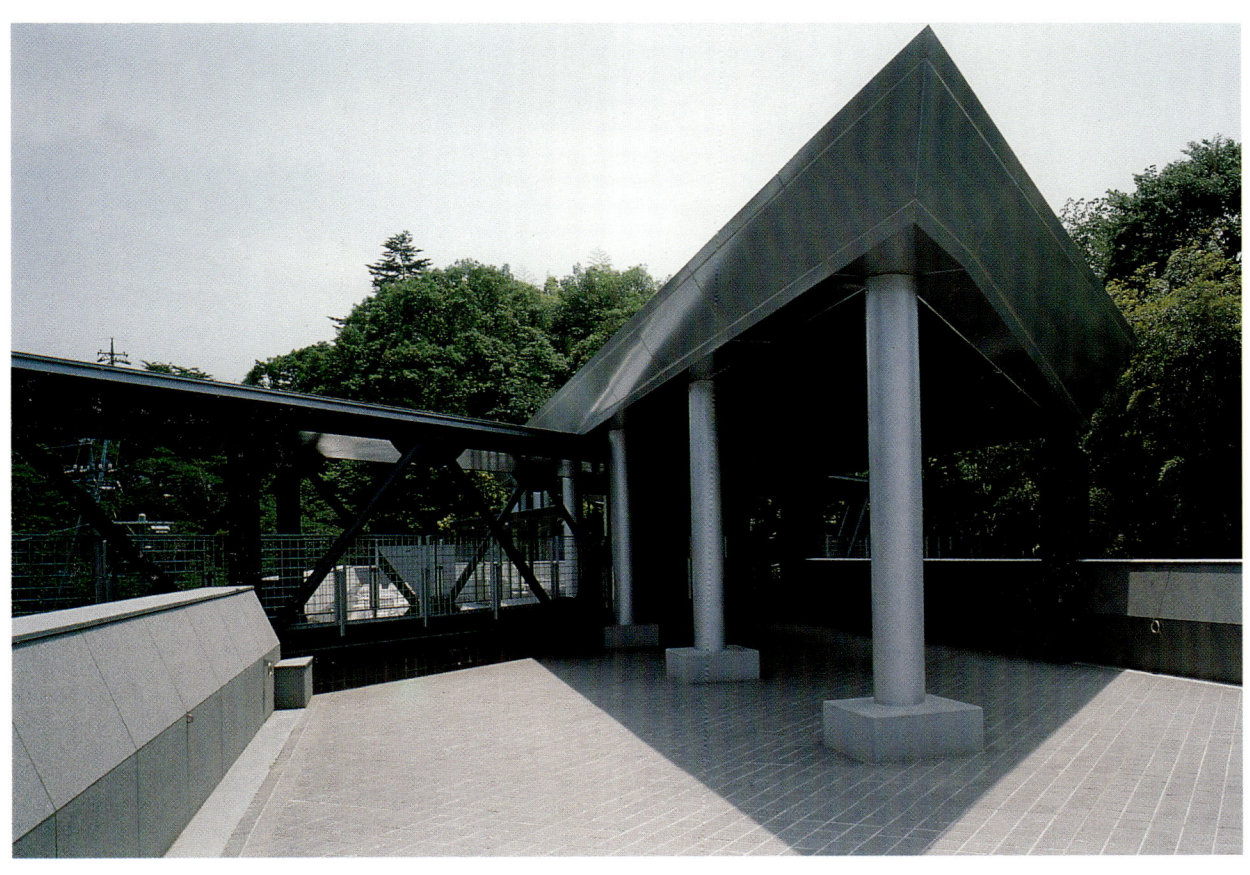

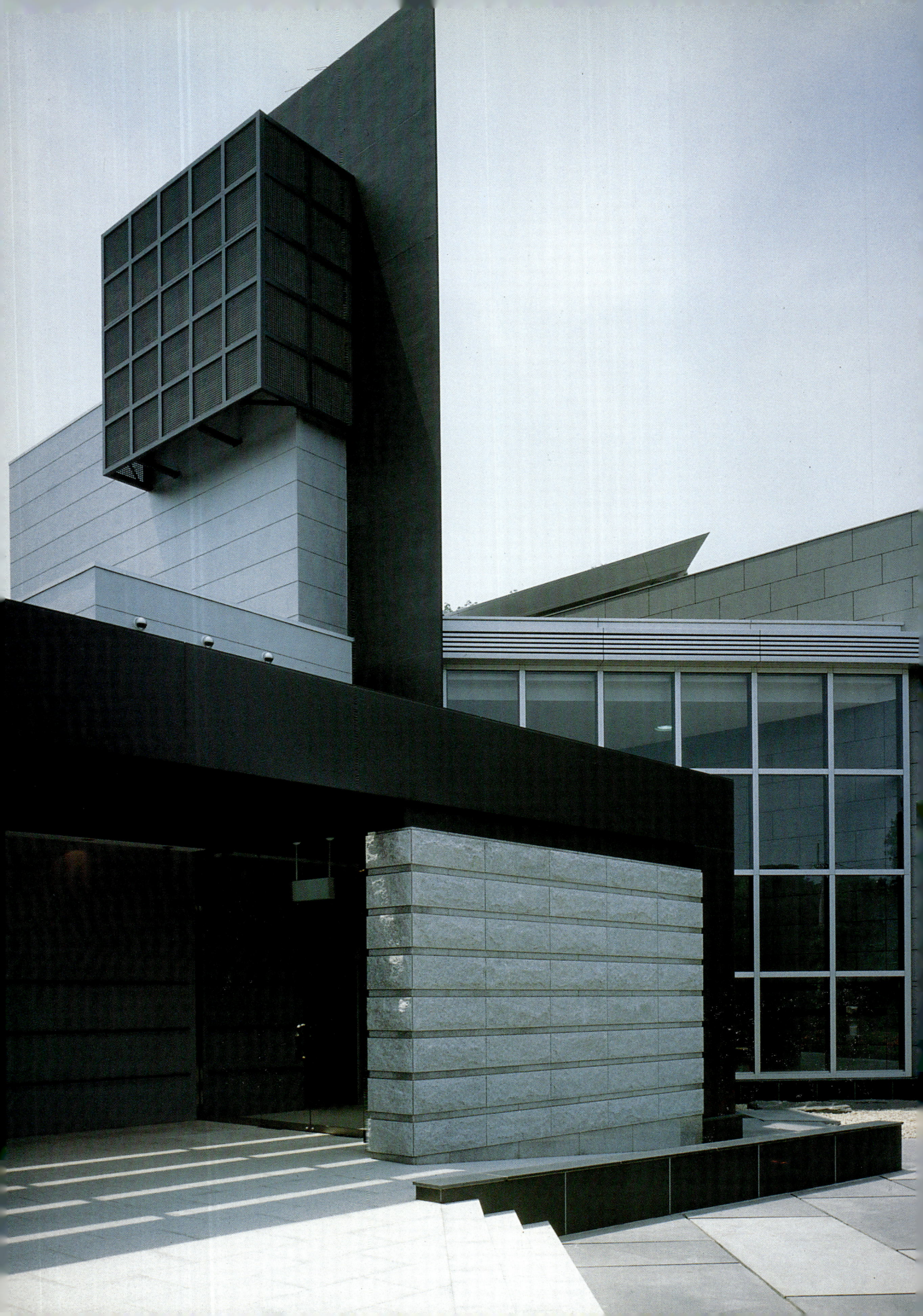

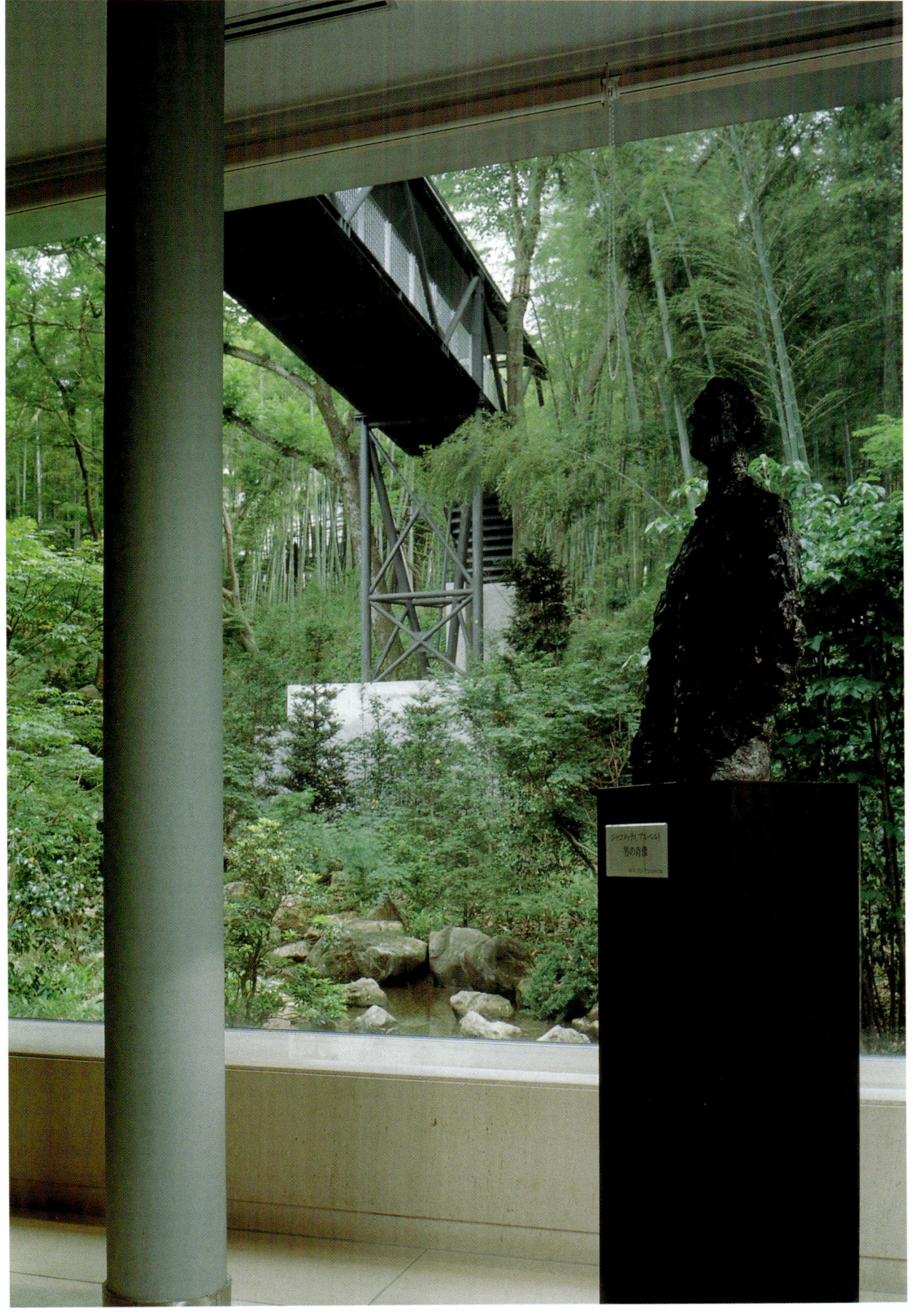

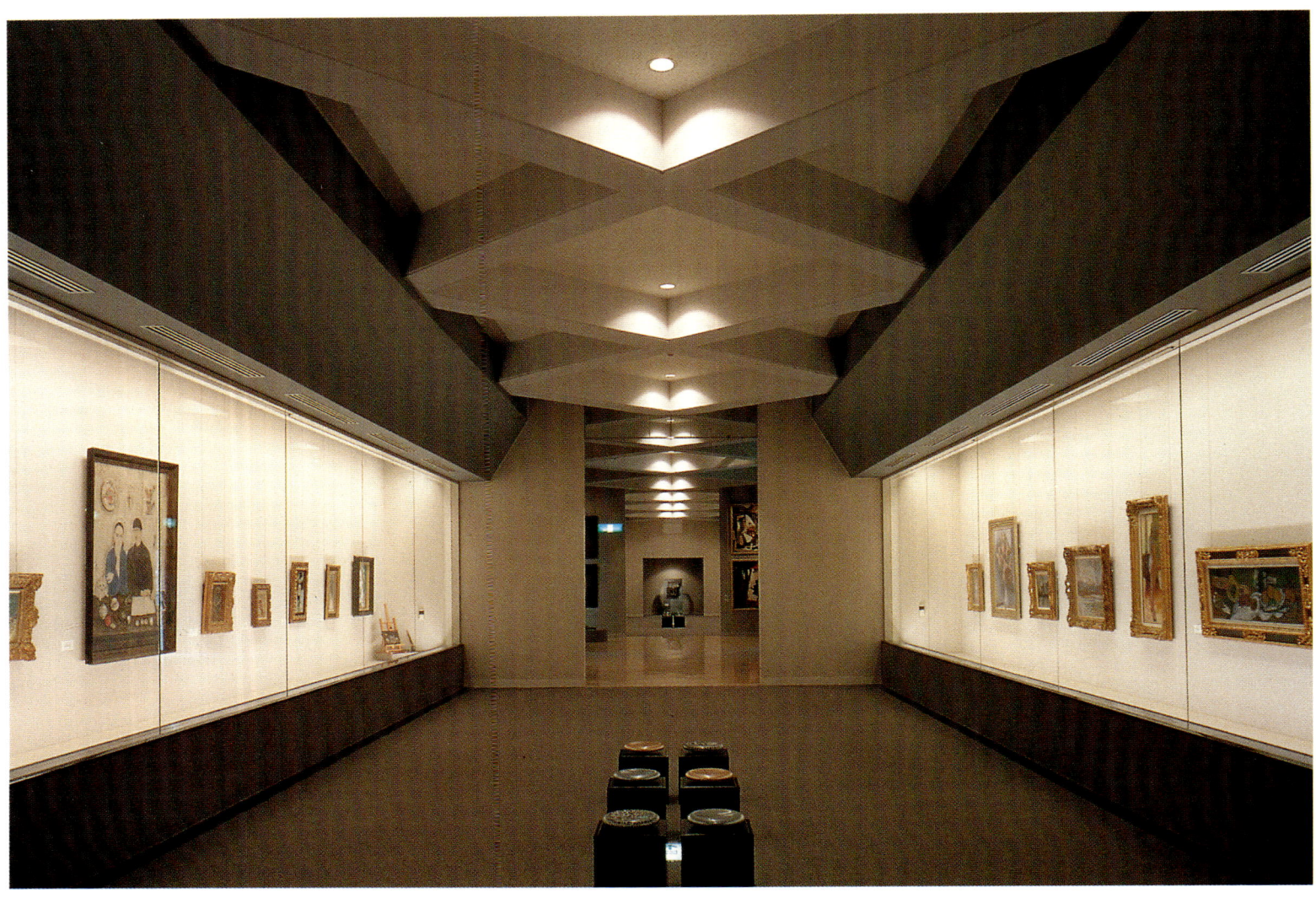

Two views of the exhibition spaces.

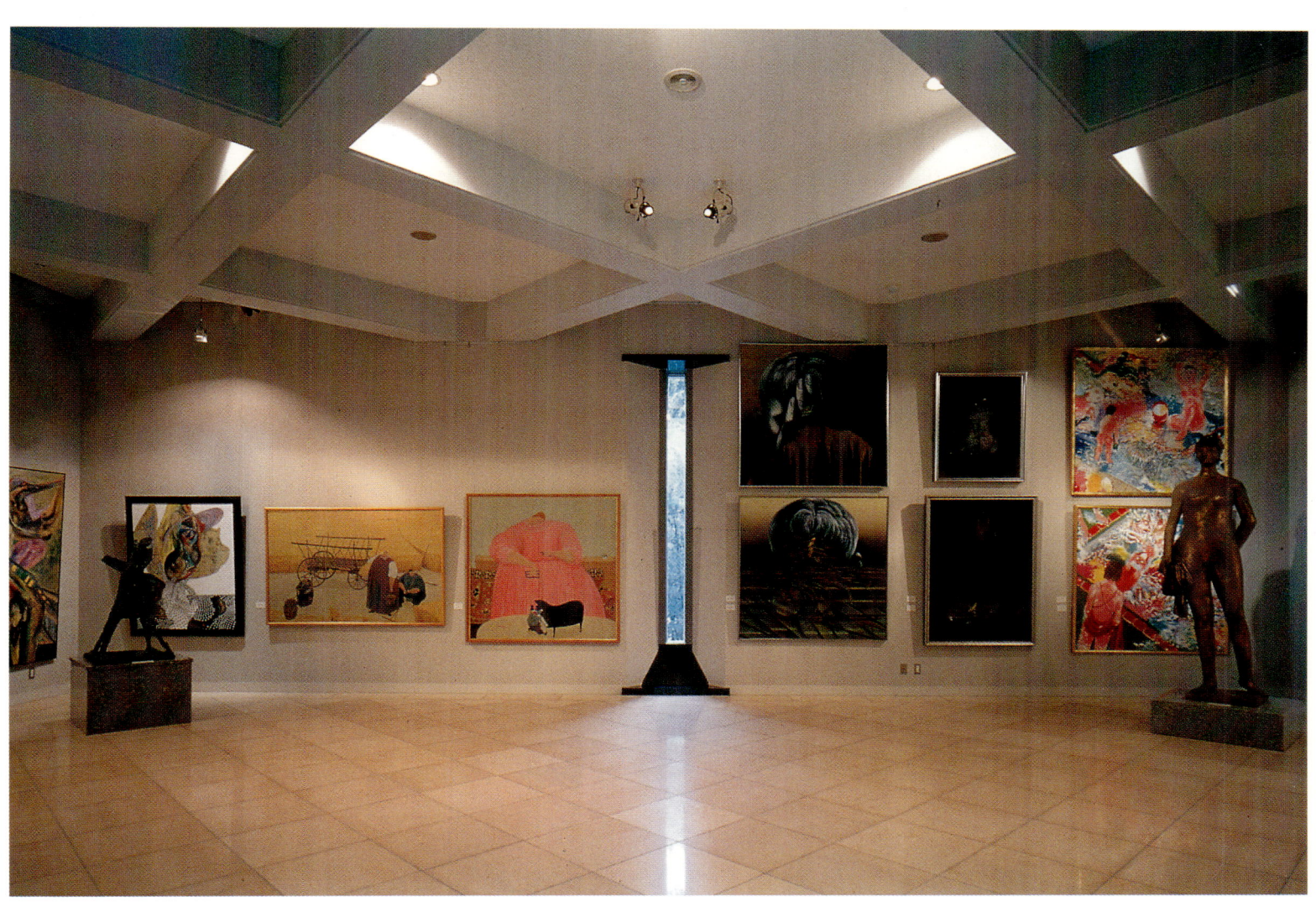

The building's architecture blends in smoothly with the surrounding landscape.

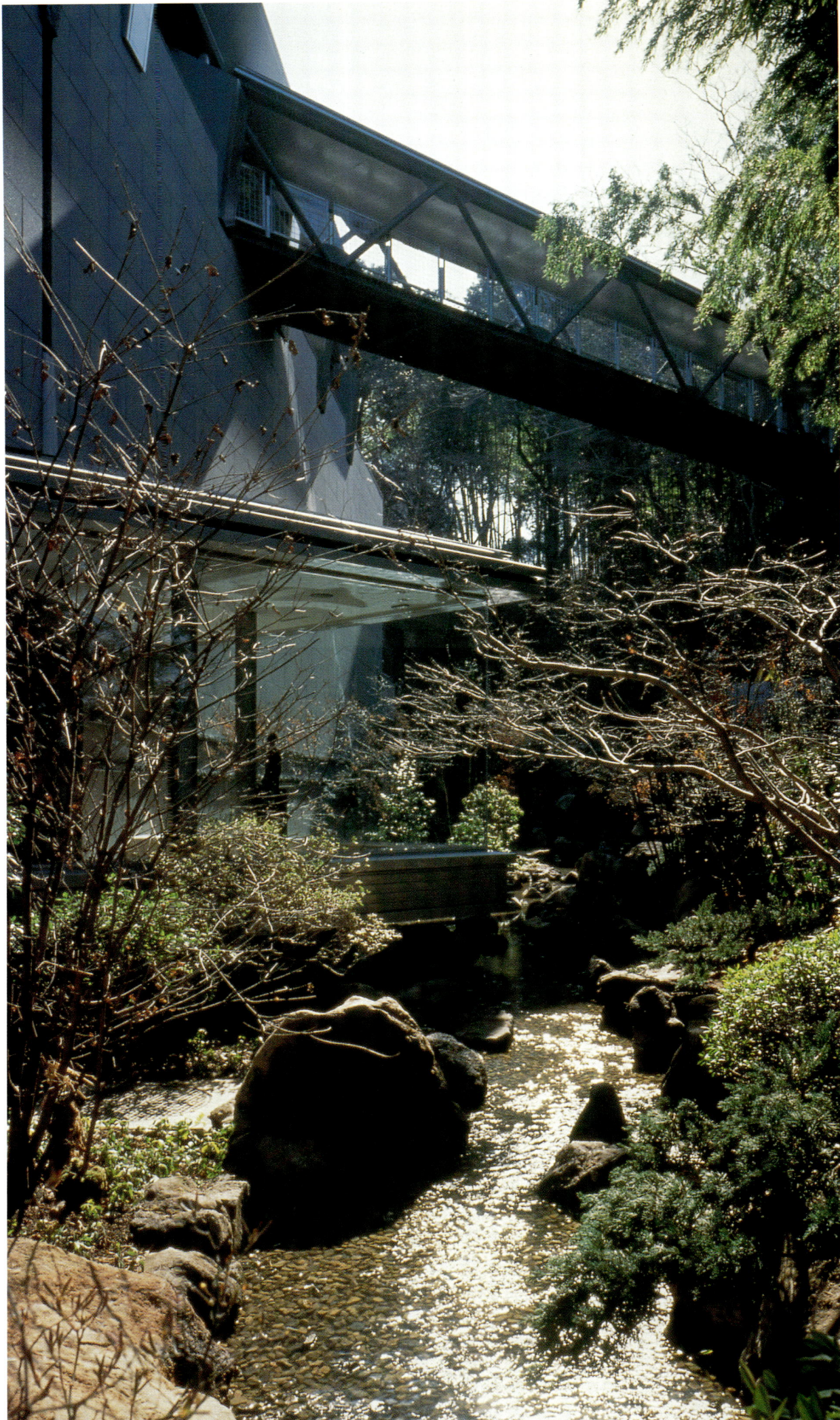

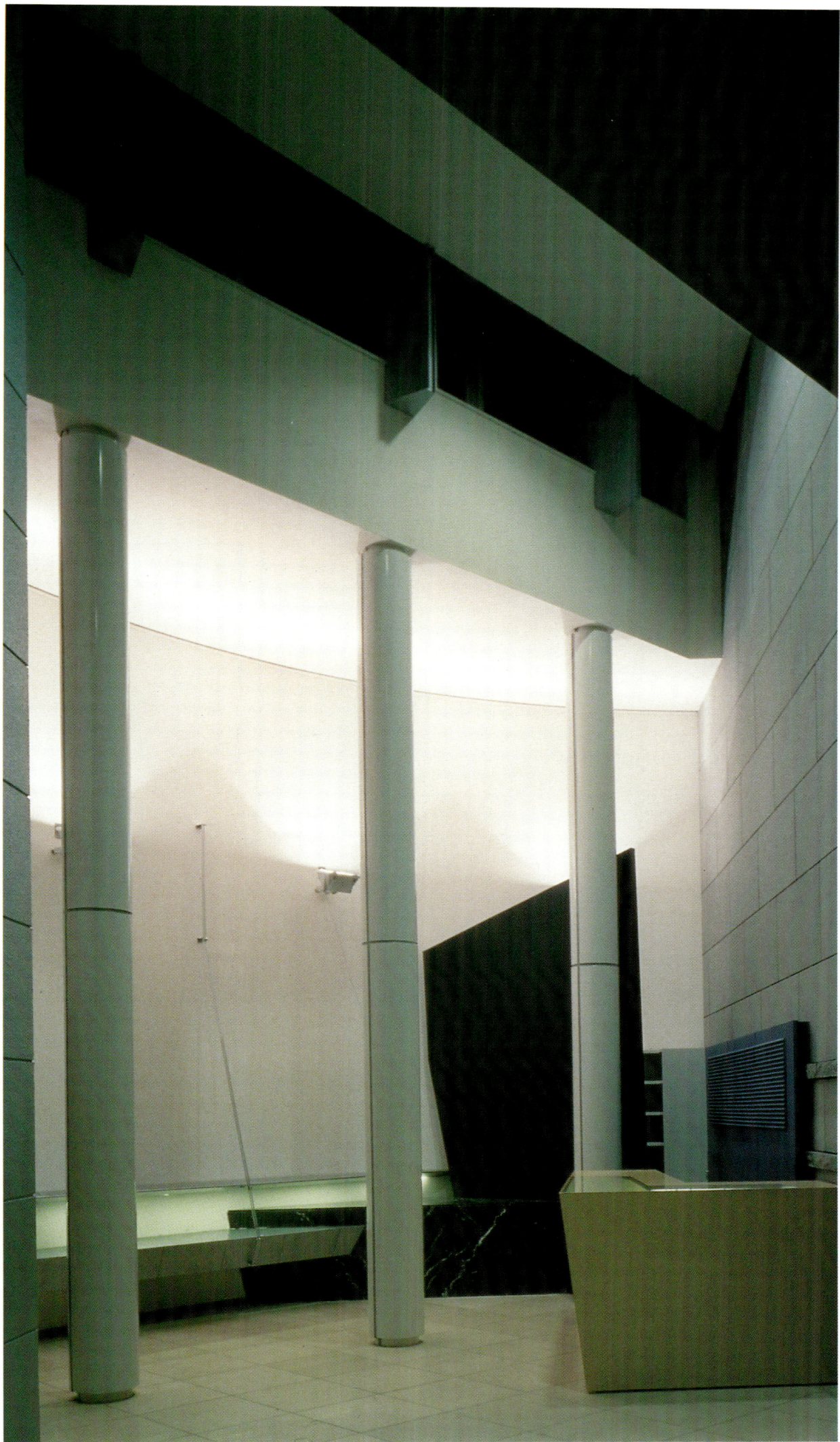

Detail of the interior space used as Museum Shop.

Australian Embassy, Tokyo

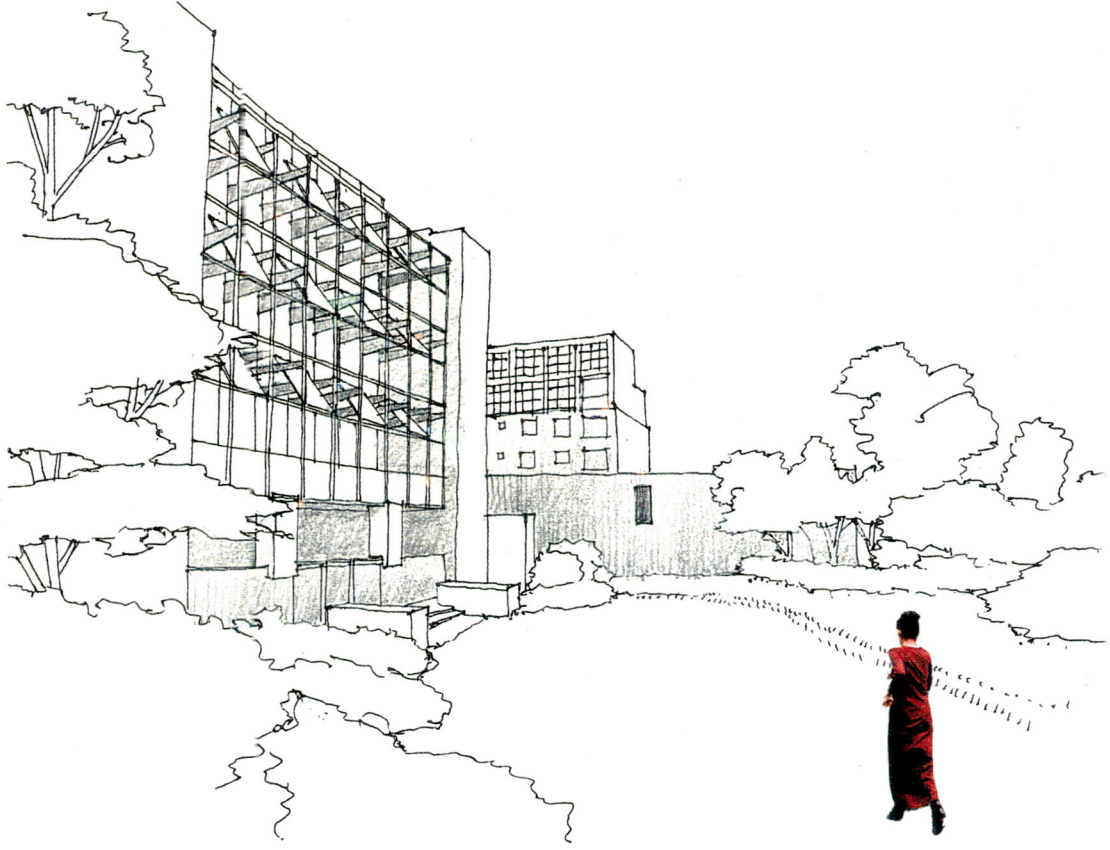

The area was once lined with palatial Daimyos' residences, and even now maintains an atmosphere of solitude and lush greenery, and is home to the embassy and commercial and government guest residences. The chancellery, ambassador's official residence, staff quarters and recreation facilities are combined around a central garden.

Along the axis that runs from the entrance to the courtyard and through the chancellery to the garden, functions are symmetrically arranged. The ambassador's residence is slightly off-axis, interpenetrating at a diagonal. The elevation is a three-layered structure, with the base in a black exposed concrete finish, the body in metal panels, and the top in a white square form. Conforming to typical Western construction methods, the grid system fuses all of the elements together, and gives the embassy a feeling of oneness. However, the form itself is not traditional, but the grids and panels and frame create a modern look, expressing the image of a young and vigorous Australia.

The value of architecture can be found in its relationship to the cultural context. The creation of architecture that has a true significance to its existence requires the examination of the significance of that architectural structure through its continuous and discontinuous relationships to time and space.

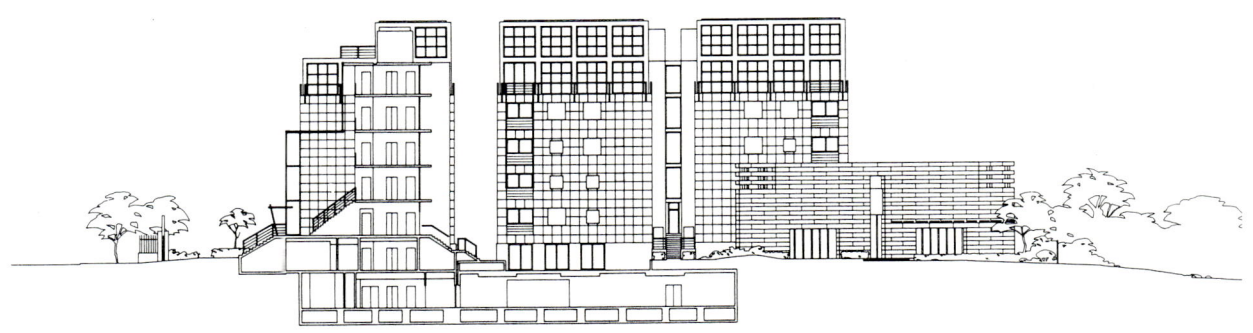

North-south section of the building through the residential block and garden to the ambassador's residence.

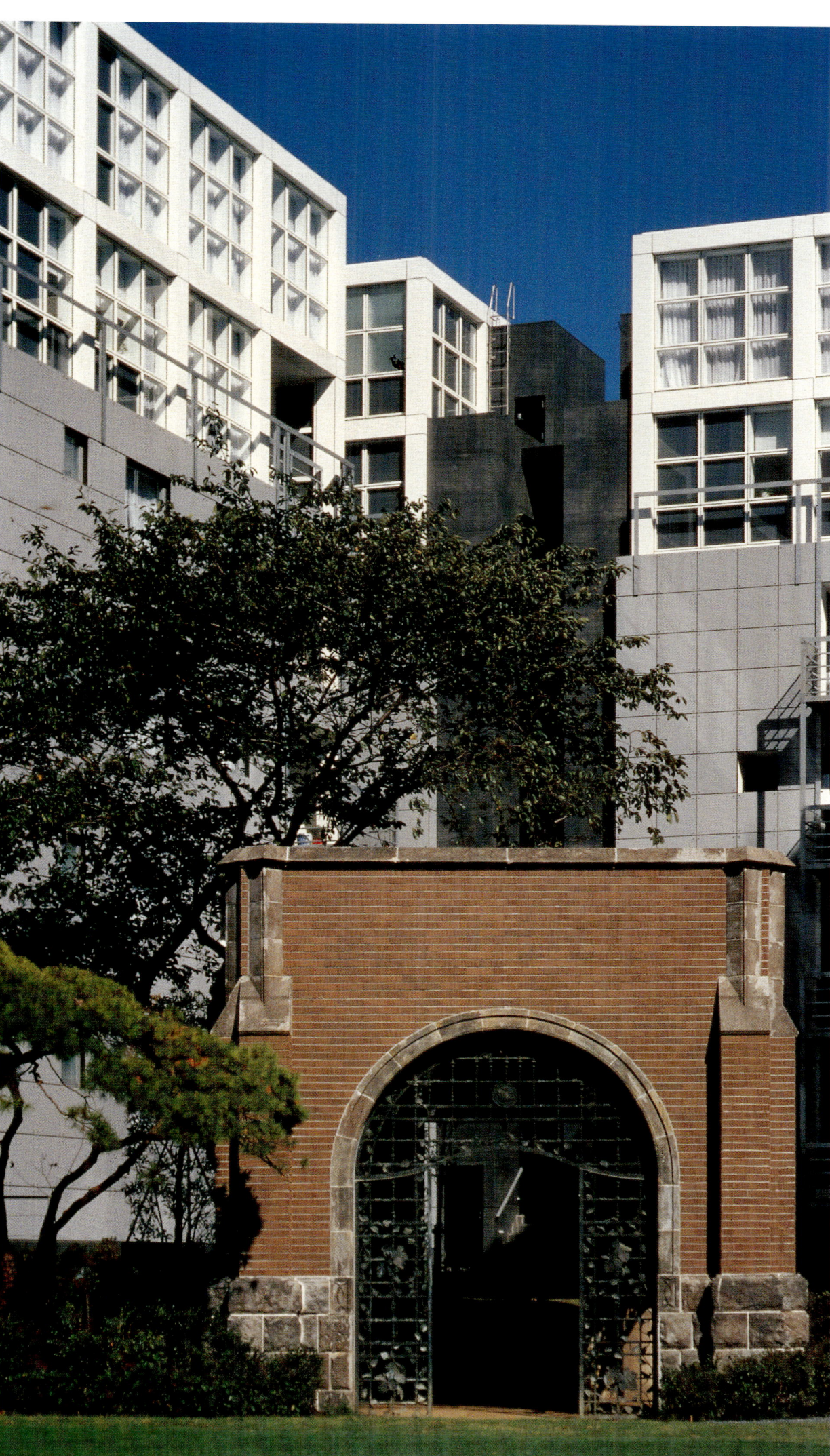

View of the former entrance.

Plan of chancery level 1, ambassador's residence level 1, residential block level 2, recreation block level 1. Opposite page, view of the complex's main facade and detail of the metal structures on the outside.

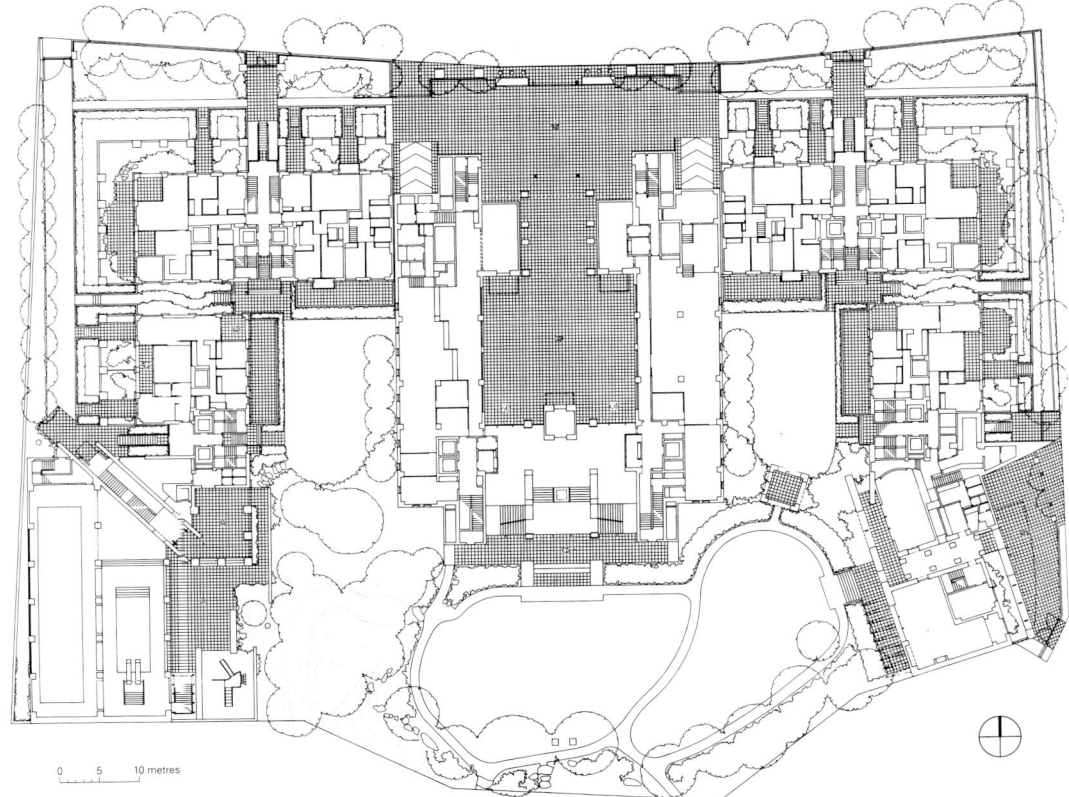

Plan of chancery level 2, ambassador's residence level 2, residential block level 3, recreation block level 2.

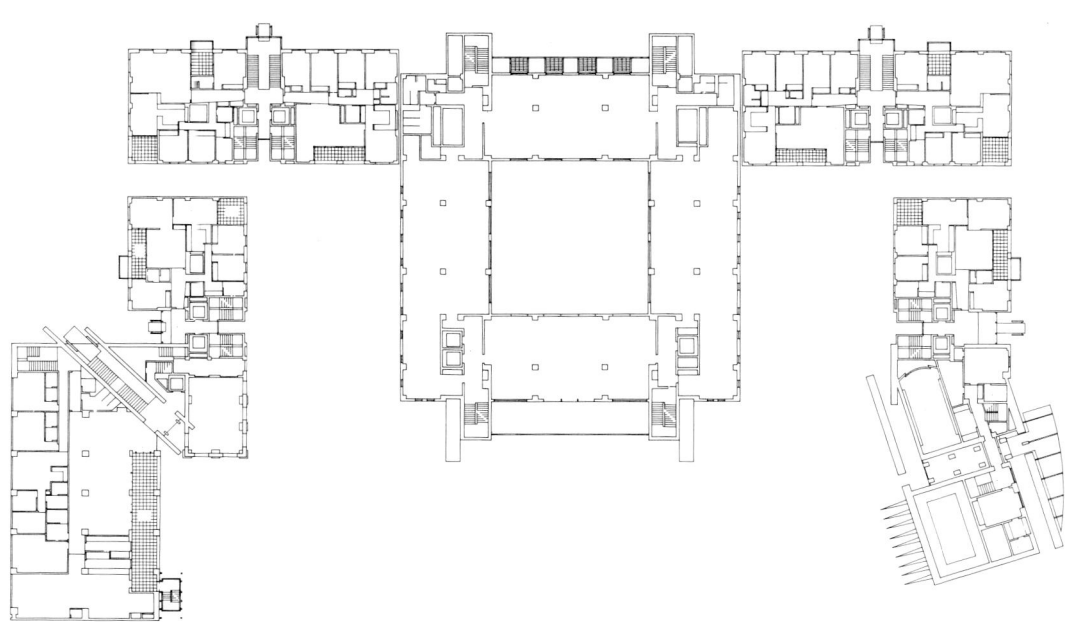

Plan of chancery level 3, ambassador's residence level 3, residential block level 4, recreation block level 3.

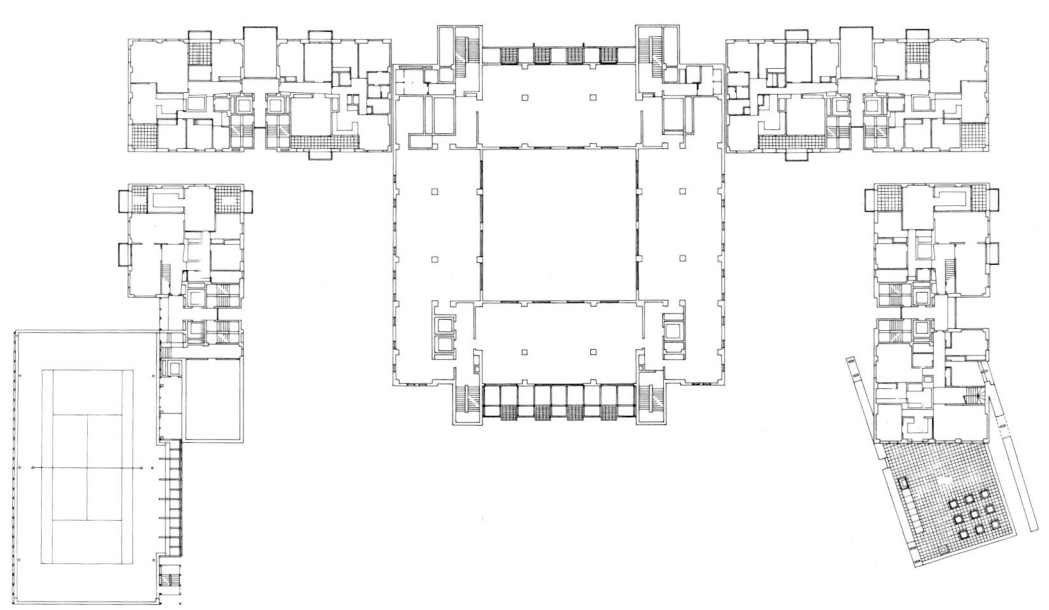

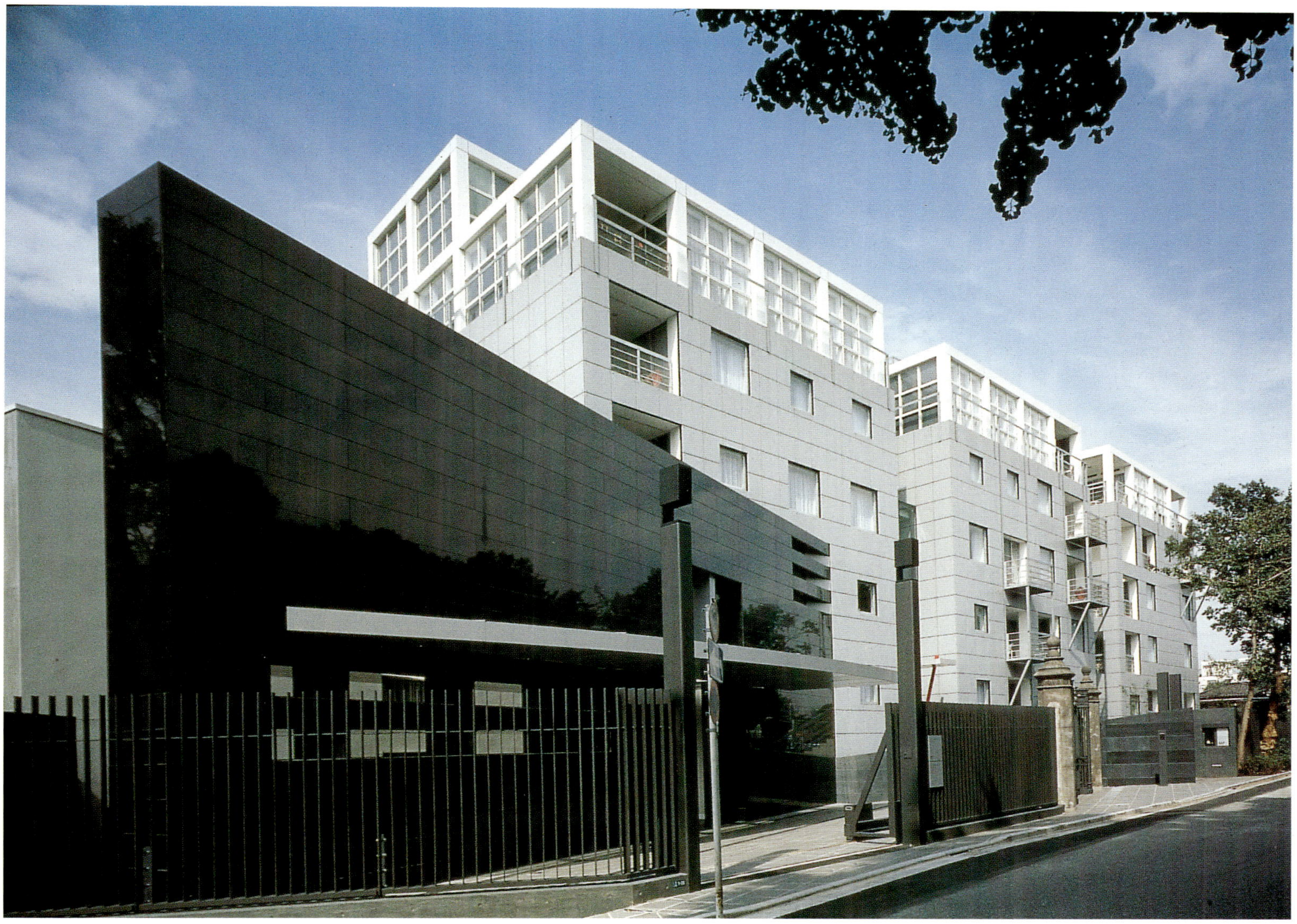

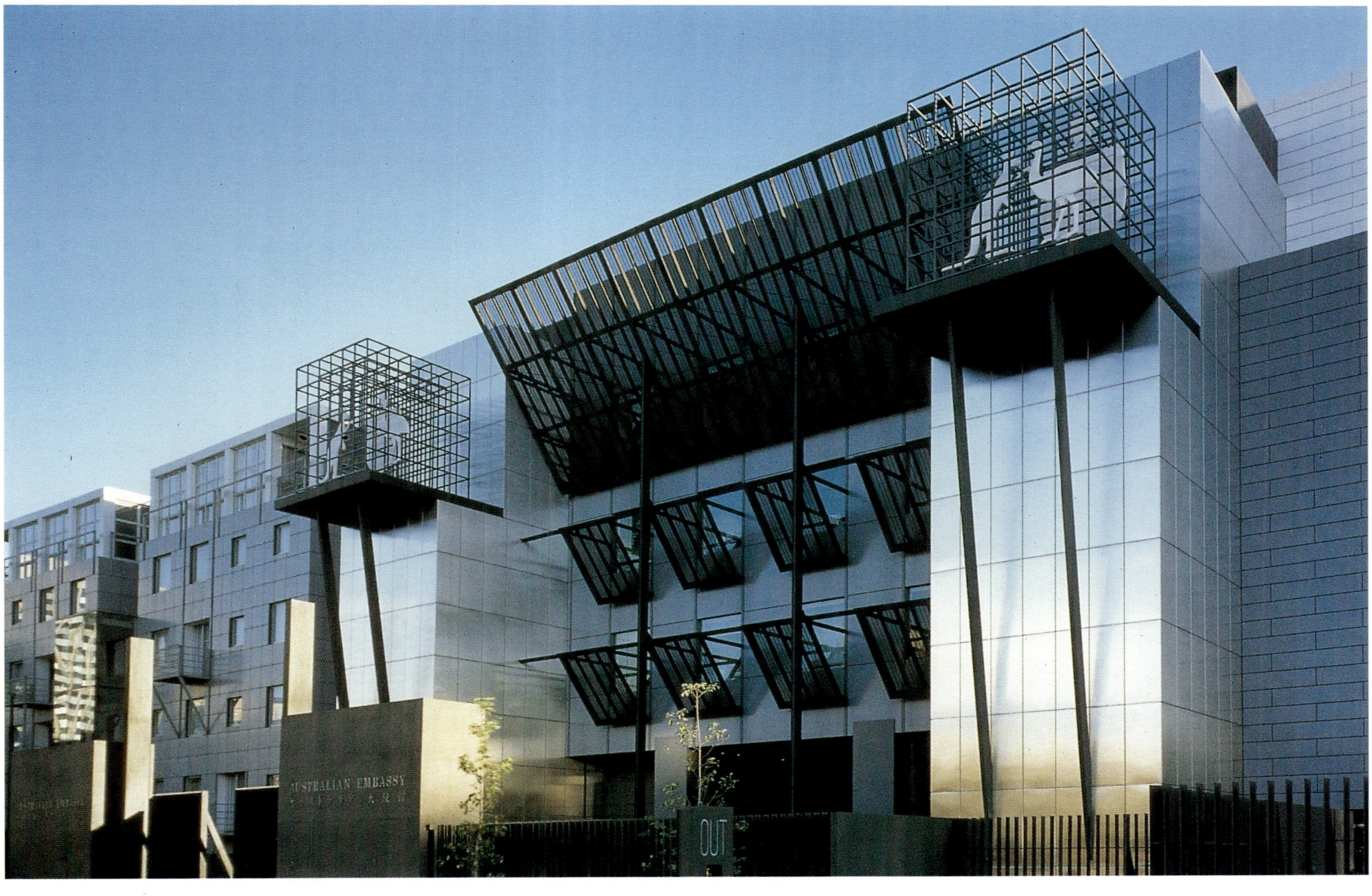

49

General views of the Embassy and, opposite page, detail of the system sheltering the facade from the sunlight. The system is made of a metal grid detached from the facade, which is also designed to link together the various building elements.

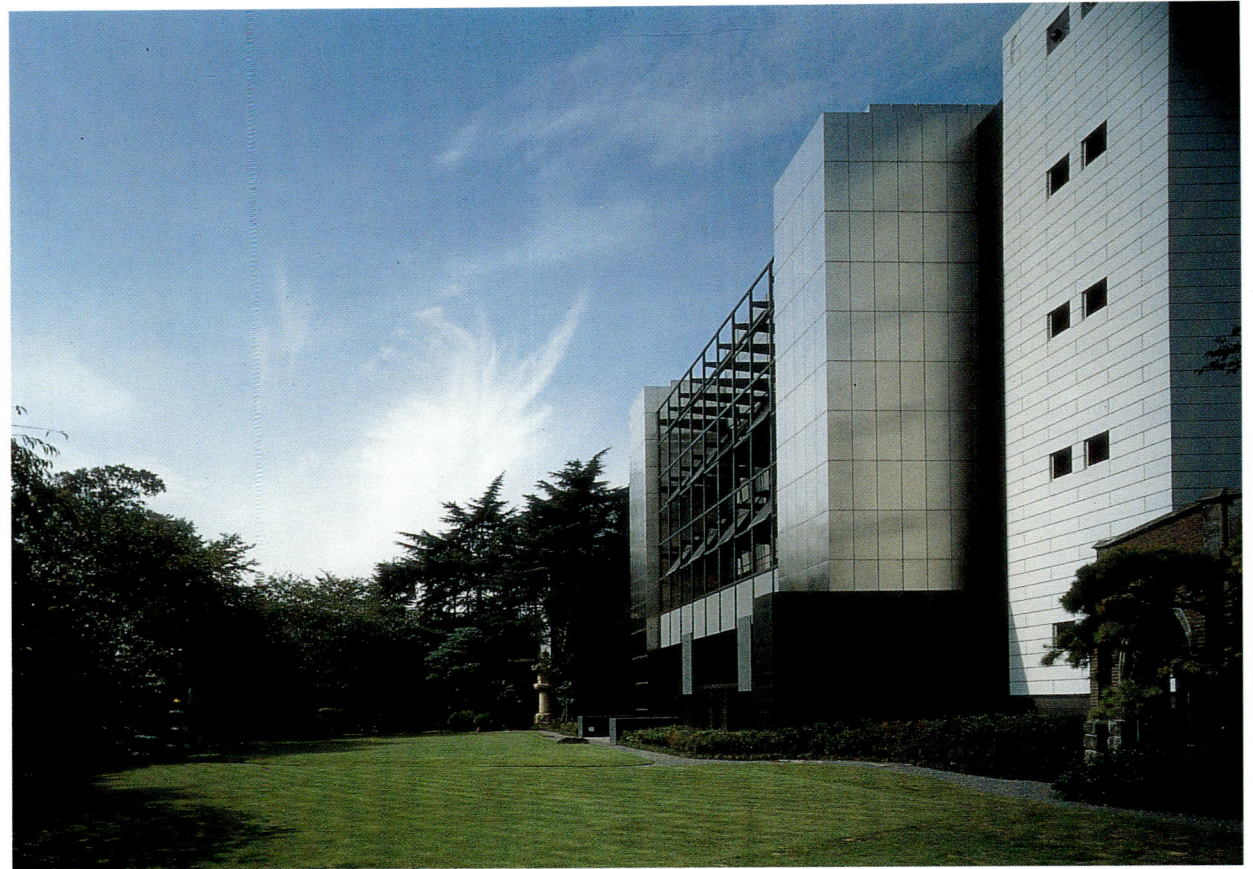

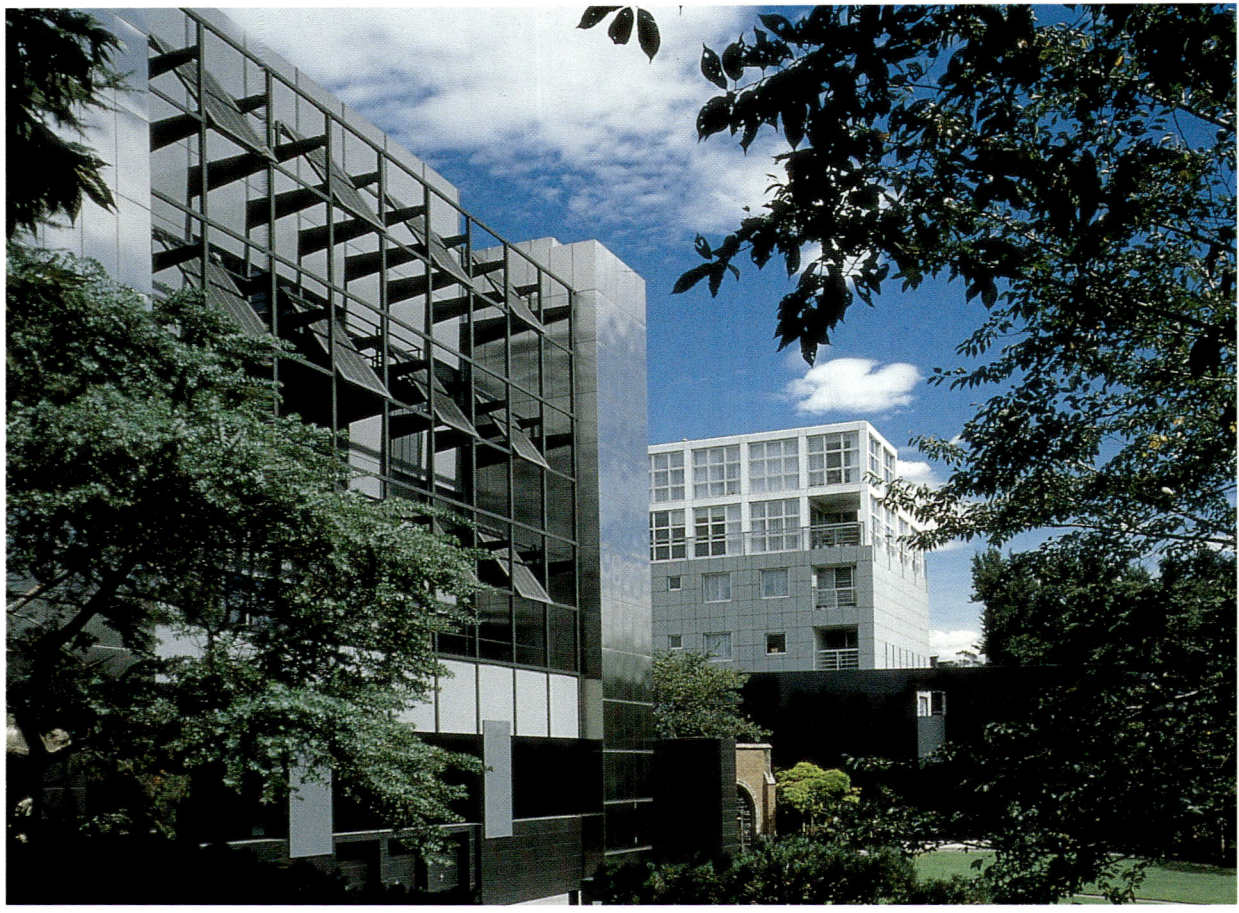

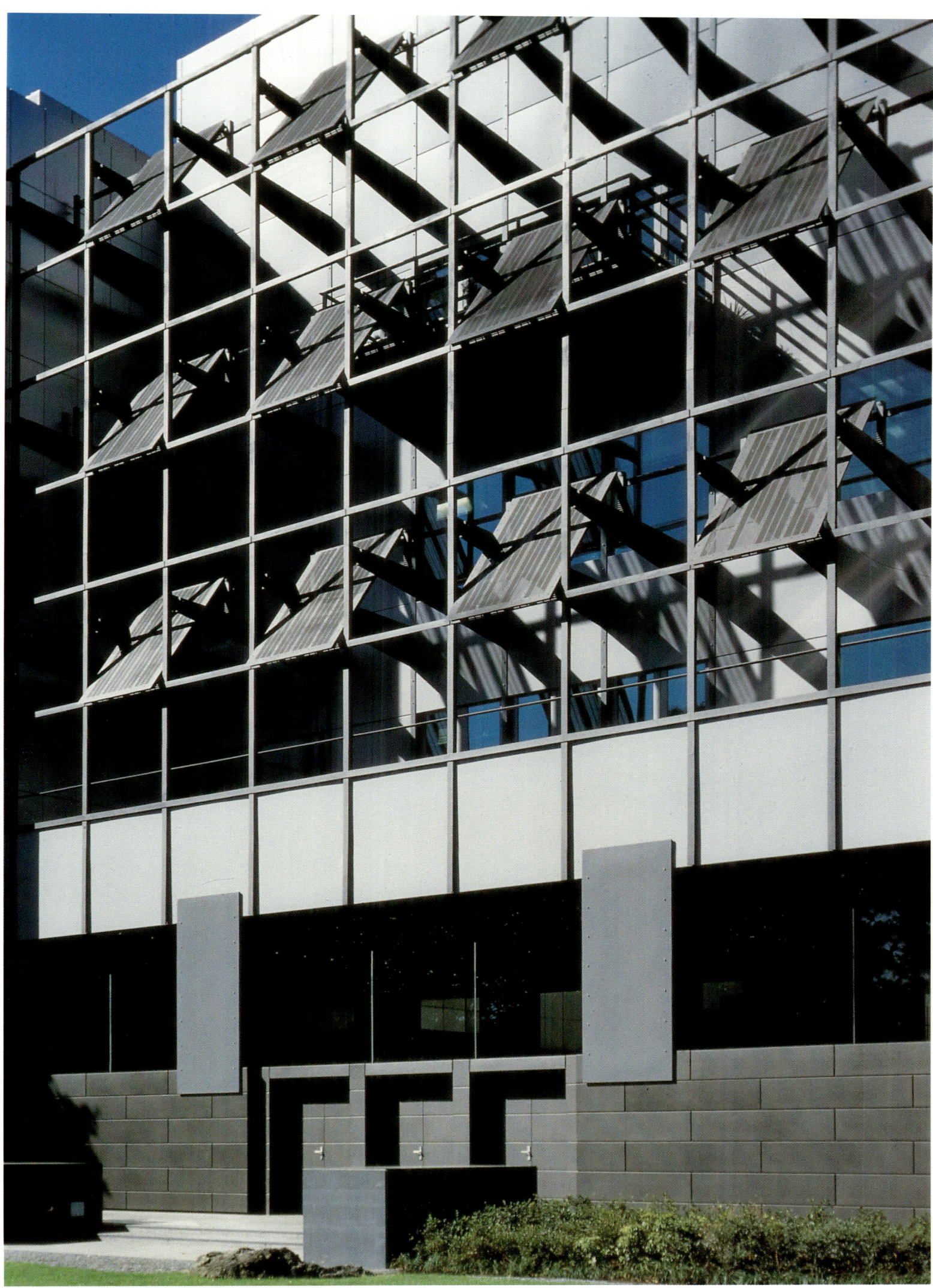

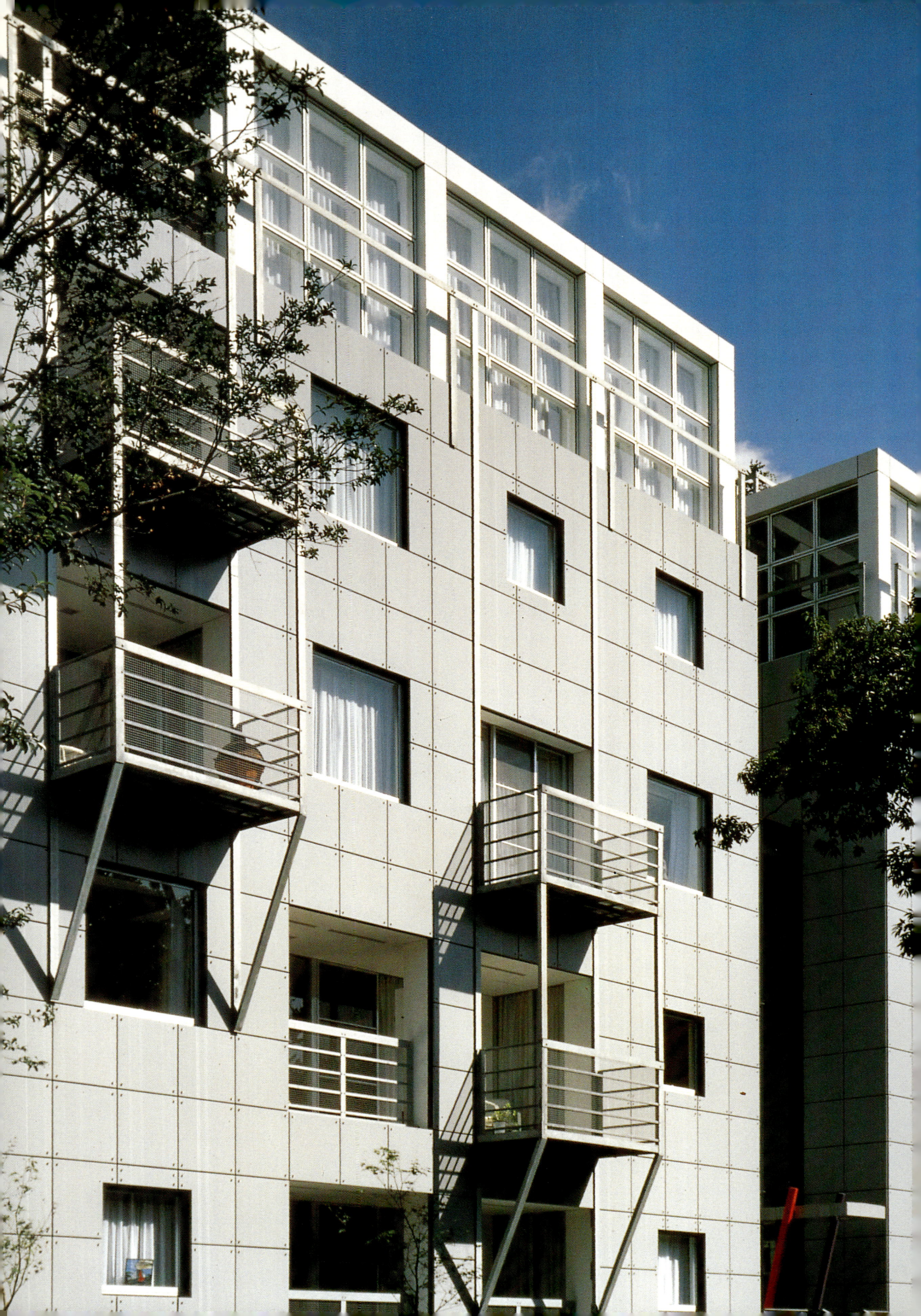

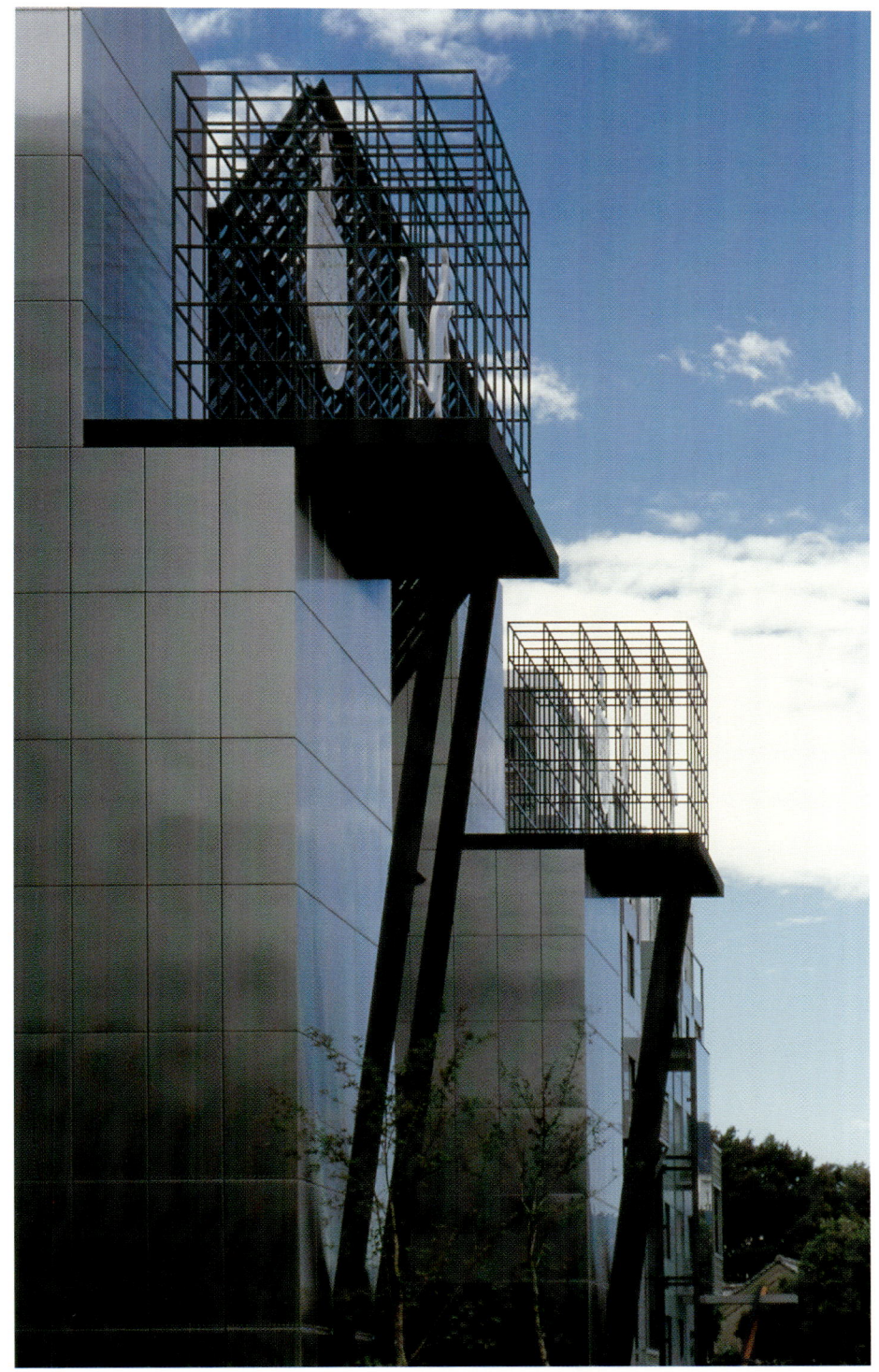

Detail of the overhanging metal structures and view of an interior space. Previous page, another view of the facade facing the road.

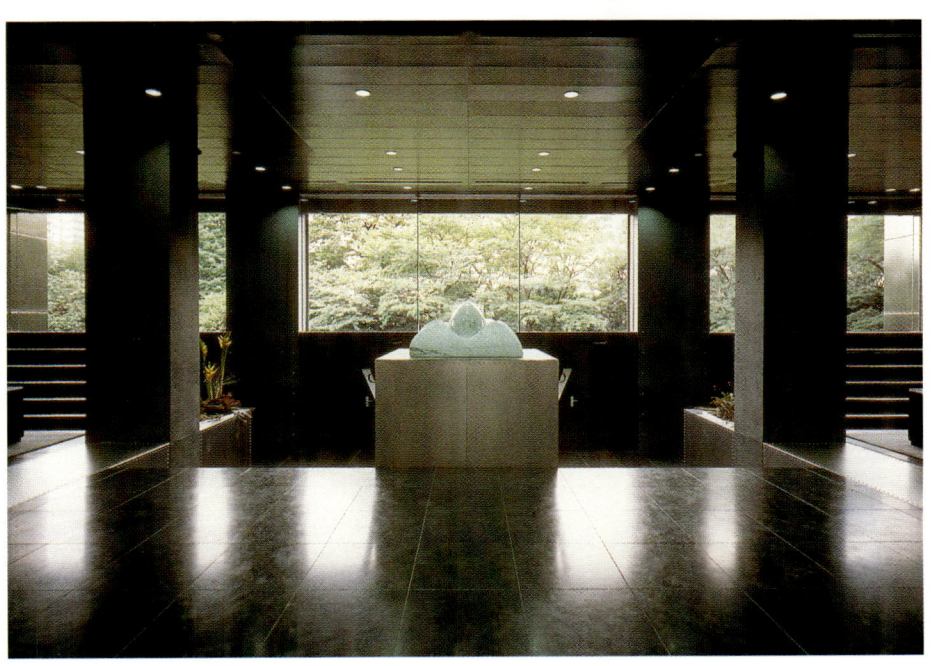

Villa-N

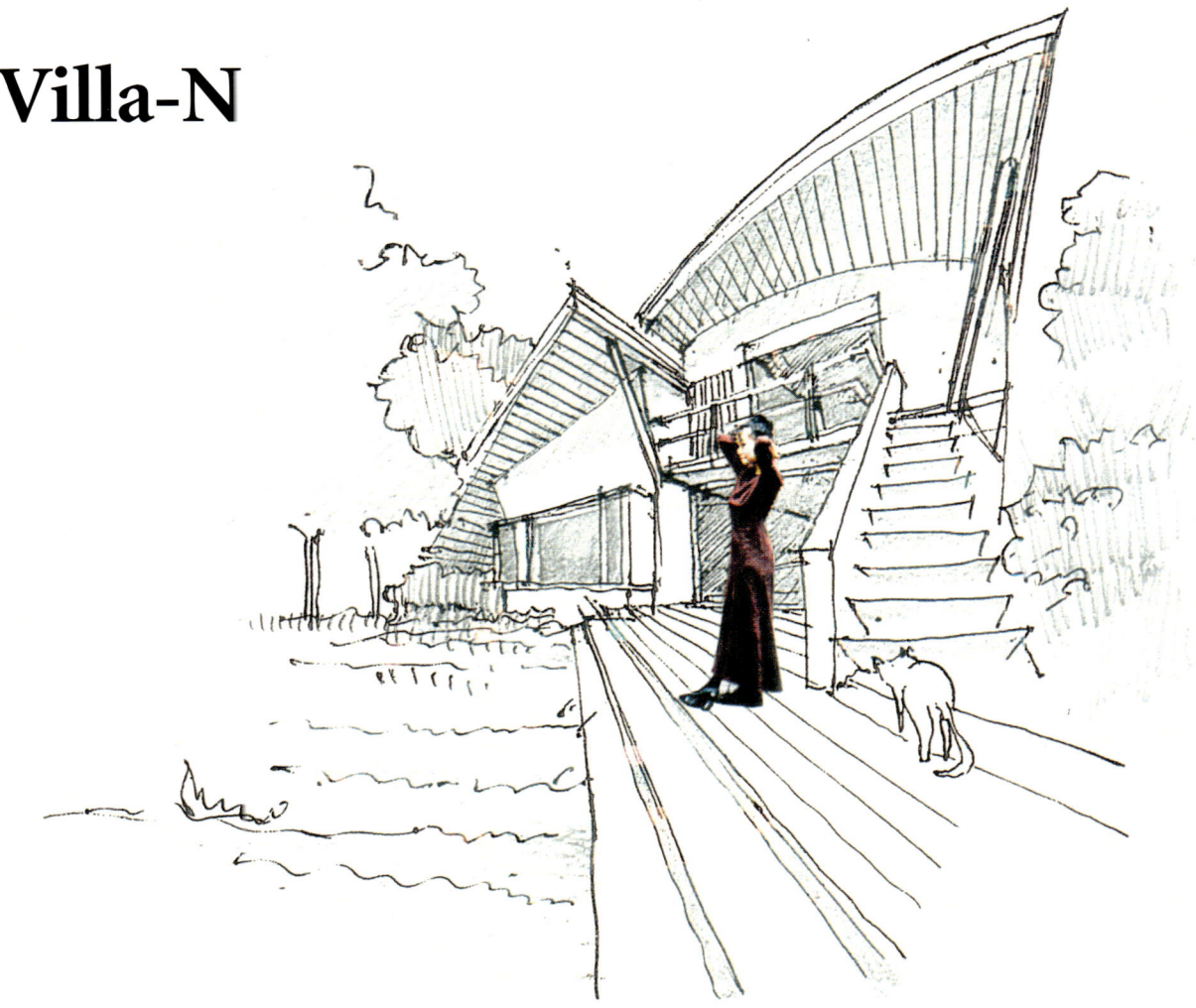

The owner had a country house on this site for many years, and knew how to enjoy the summers here.
The two roofs which appear through the clusters of trees have a feeling of continuity, as if a single roof had been divided and separated. The freestanding north and east walls are used to form a space that opens out towards the south-westerly exposure of the site. The living room is a tranquil space with a picture window that looks out onto an expanse of greenery. Parties and other gatherings can easily flow out from the terrace.
The second floor contains the master bedroom, children's rooms and guest rooms.
Natural materials have been used unsparingly, and unstinting effort put into the painting, in order to bring out the full flavour of the materials. This is because, when the country house is to be used as a place of relaxation, if the house itself is too strident, it will be conducive to relaxation. The country house should be a place to rest, in an atmosphere of warm and carefree gentleness, where body and soul can receive the unseen blessings of nature, and burn off excess energy.

Plan of first floor and, right, plan of second floor.

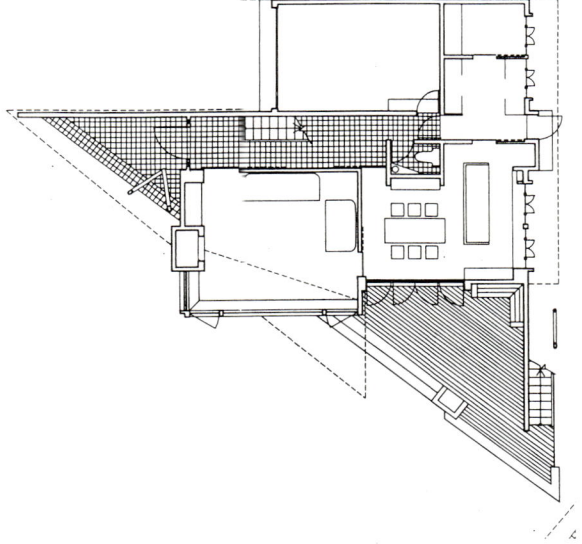
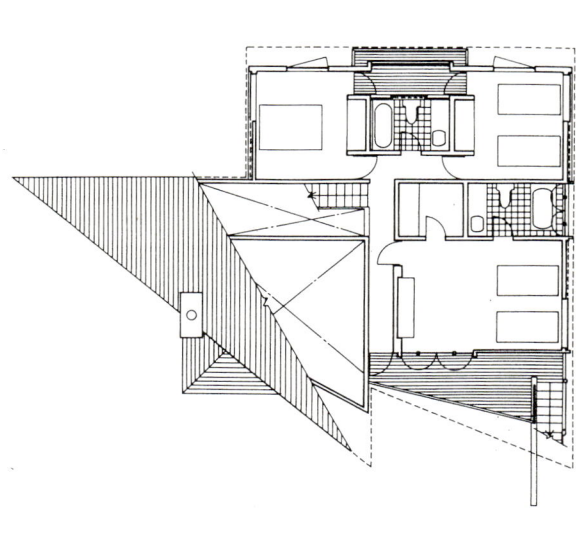

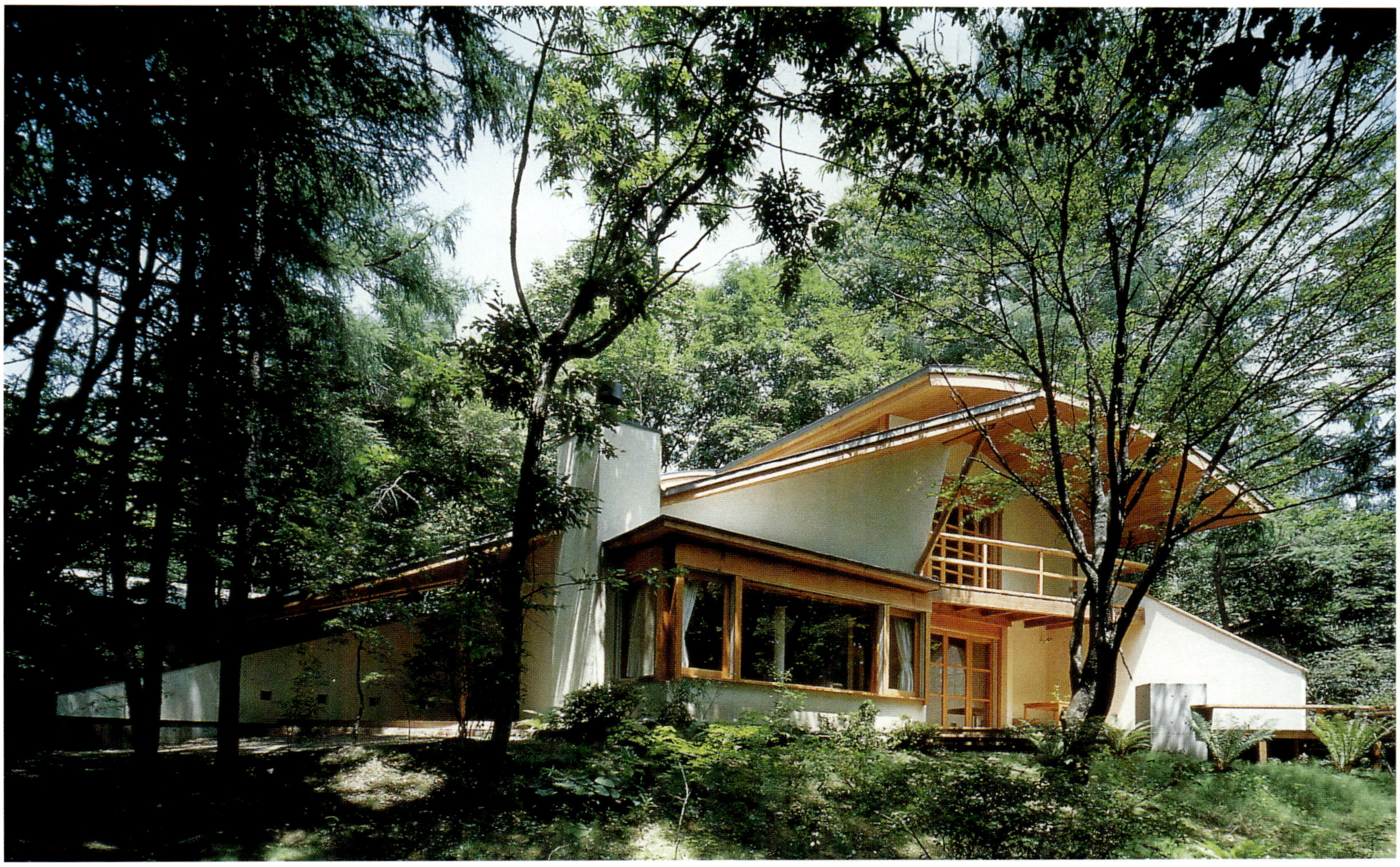

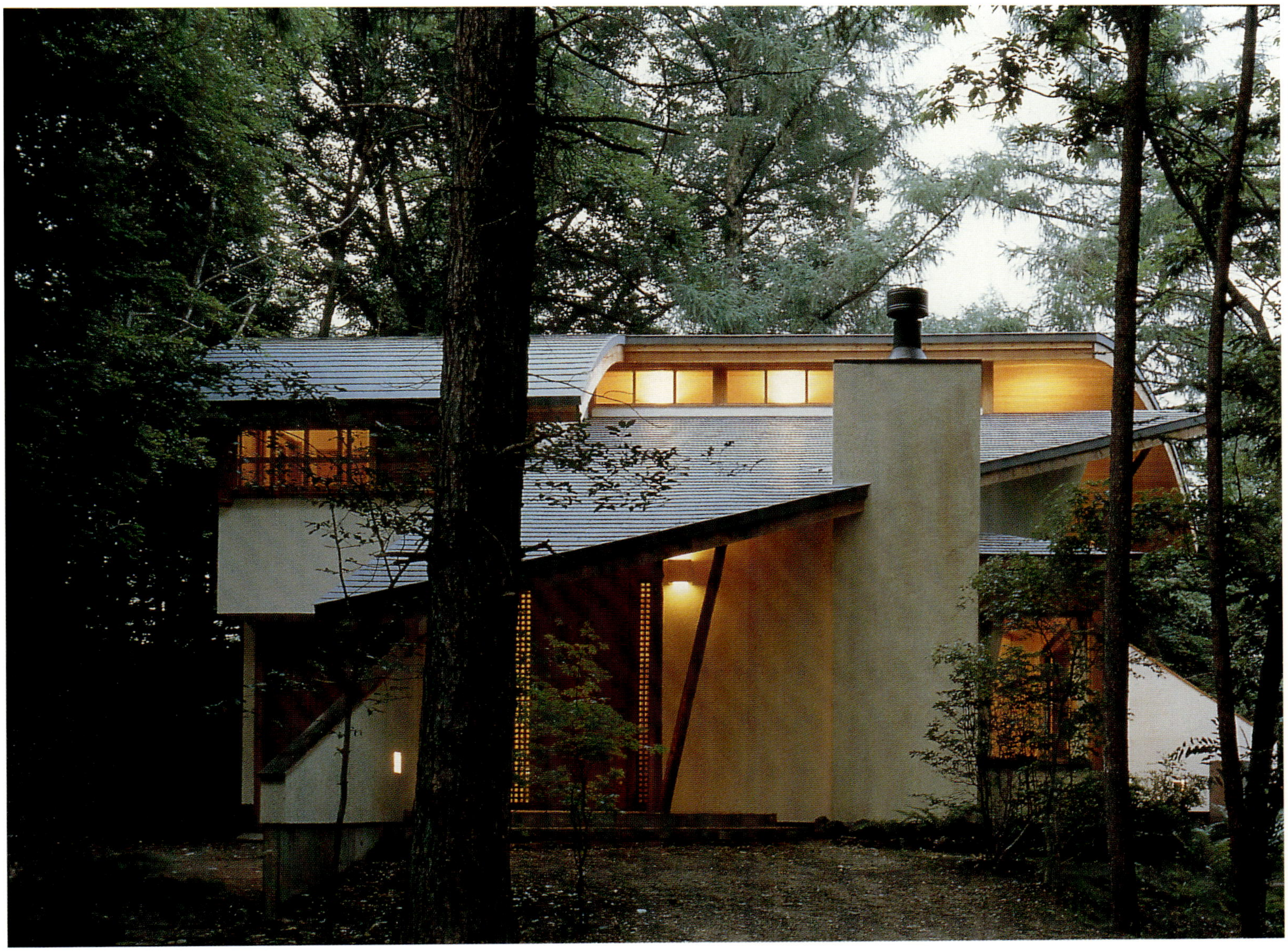

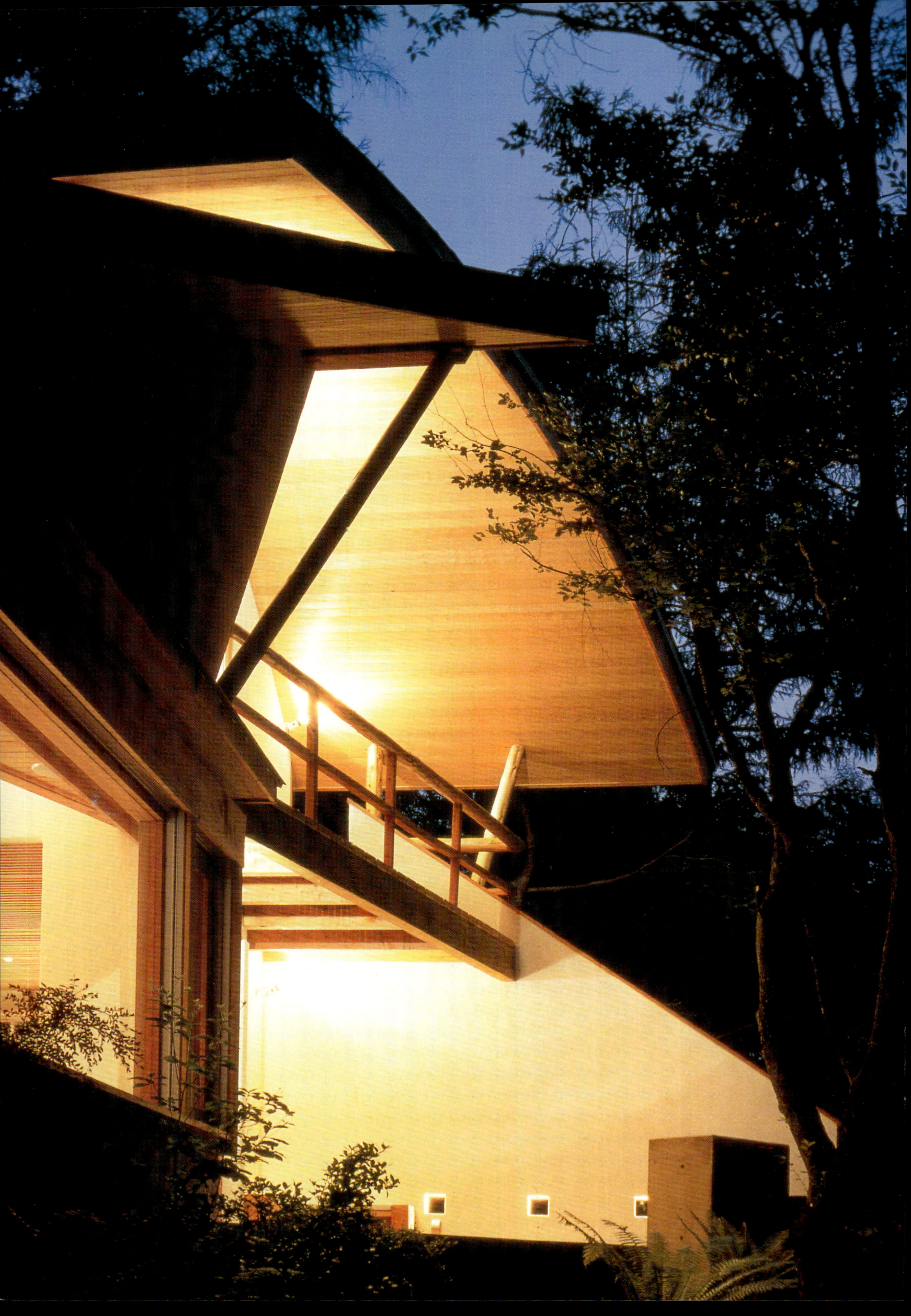

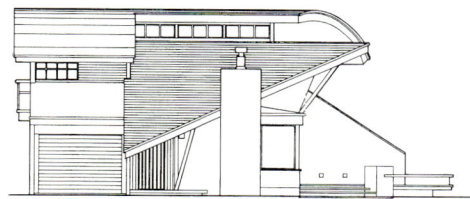
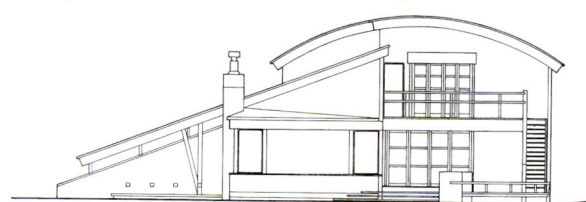

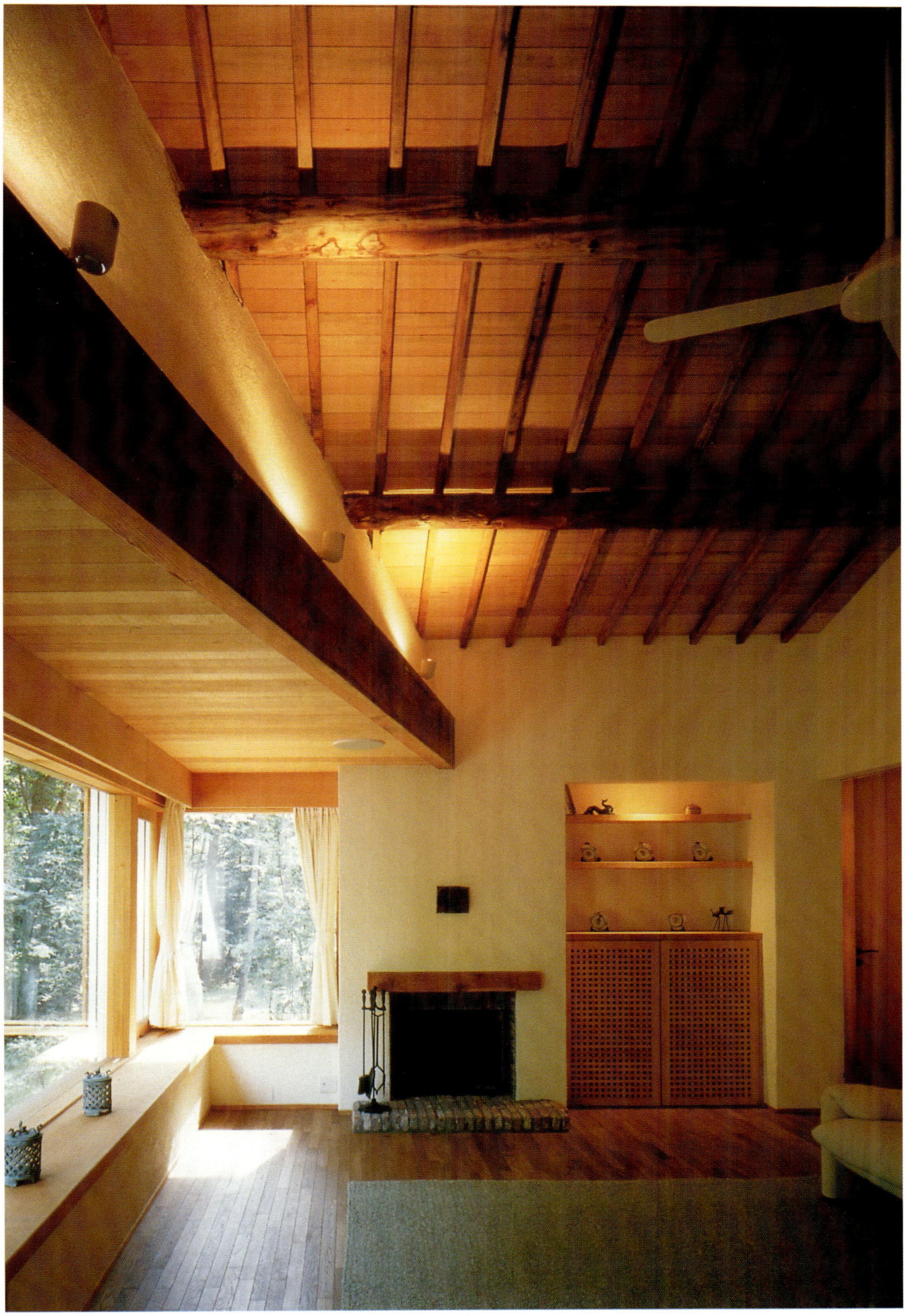

Two sections of the building and a view of the ground floor living room.
Previous pages, views of the building buried in greenery.

The natural wooden staircase leading to the first floor where the bedrooms are located.

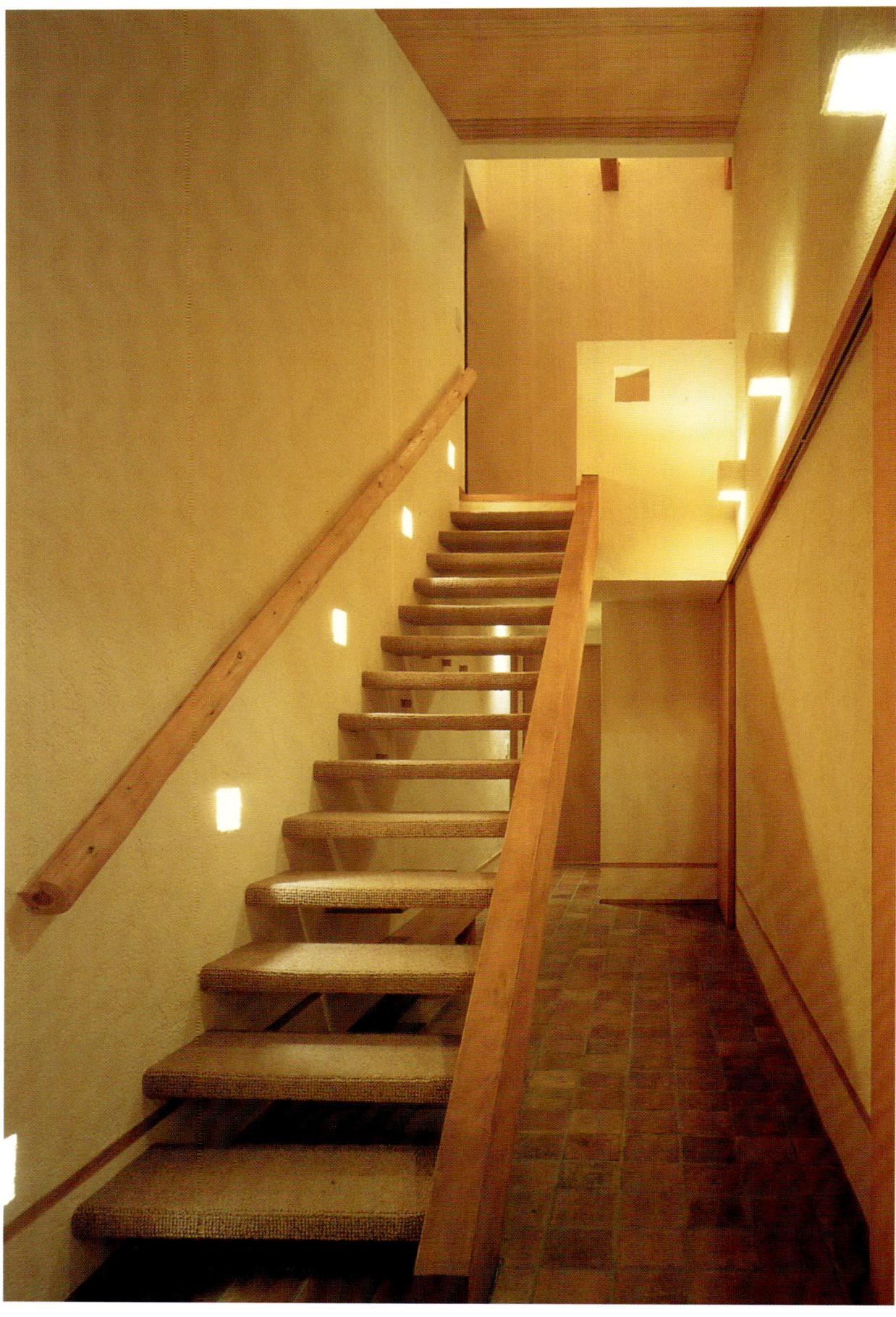

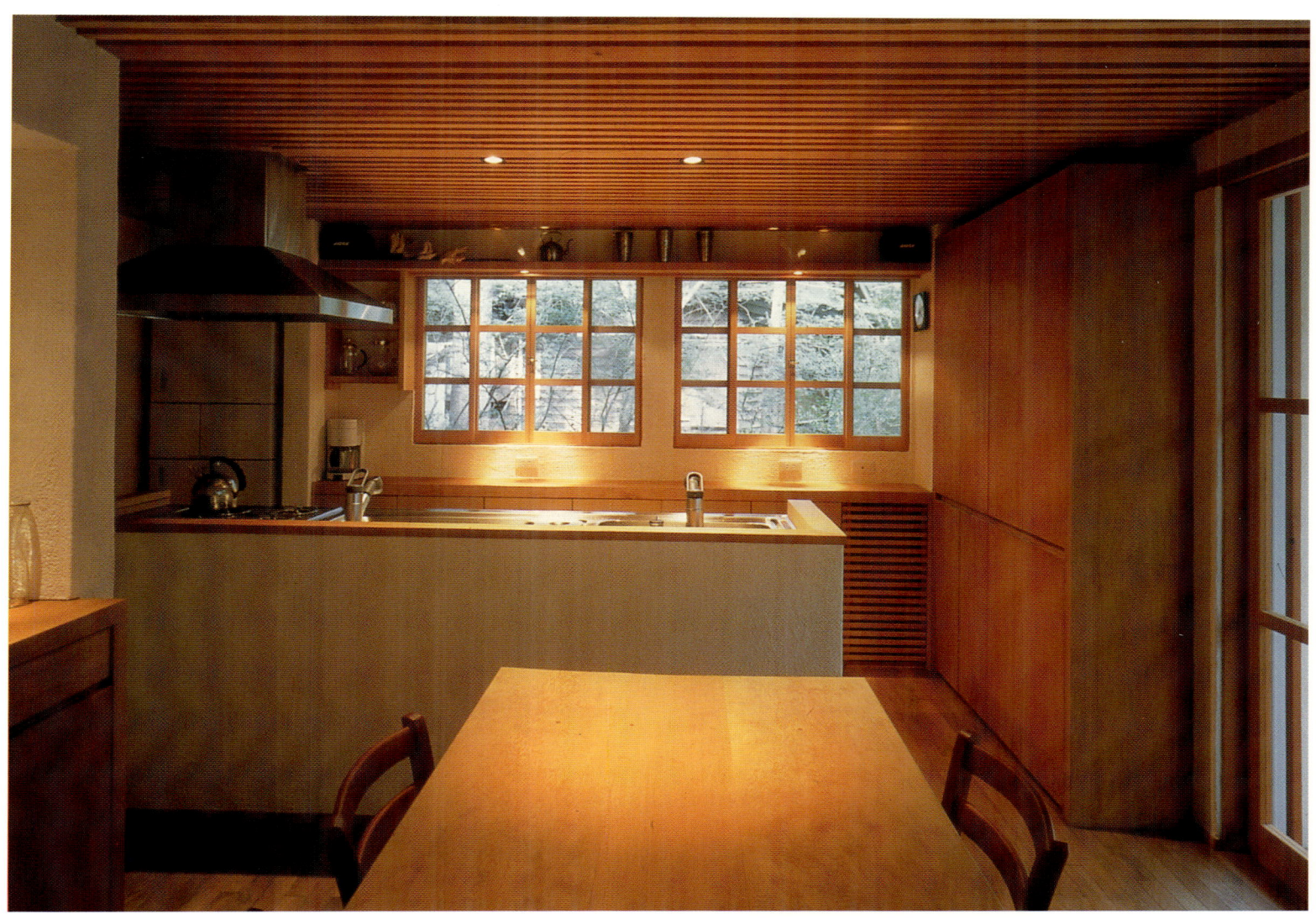

The ground-floor kitchen showing the wide glass window overlooking the garden.

Sirocco

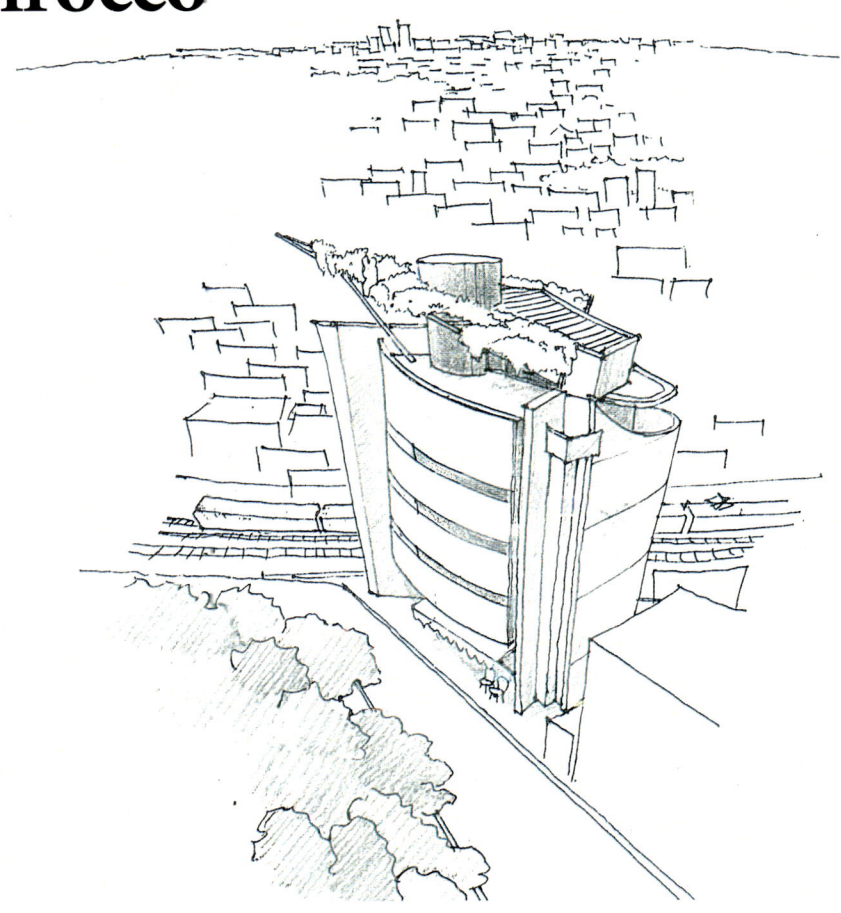

This building functions as the centre of activity for a food related company, and is the materialisation of a forward looking CI. The plan was to have the fourth and fifth floors used as the company headquarters, the third floor as an area for roasting coffee beans and storing foodstuffs, the second floor as the restaurant kitchen, and the basement as a newly opened restaurant venture.
Particular features are the fifth floor penthouse and first floor pilotis.
The penthouse is an extremely open space which affords an all-round panorama. The wisteria trellis will eventually be covered with green as the wisteria grows.

The first floor pilotis serves as a café which opens onto the street and a park, and as the lead into the restaurant and building. Other spaces are contained behind the mask-like facade.
Any single architectural structure, as long as it is part of a city, must relate to that city not only in economic and production terms, but also on a cultural level. Even though the building is the property of a particular enterprise, it is also charged with a certain public quality. A building is linked to various levels of systems, and has the potential to stimulate relationships. In this sense, a building is like a concentrated fragment of the city, a 'city in miniature'.

Typical floor plan and, right, plan of the fifth floor penthouse.
Opposite page, model of the building.

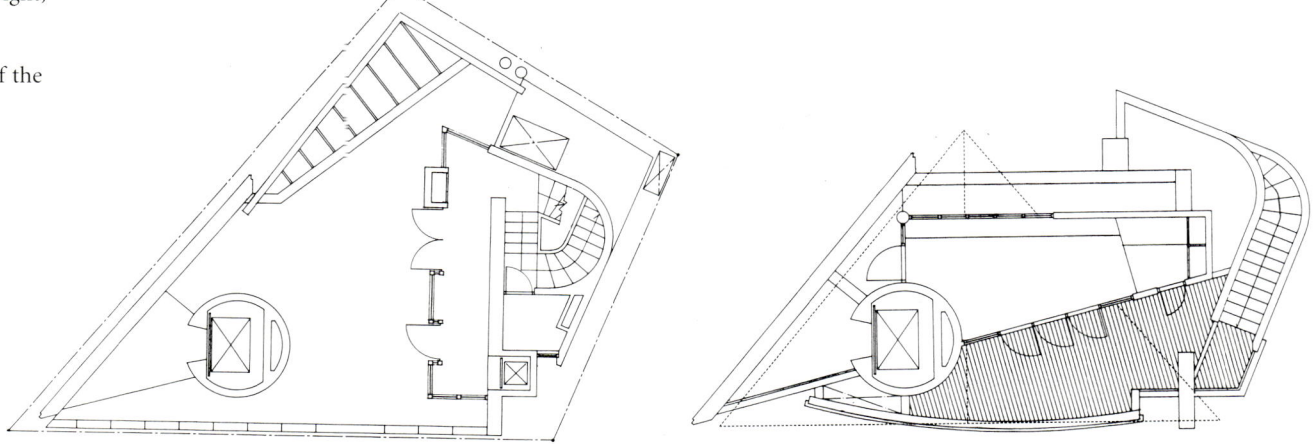

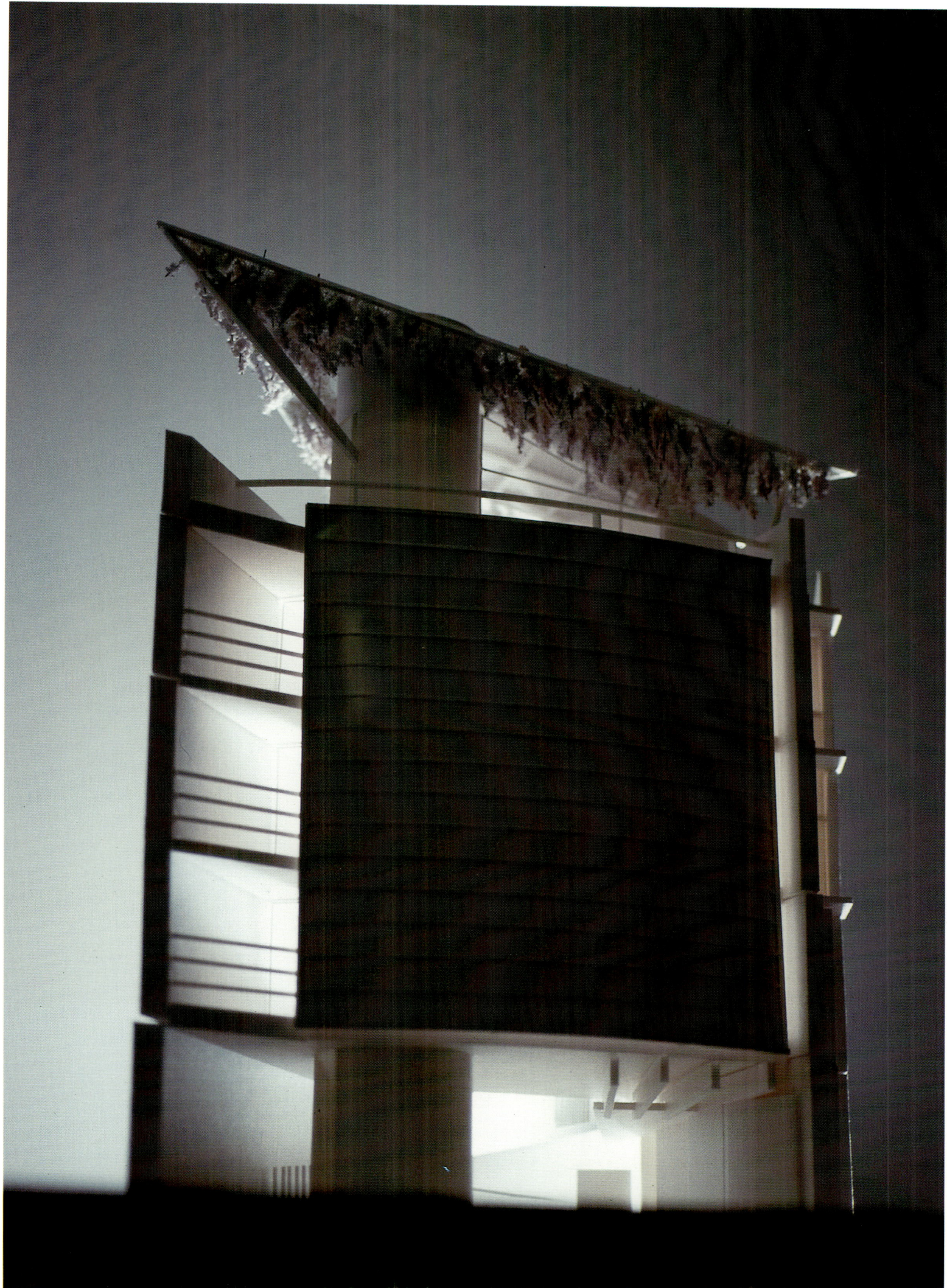

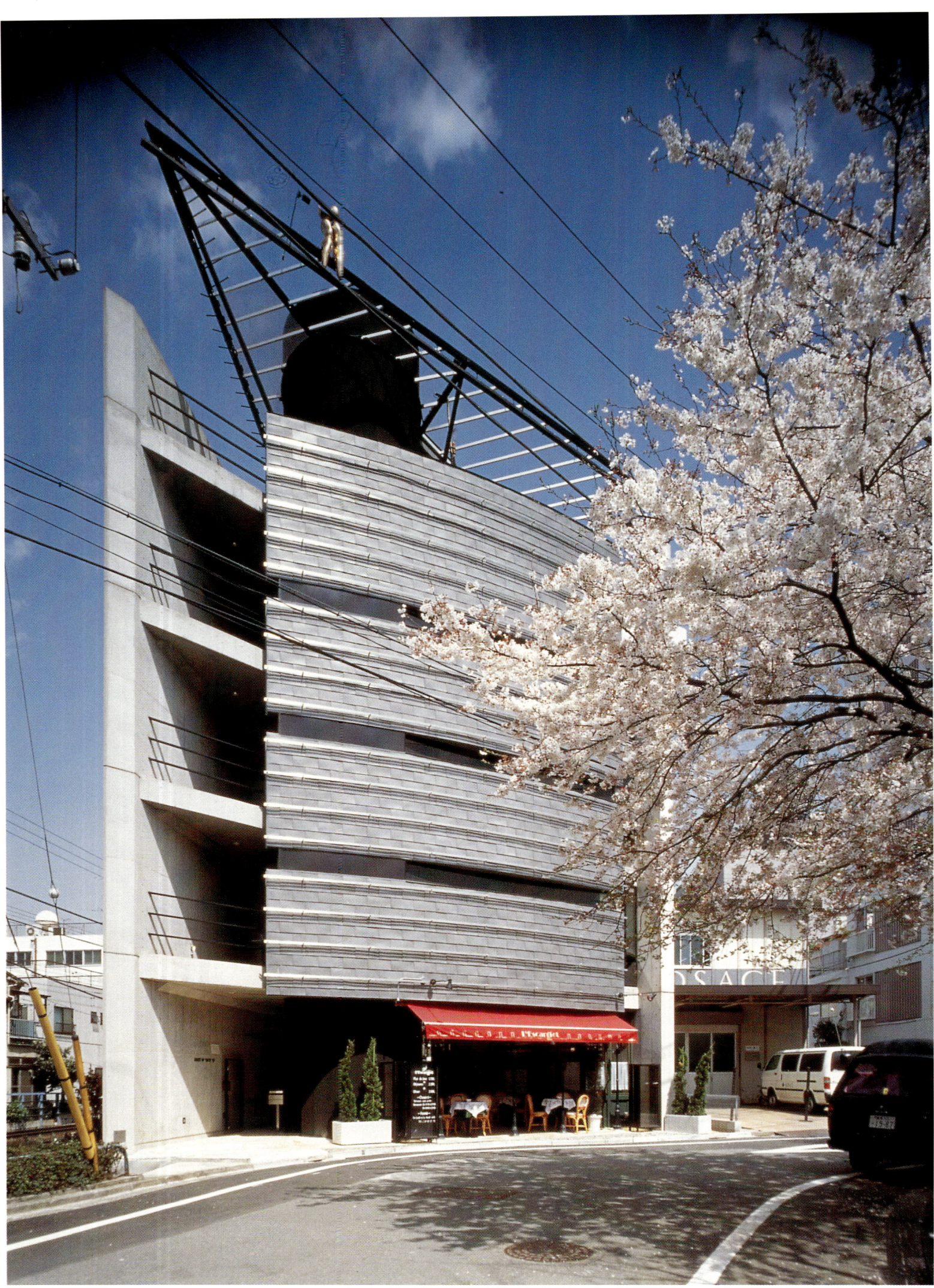

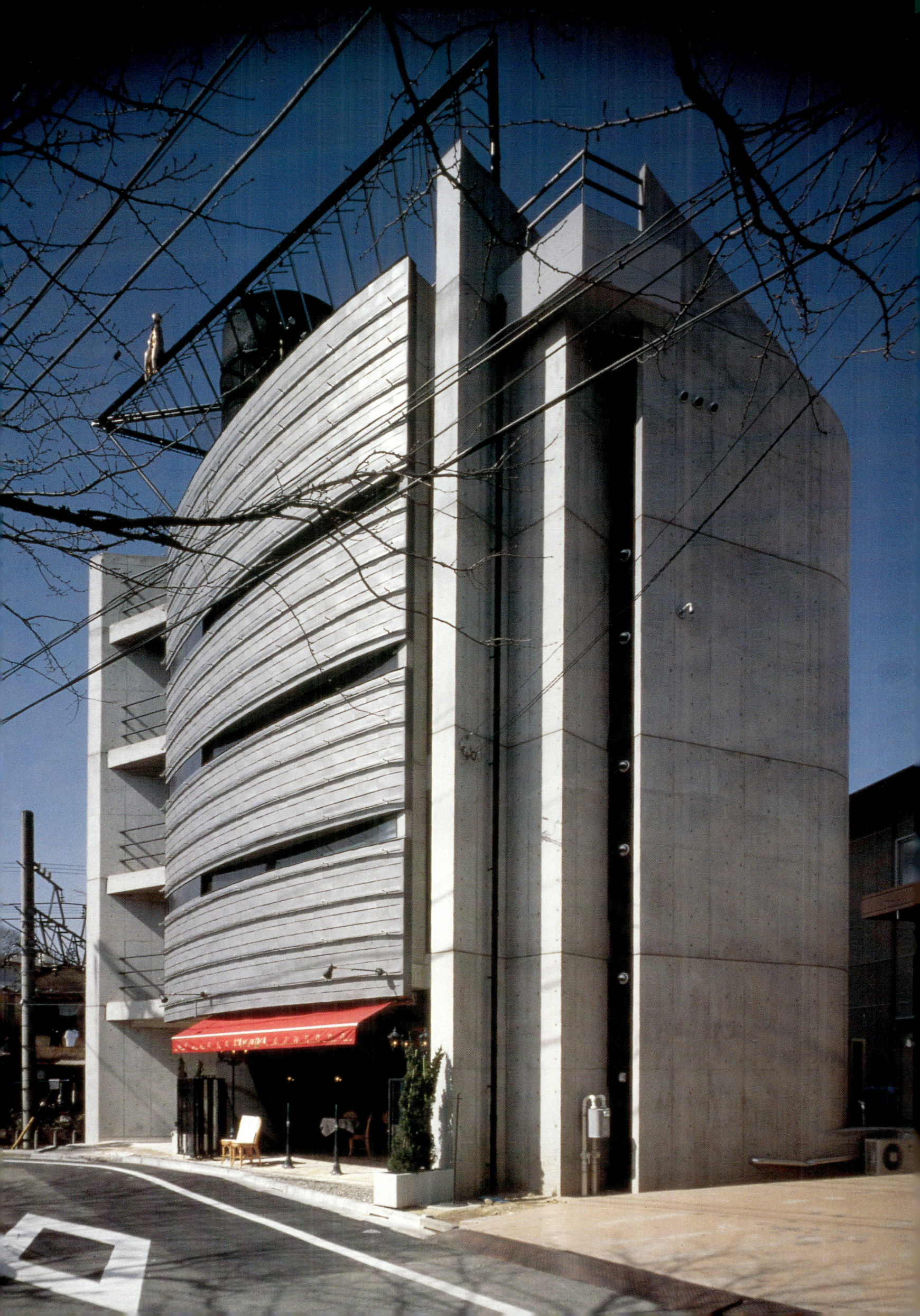

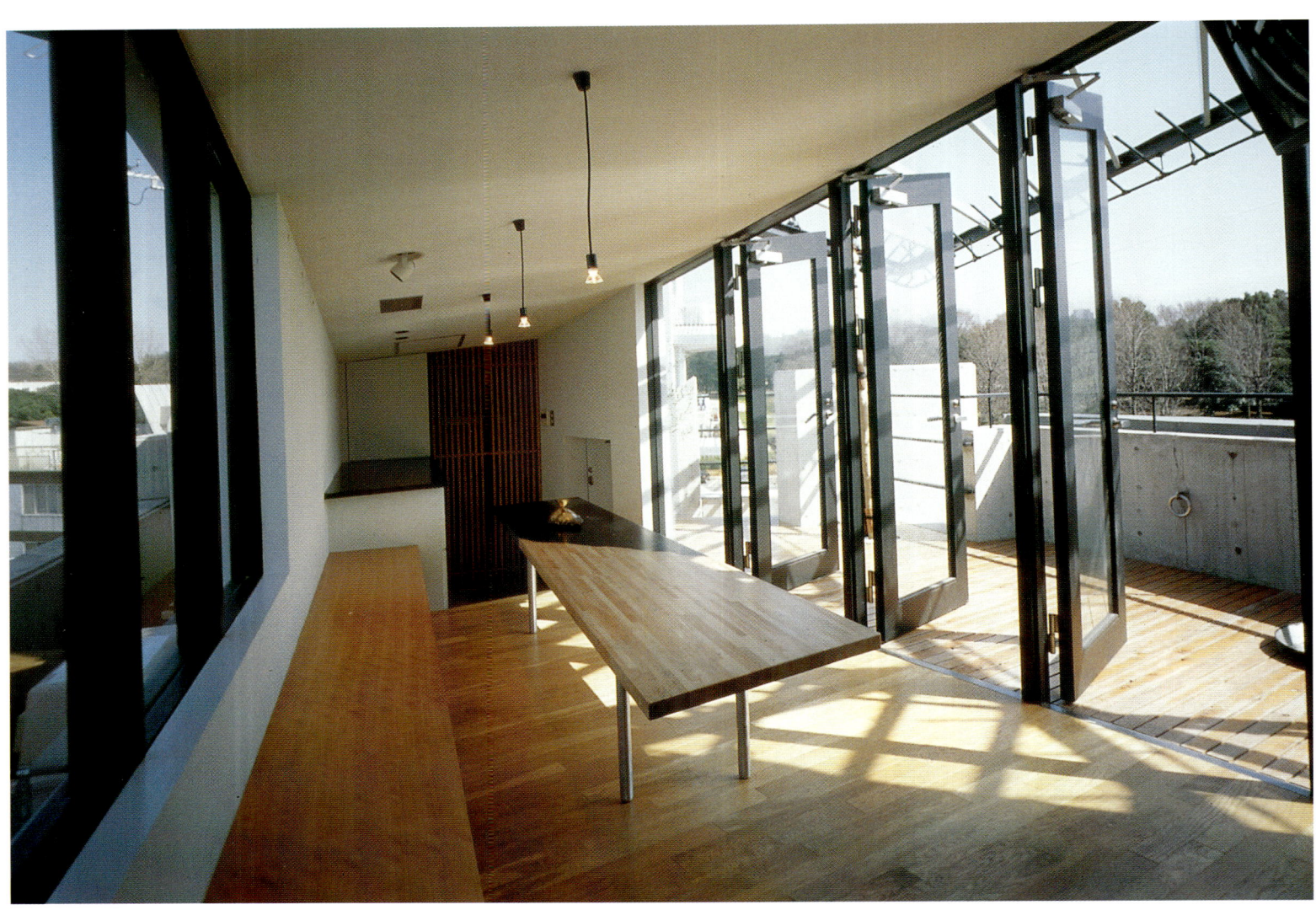

Previous pages, two views of the main facade of the building with the café opening onto the street. These pages, two views of the fifth floor penthouse and its terrace, which affords an all-round panorama.

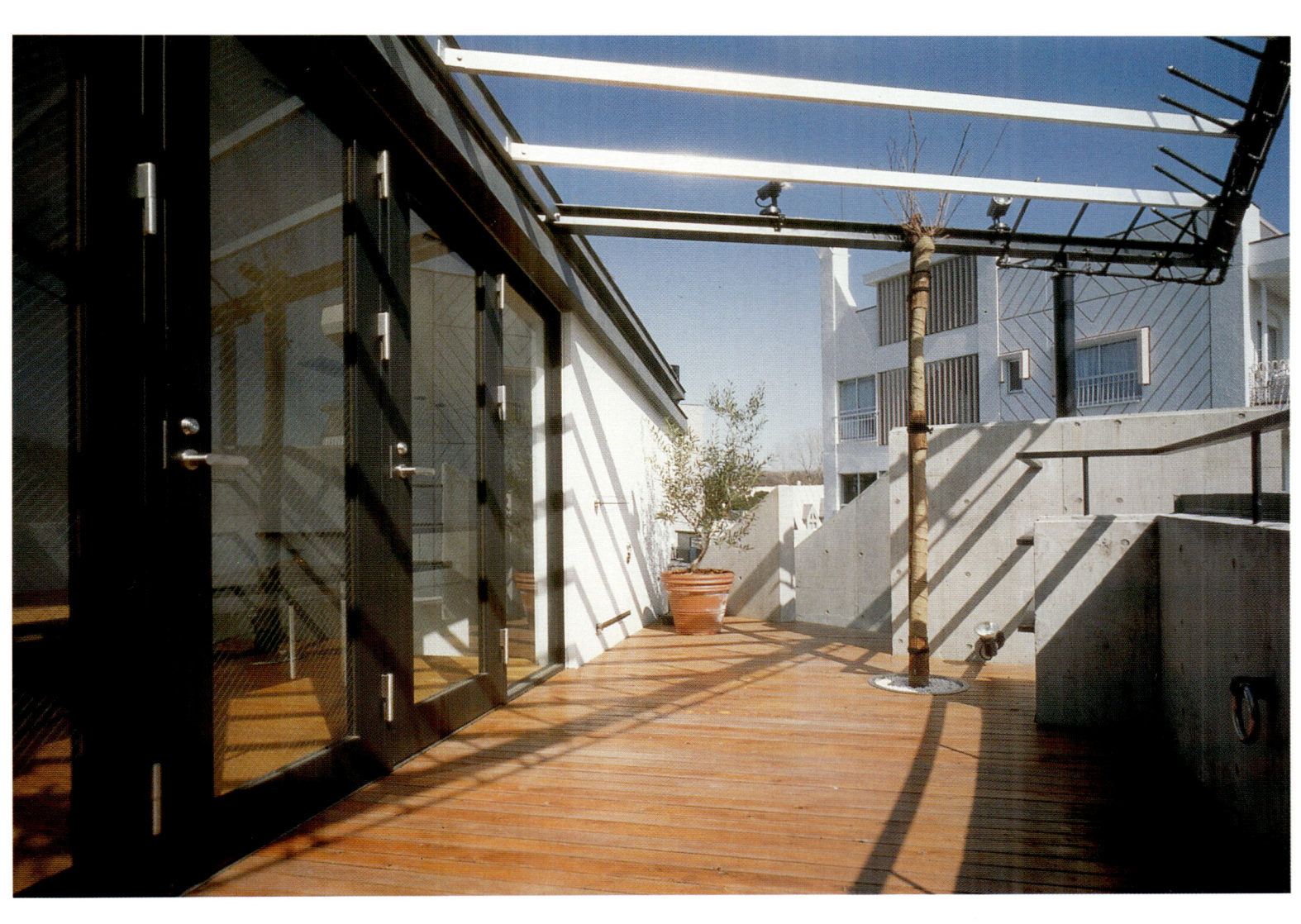

Yamanashi Prefectural Nursing Junior College

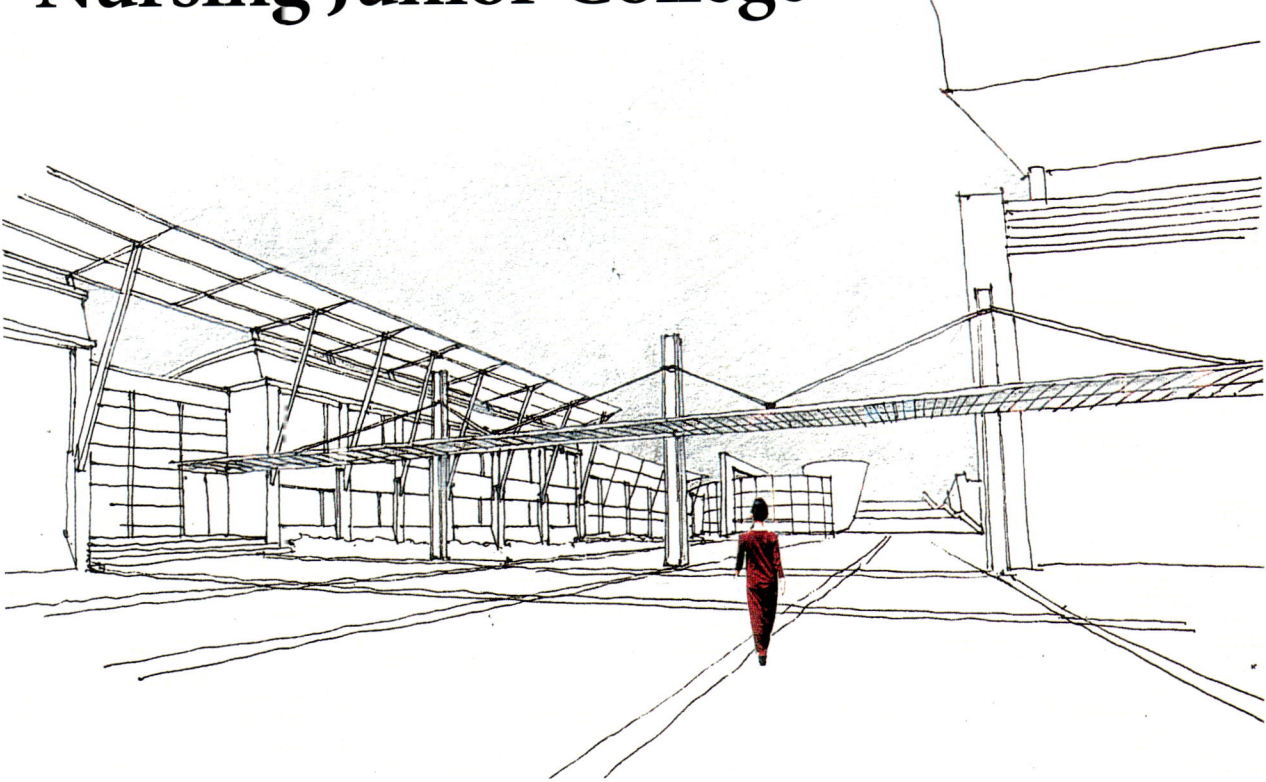

This project came about as a result of extension planned after the upgrading of an existing nursing academy in Yamanashi prefecture to a nursing college. The existing facility was like a junior or high school, with classrooms and playing fields, in other words, only those elements necessary to satisfy the educational curriculum requirements.

The task was to complement the building with a main facility, research laboratories, library, lecture hall, etc., to create a spacious educational environment.

At the planning stage, the aim was to create a campus plaza in the centre of the school grounds, to lay out the individual facilities carefully, and to create an open design for the plaza.

The campus plaza is a place where extra-curricular informal communication can begin, and where all manner of meetings and discovery can take place.

First floor plan.

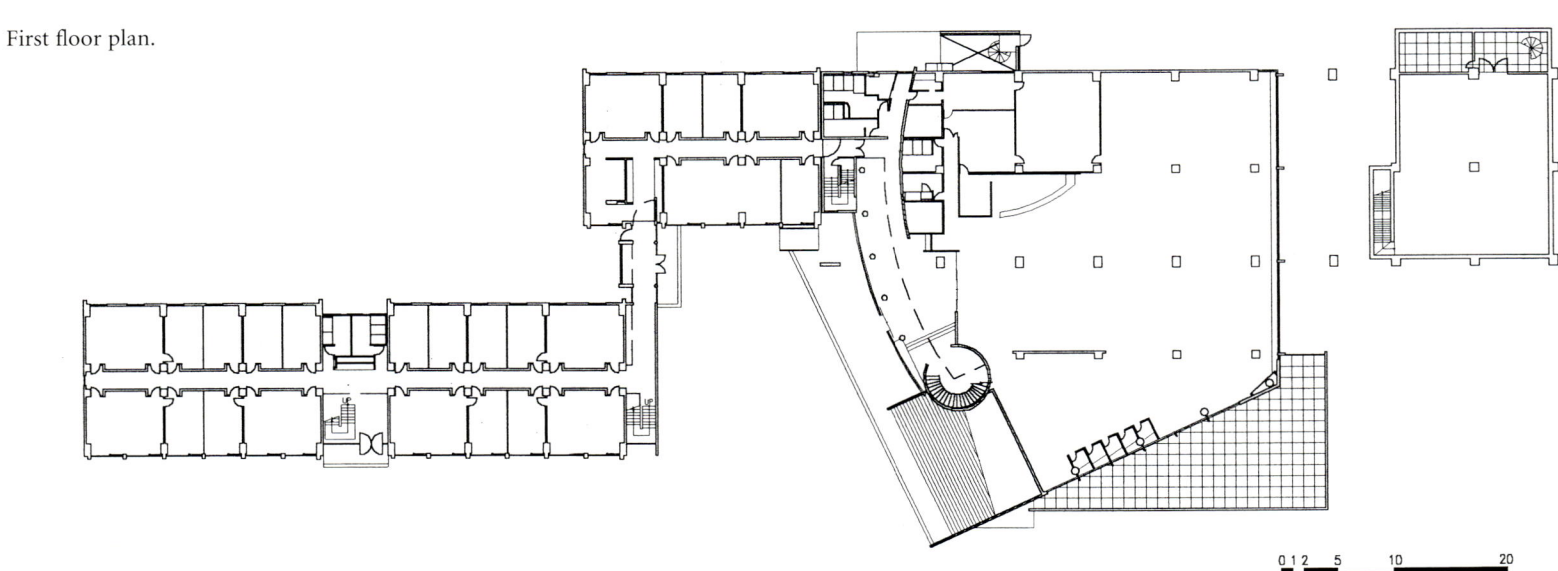

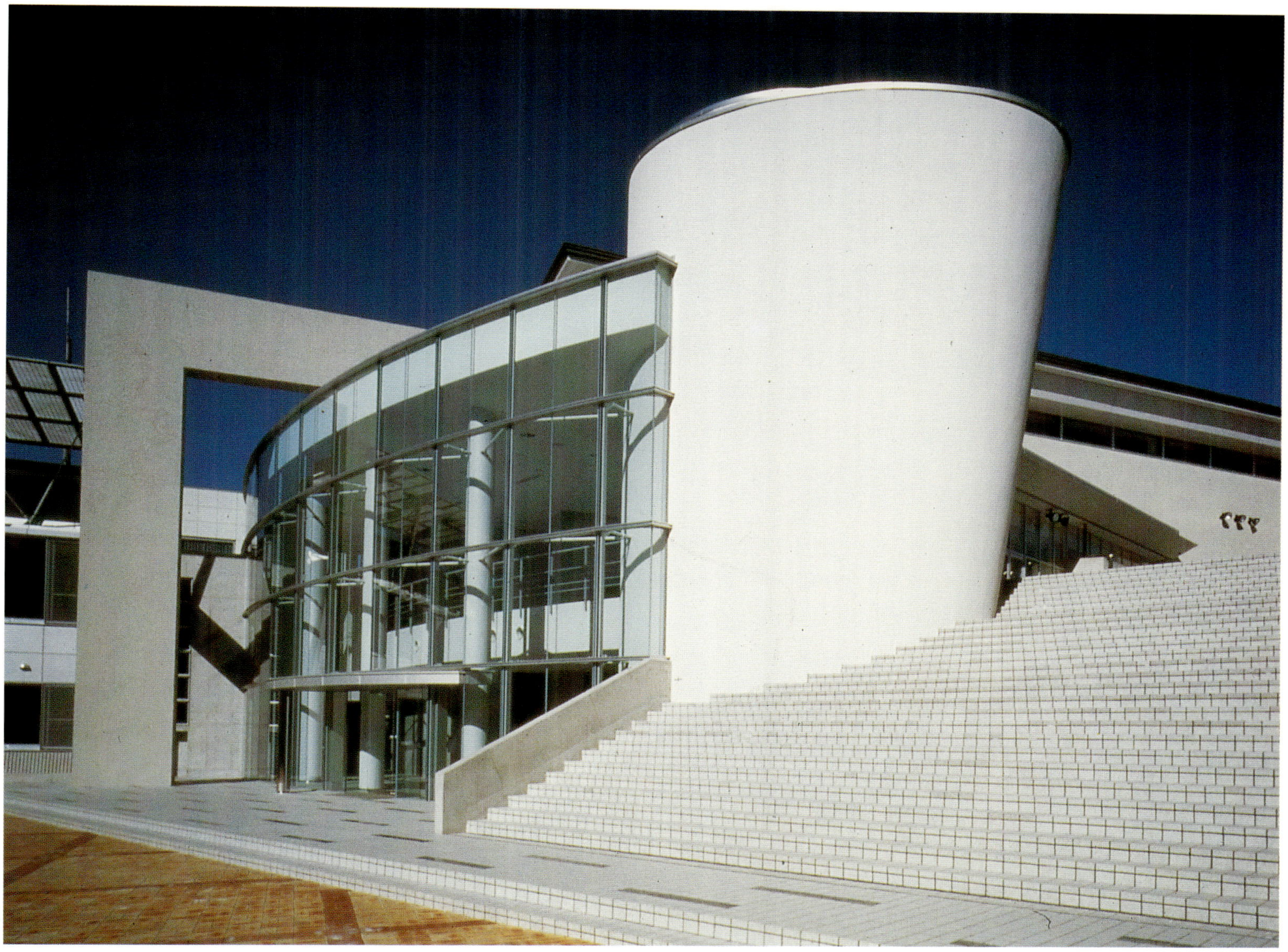

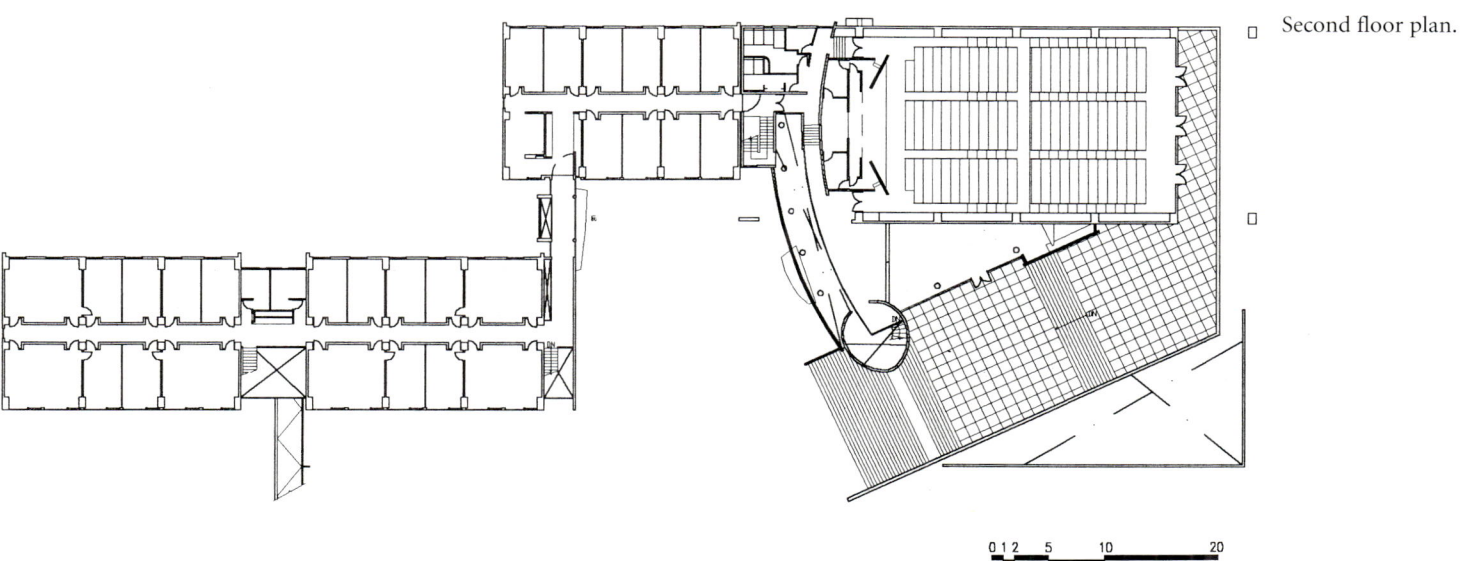

Second floor plan.

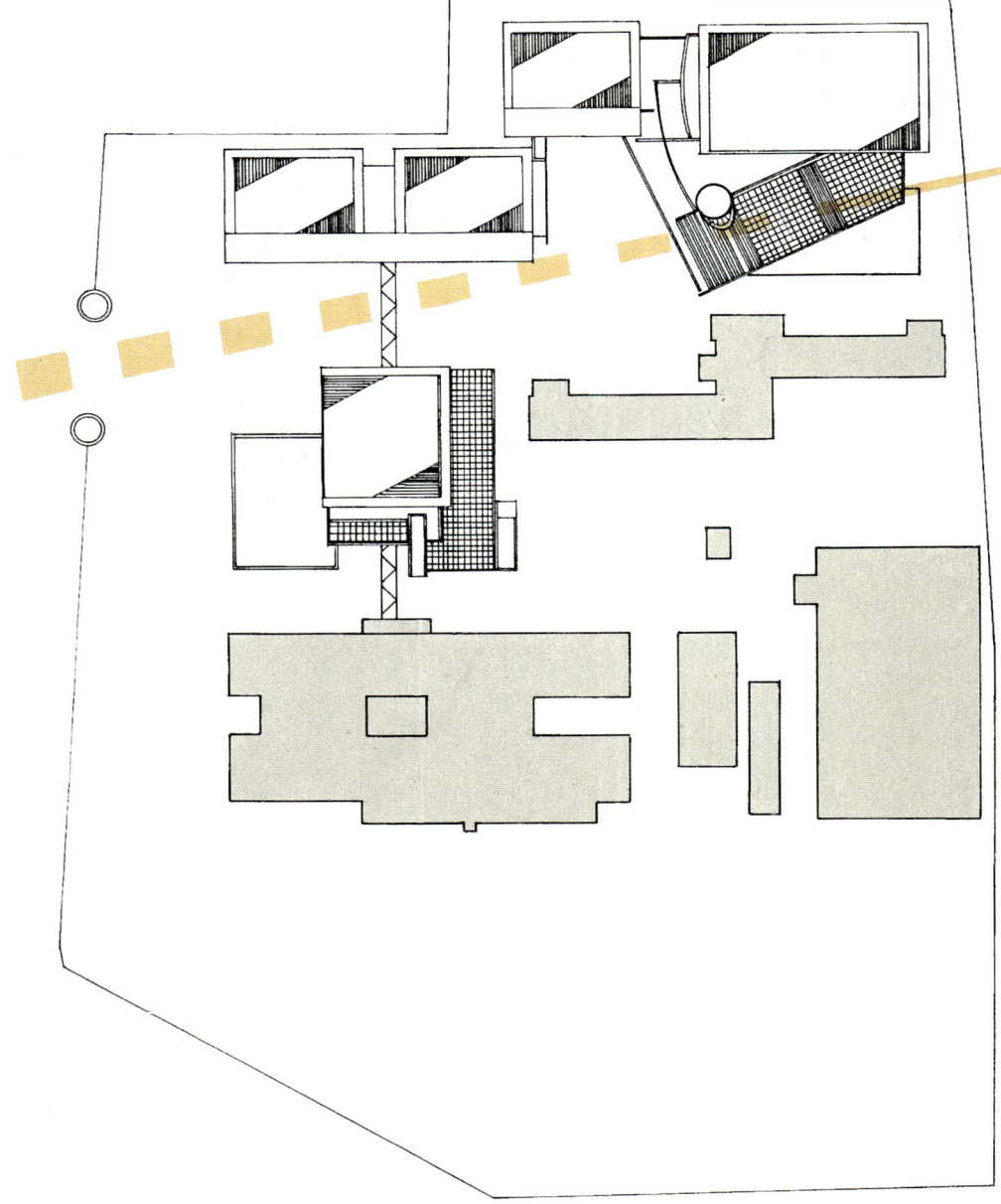

Site plan and sections of the building used for the laboratories and the offices.

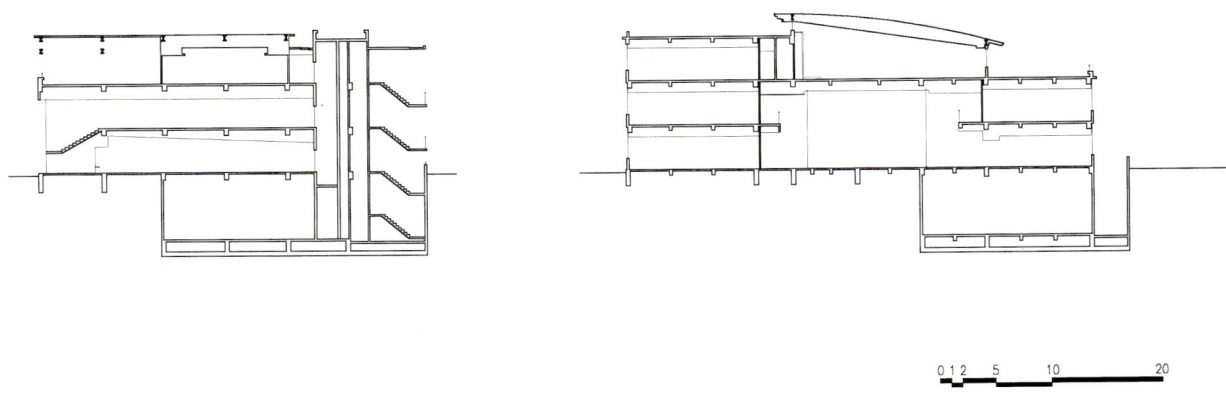

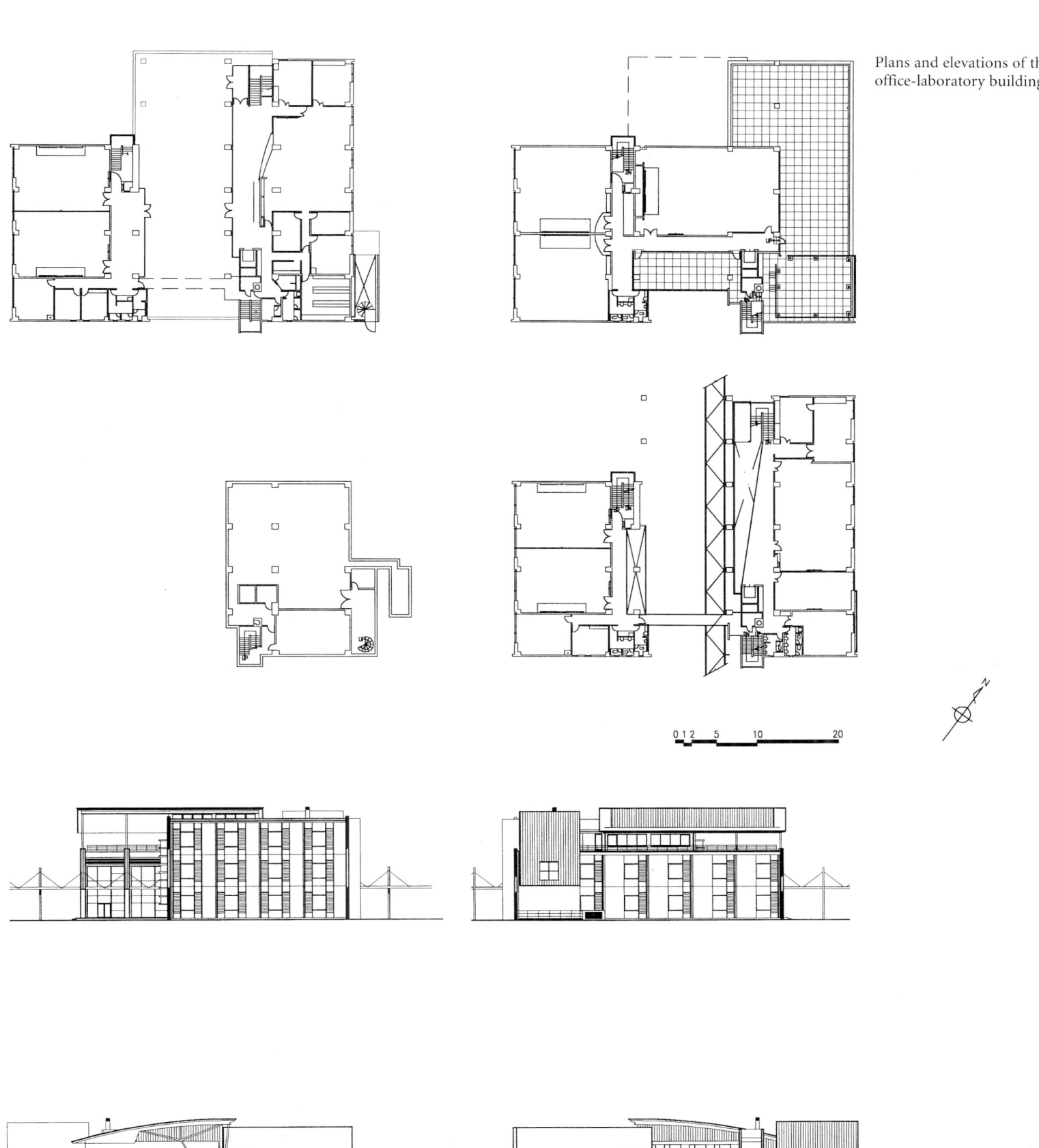

Plans and elevations of the office-laboratory building.

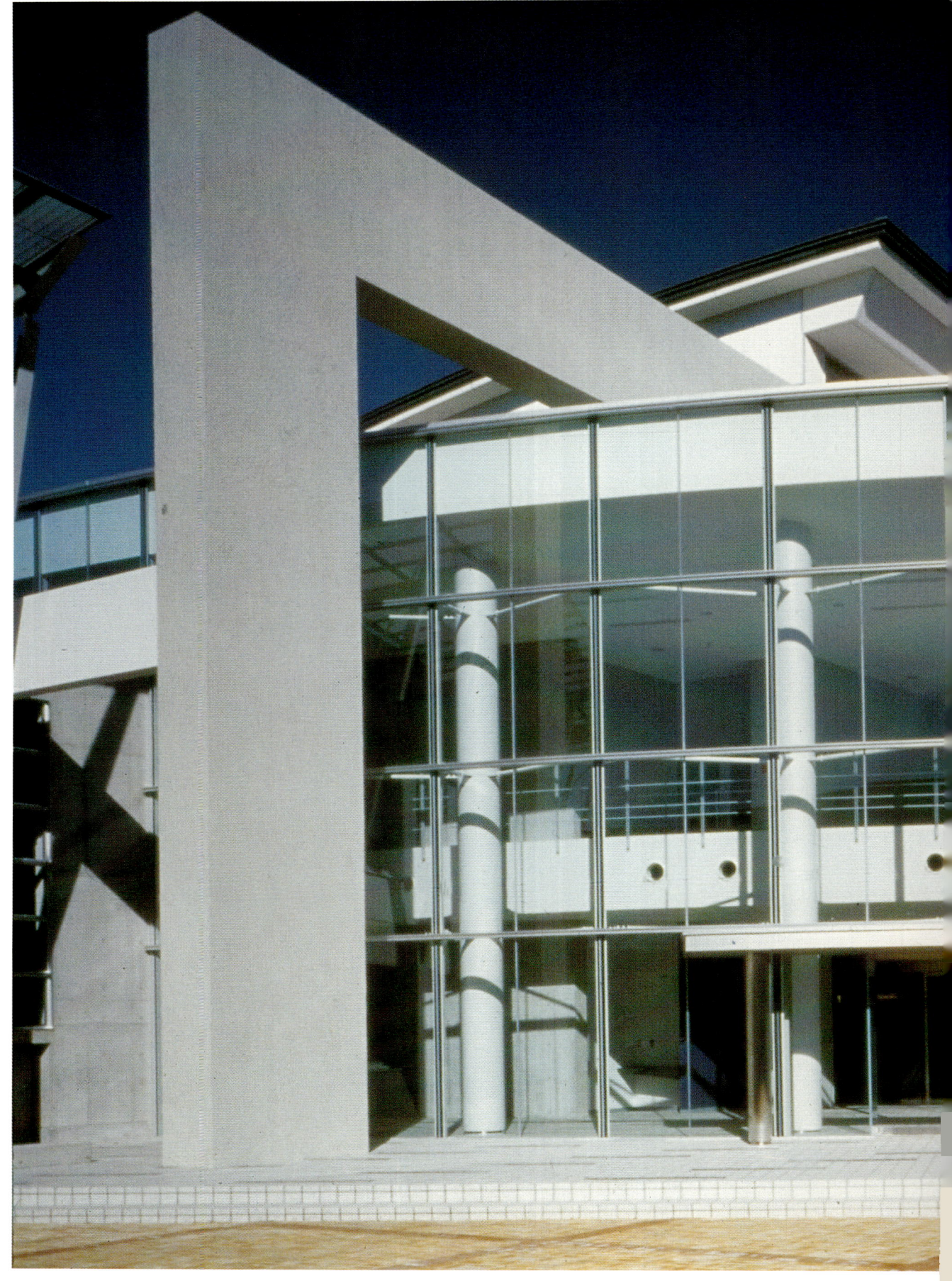

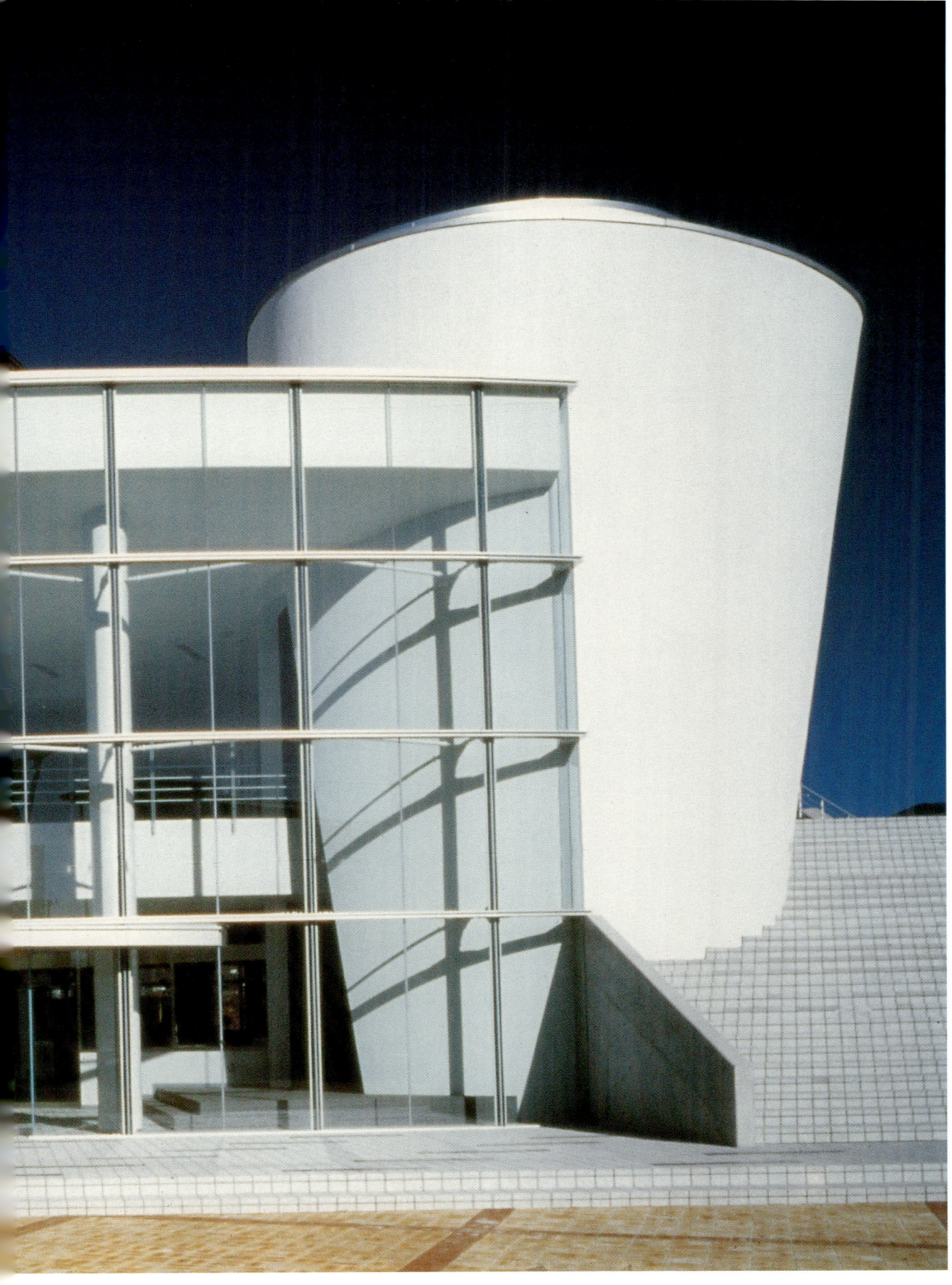

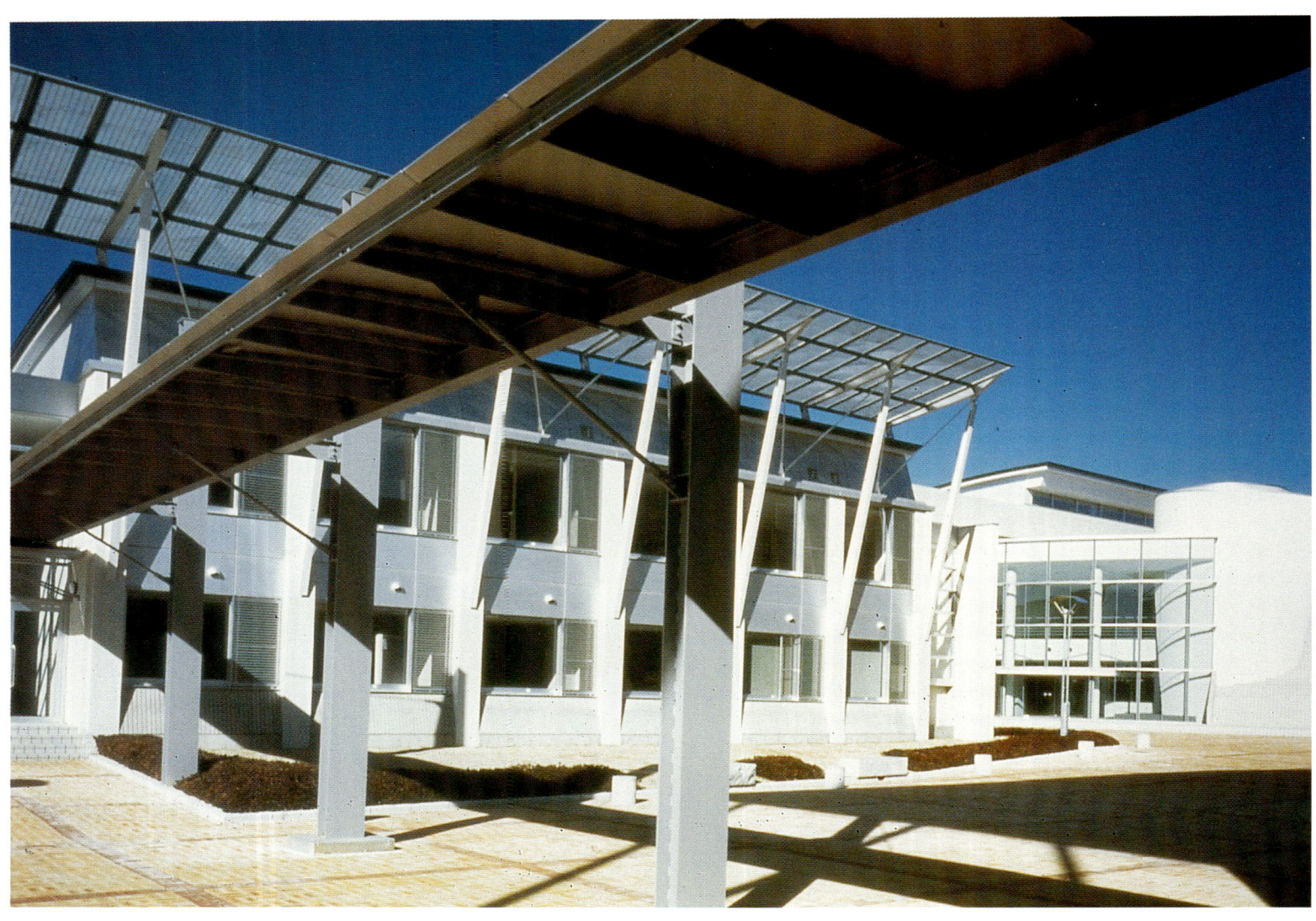

The school entrance seen from the walkway connecting the various buildings on the complex.

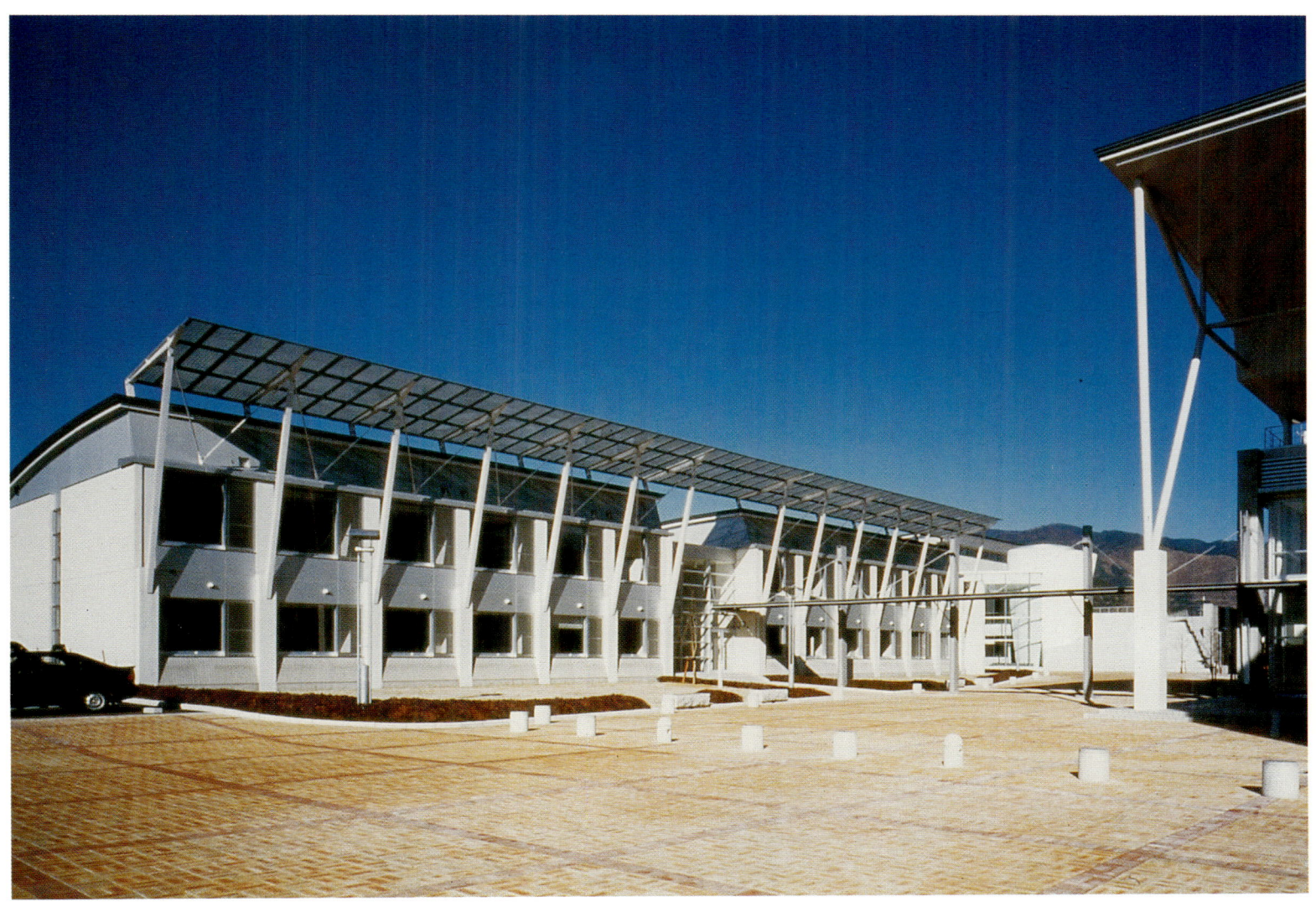

The block housing the classrooms, showing the glass windows letting in natural light from the outside.

Right and opposite page, details of the tower and of the stairway marking the entrance to the complex and the inside of the glass lobby.

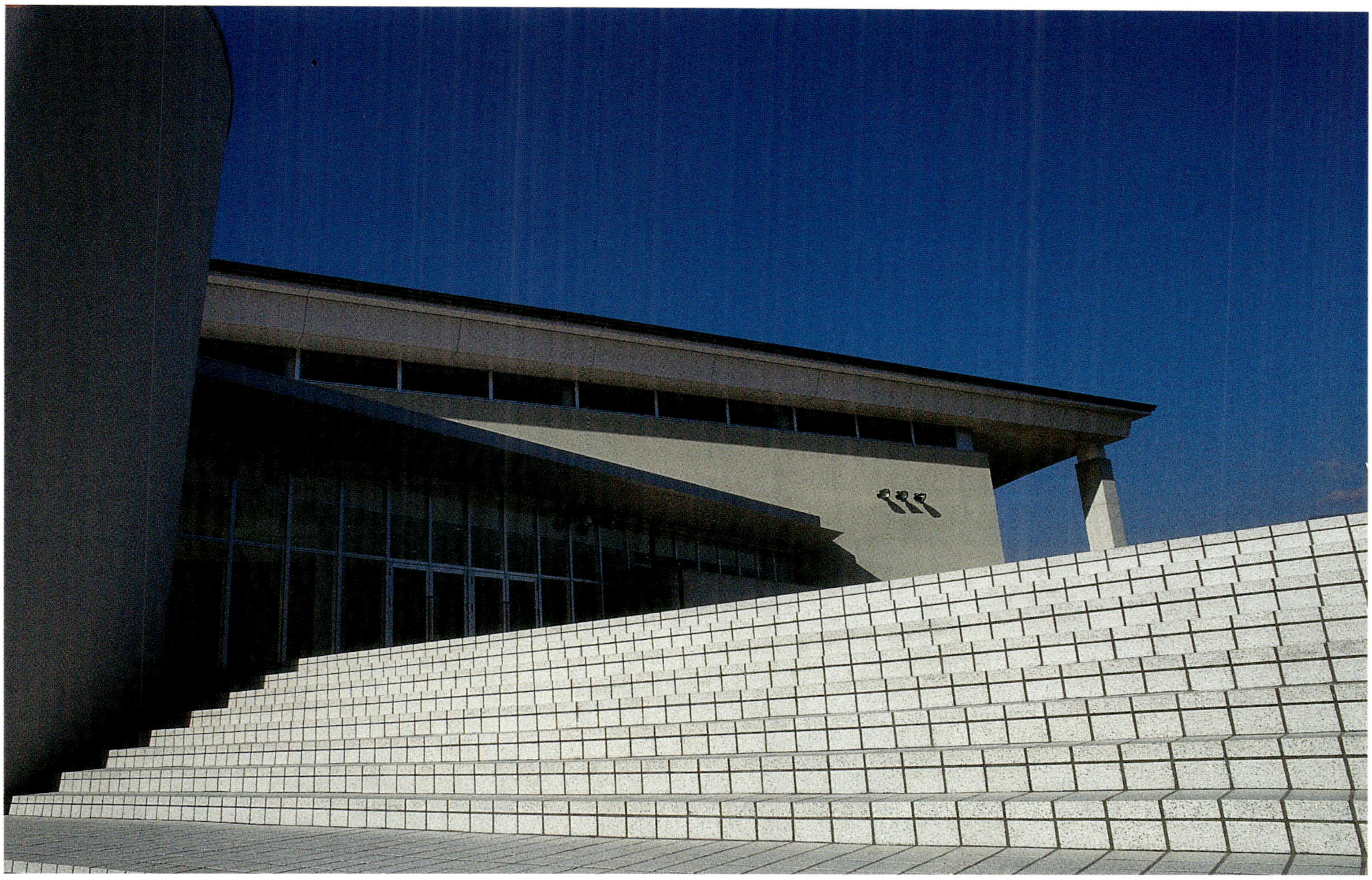

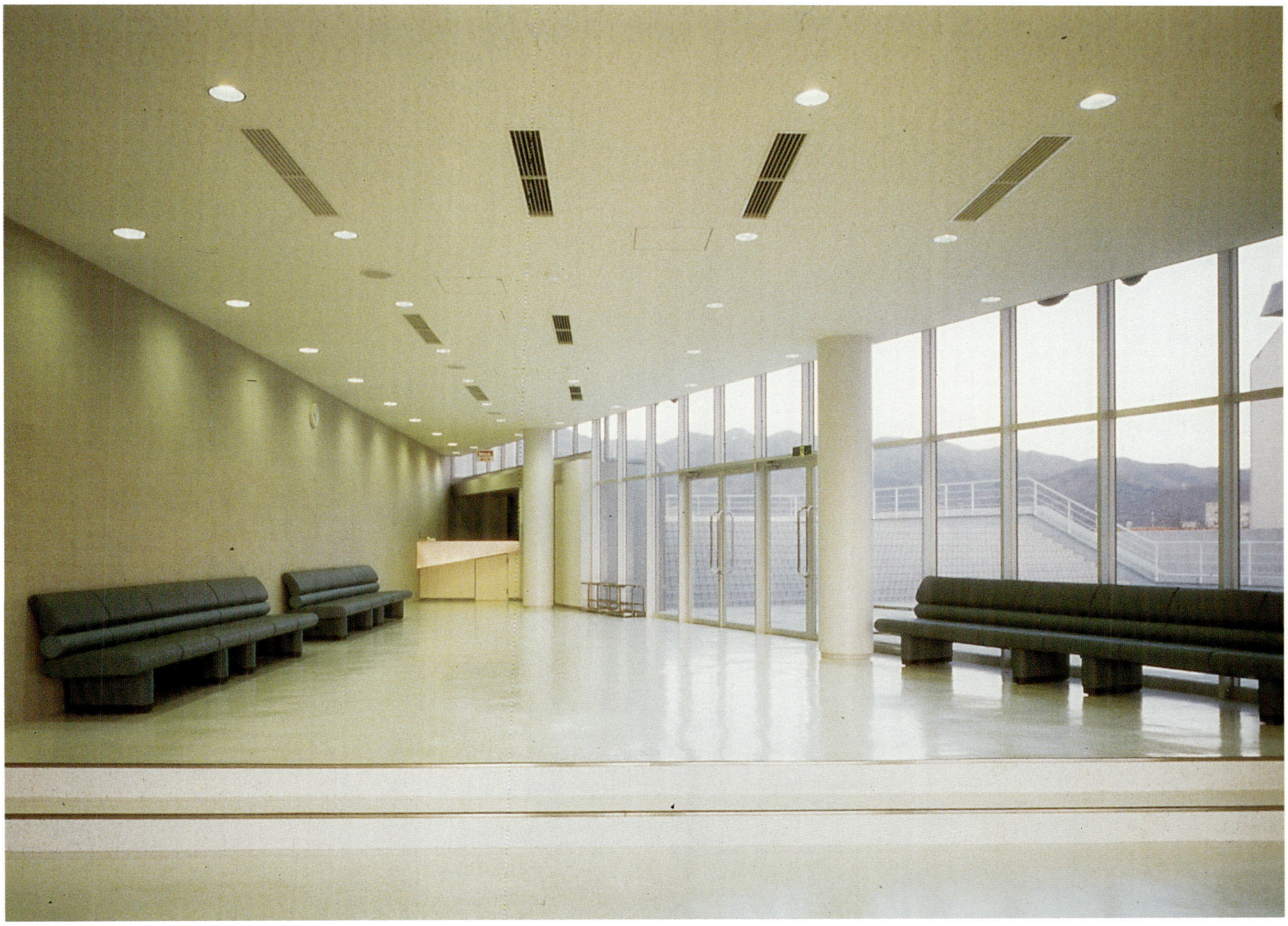

Tokyo Metropolitan Office, Niijima Branch

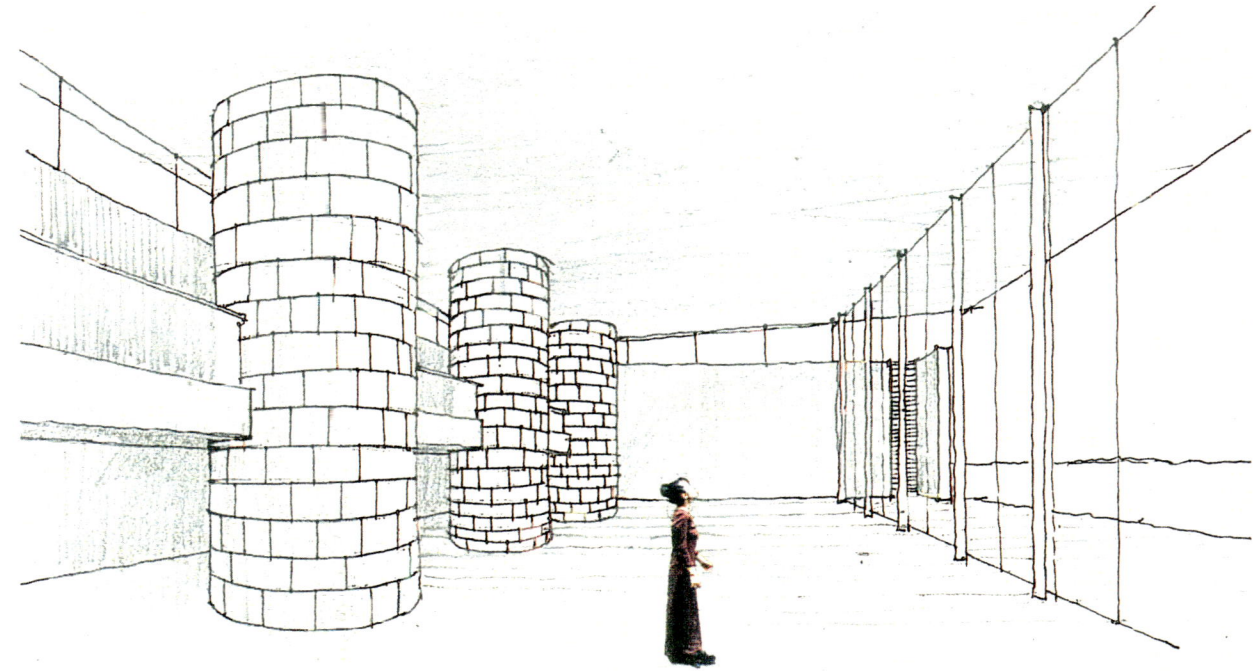

Niijima is a small island lying some 158 km off the mainland, with a population of 2,383.
In summer, the island throbs with crowds of young people, but it is usually a very quiet place. Exposed as it is to the sea, the inhabitants are constantly engaged in a struggle with typhoons and other severe natural elements.
This project was to combine a branch of the Tokyo Metropolitan Office, and a public health centre.
The huge cantilevered roof, supported by three pillars made of locally obtainable fireproof stone, covers an entrance hall, and welcomes in the people. This hall maintains maximum continuity with the square in front, and provides the first floor health centre and the second floor metropolitan office.

Plans of the first floor and second floor.

Key 1 (left)
1. Counselling Room
2. Conference Room
3. Women's Rest Room
4. Men's Rest Room
5. Meeting Room
6. Office

Key 2 (right)
1. Entrance
2. Parking
3. Women's Rest Room
4. Men's Rest Room
5. Multi-Purpose Room
6. Clinic
7. Office

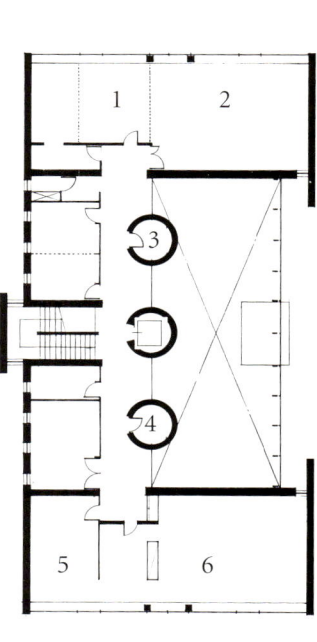
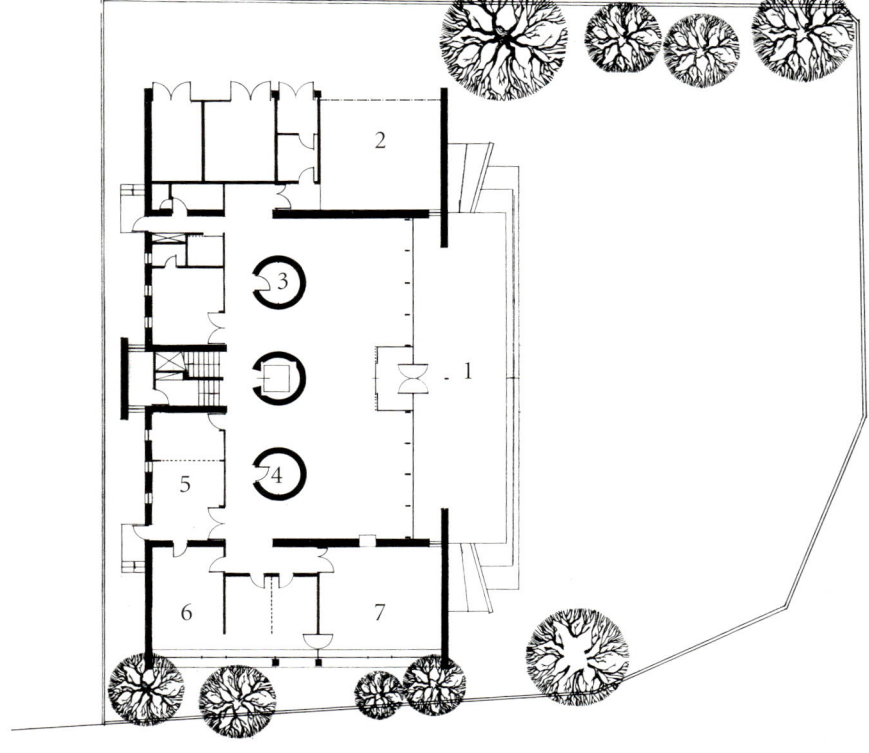

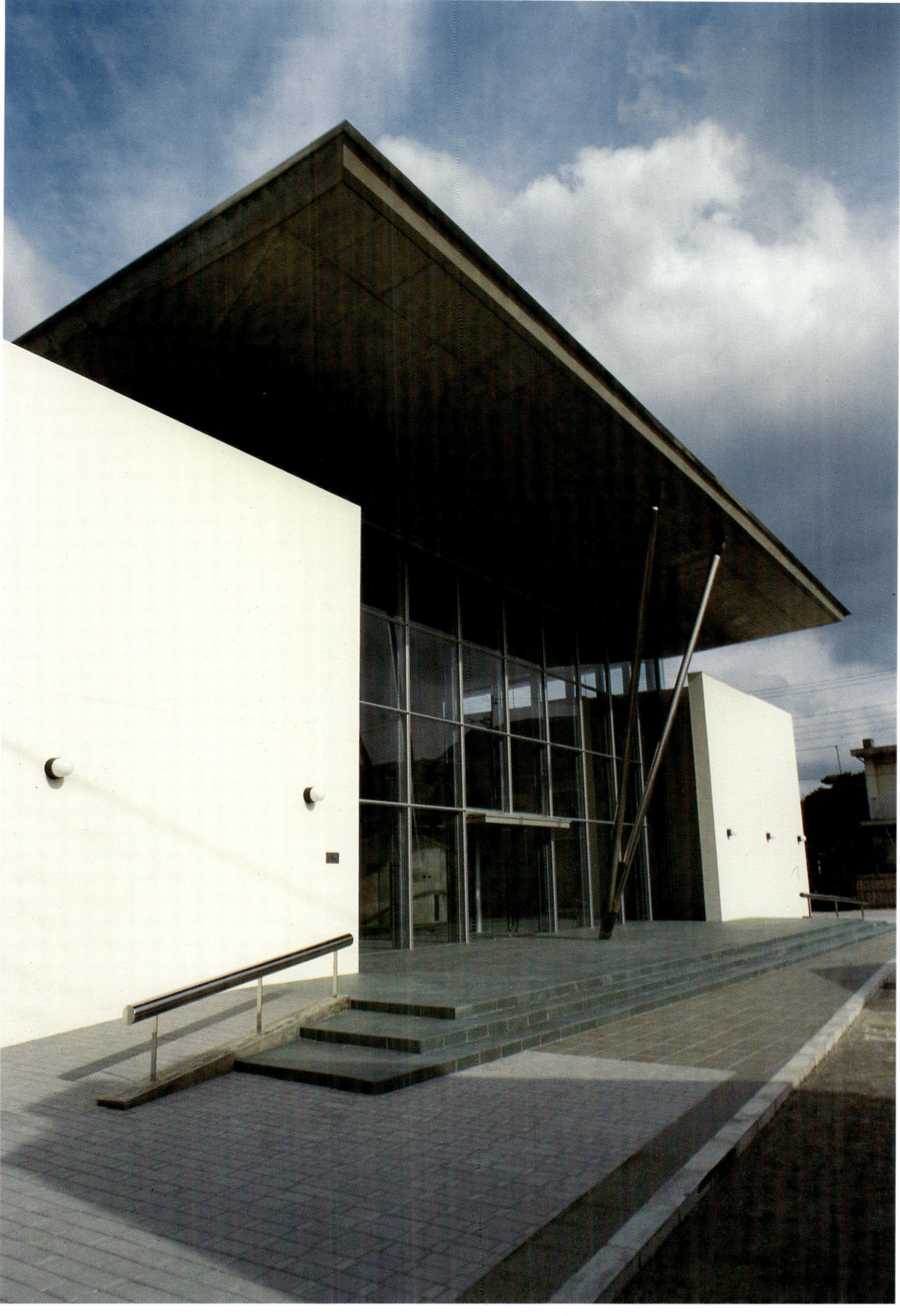

This page and next pages, two views of the main facade and entrance lobby.

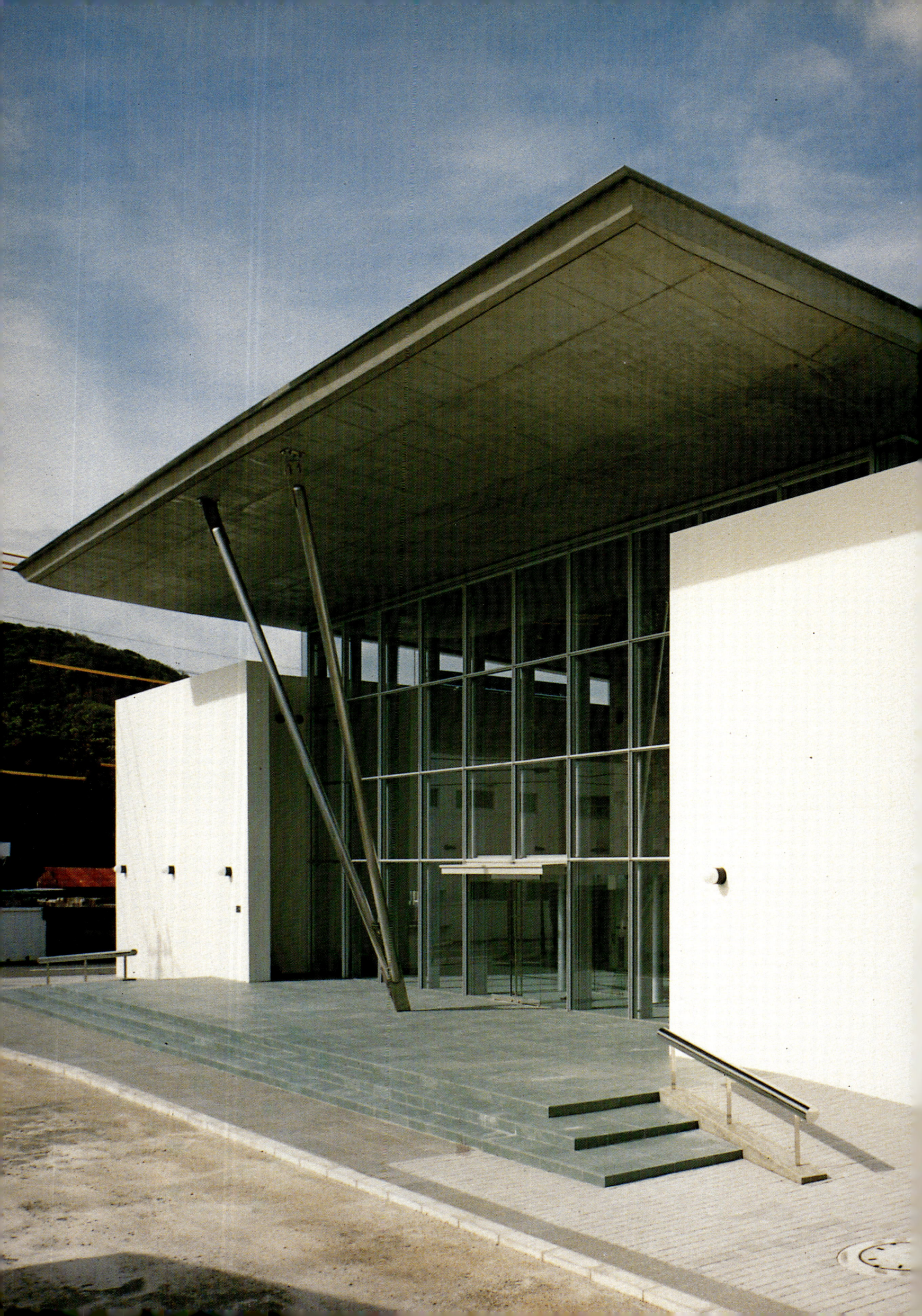

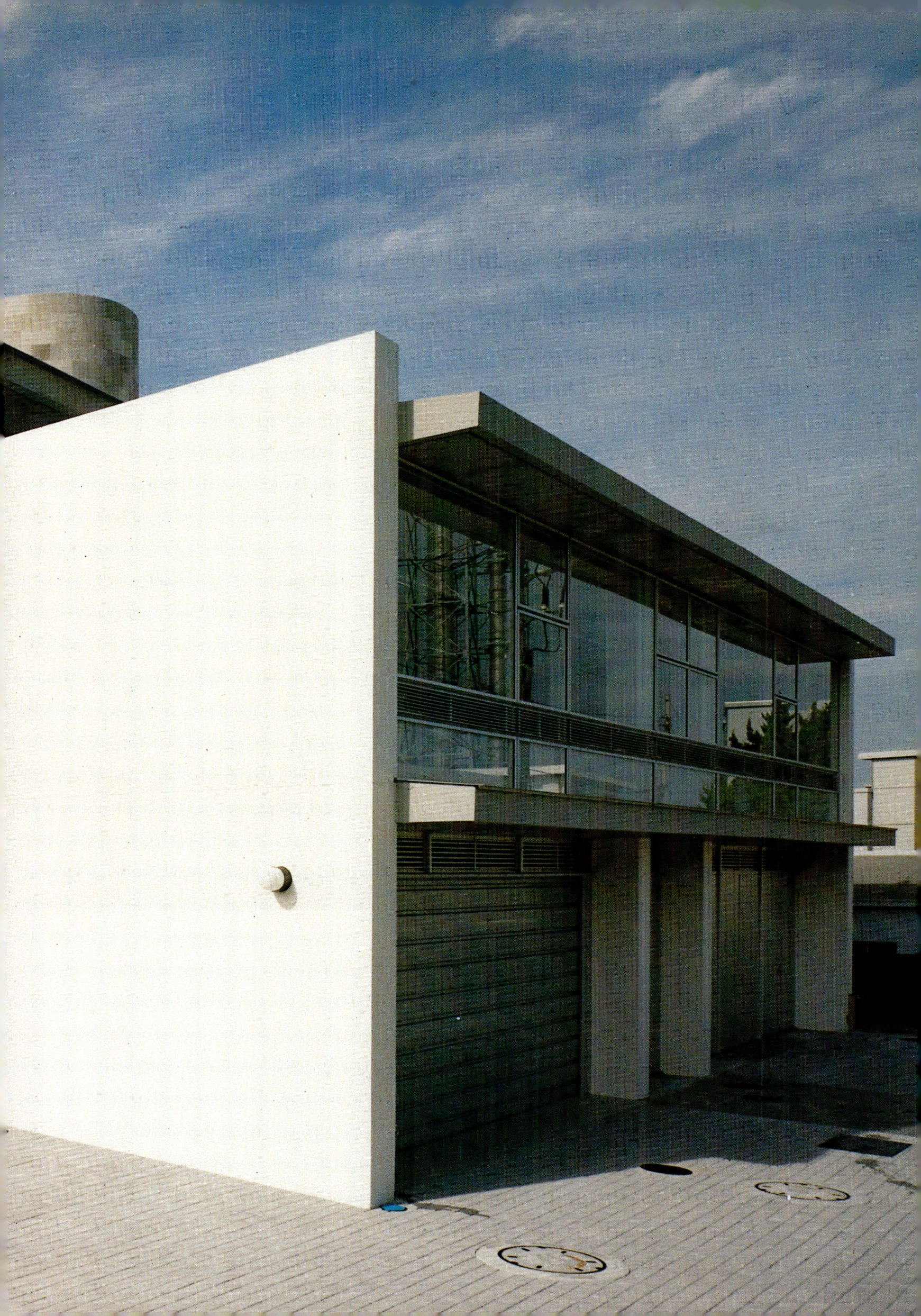

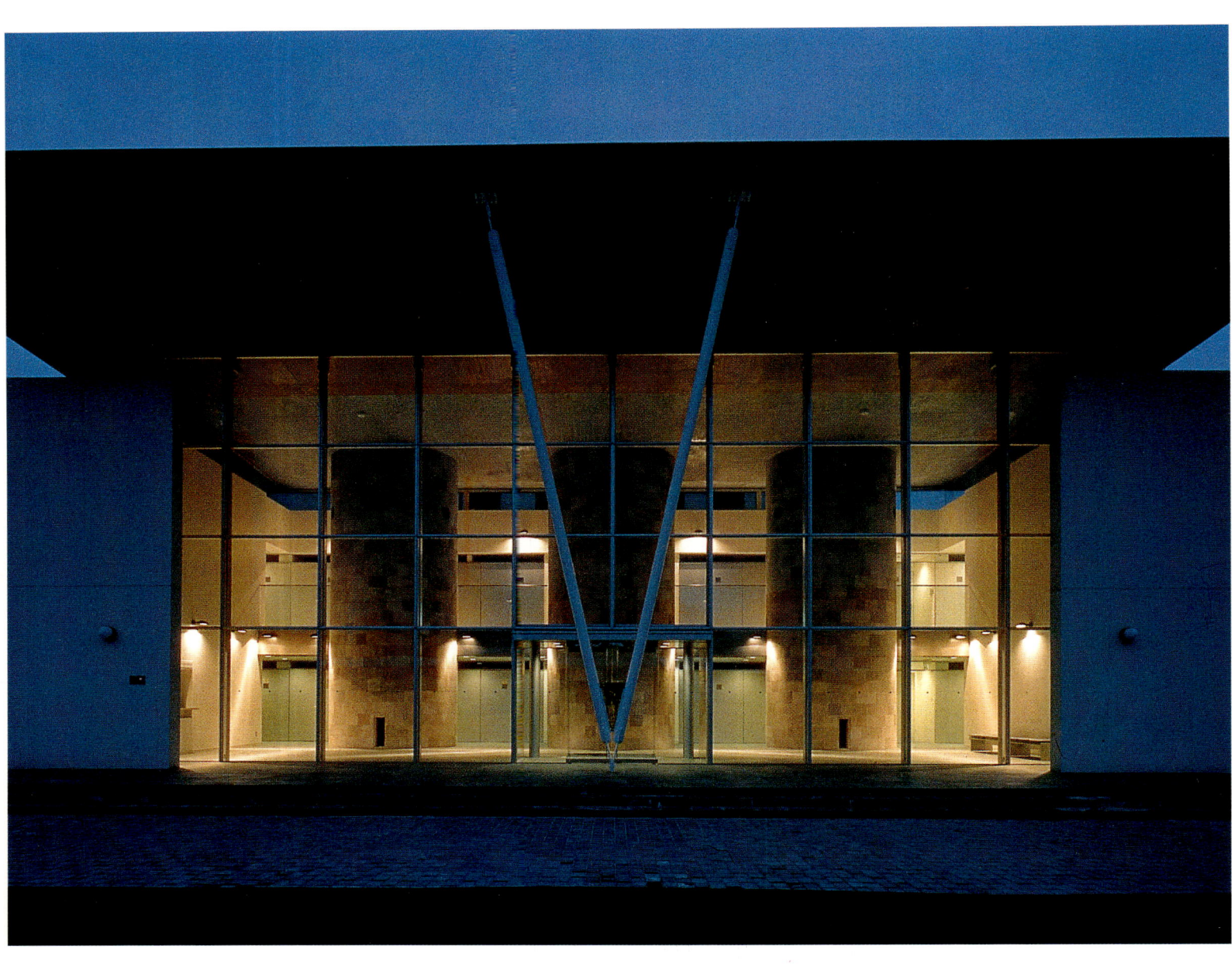

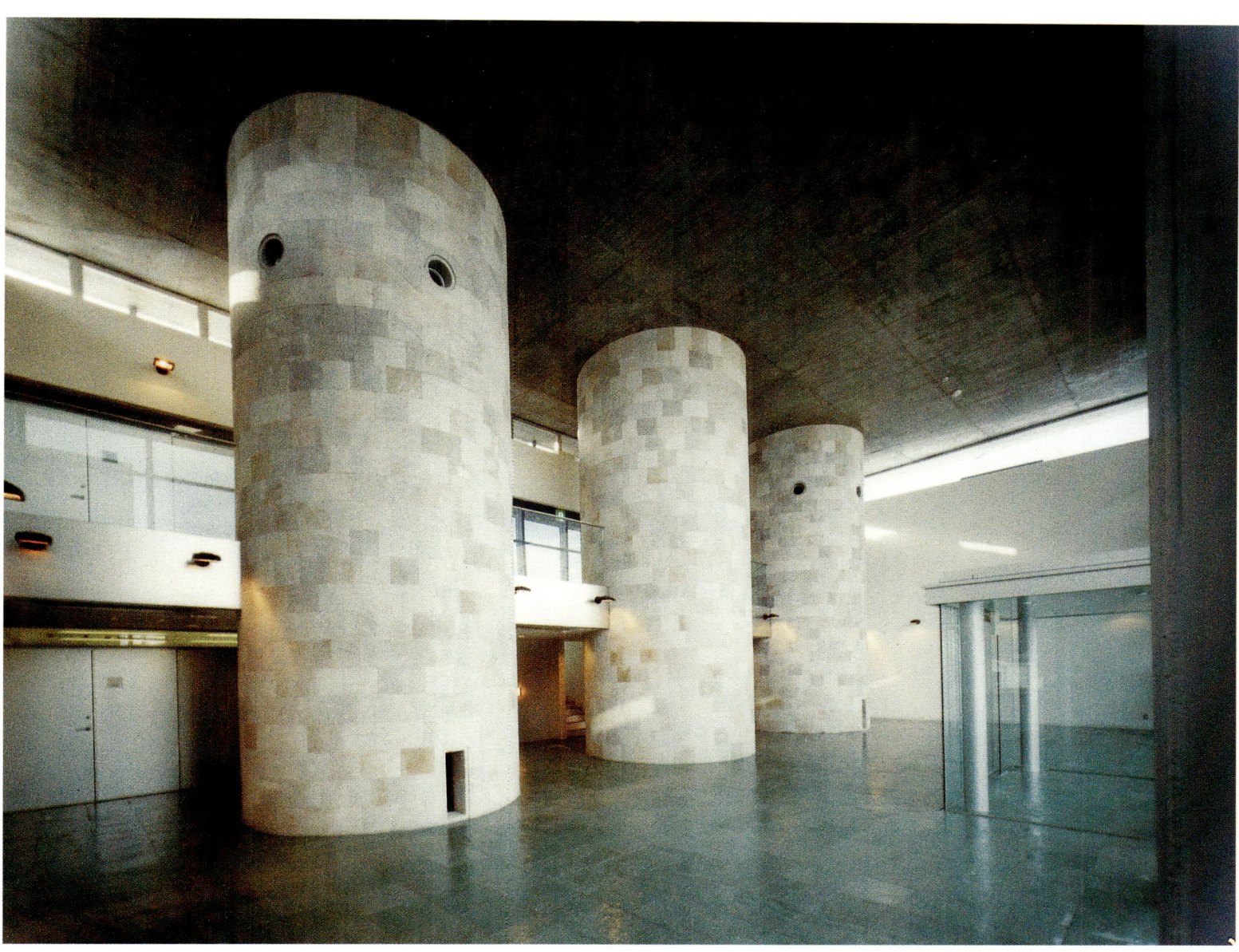

View of the three blocks holding the rest rooms and elevator.

F-House

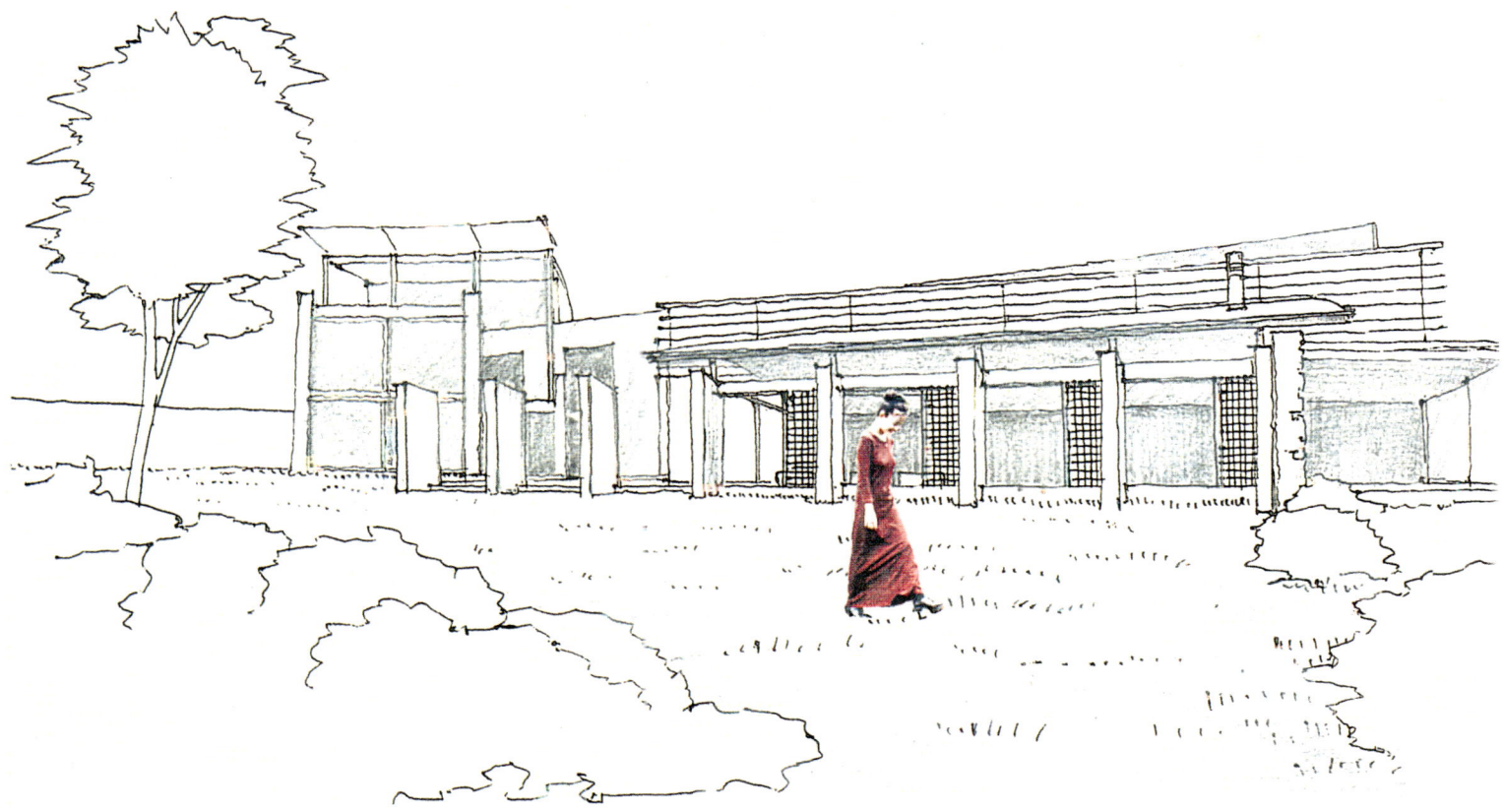

I decided to follow the style of the traditional Japanese mansion, and encompass the entire perimeter of the site with a wall, and to create a formal garden within these confines, with an open building in relation to the garden.

The entrance zone, living zone and sleeping zone were arranged in south facing form, running along the east-west axis of the property.

A variety of scenes unfold as the occupants move through the residence. The living room flows naturally from the dining room, with a difference in levels, expanding out to the terrace and formal garden. The bedrooms are angled so as to encompass a basin, and are planned so as to separate the public and private zones, while at the same time causing them to stand out in relationship to each other.

Many large sliding doors are used to present continuity between interior and exterior space, and to bestow plentiful spaciousness and change.

These individual spaces combine in mutual relationships to form a single whole, and that whole is the traditional Japanese mansion.

Plan of the first floor of the villa.

1. Main Entrance
2. Living Room
3. Terrace
4. Bedroom
5. Closet
6. Terrace
7. Bathroom
8. Kitchen
9. Closet
10. Back Yard Entrance
11. Japanese Style Room
12. Car Parking Space

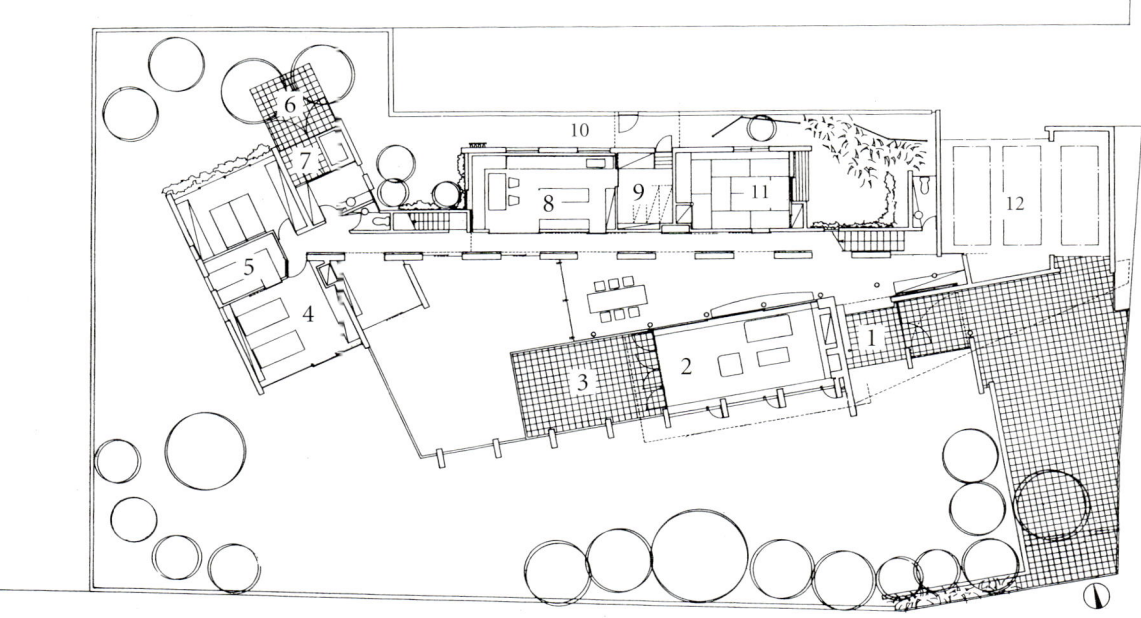

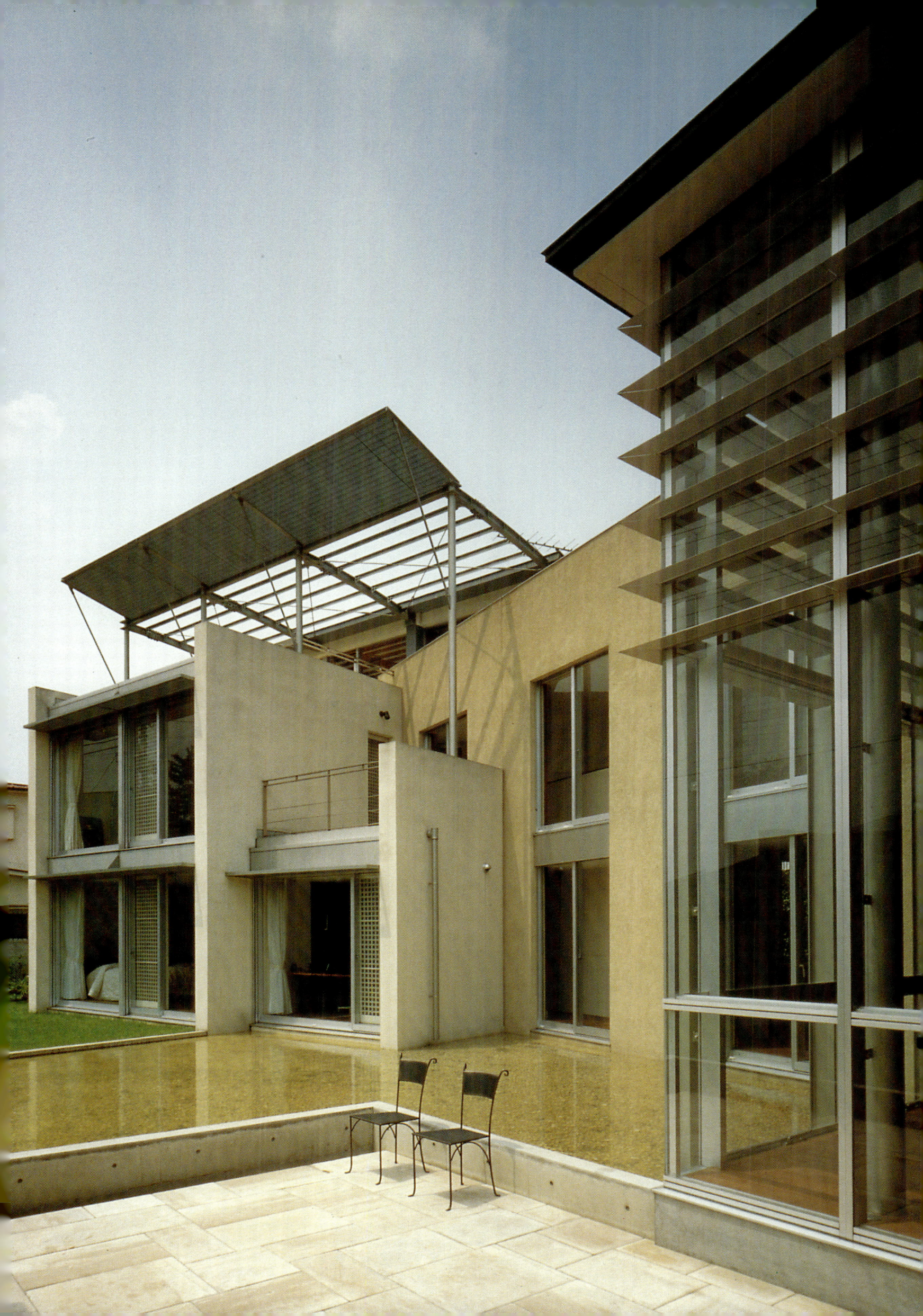

Plan of the second floor and south elevation.
Bottom of page, nighttime view of the villa. Previous page, view of the roof terrace.

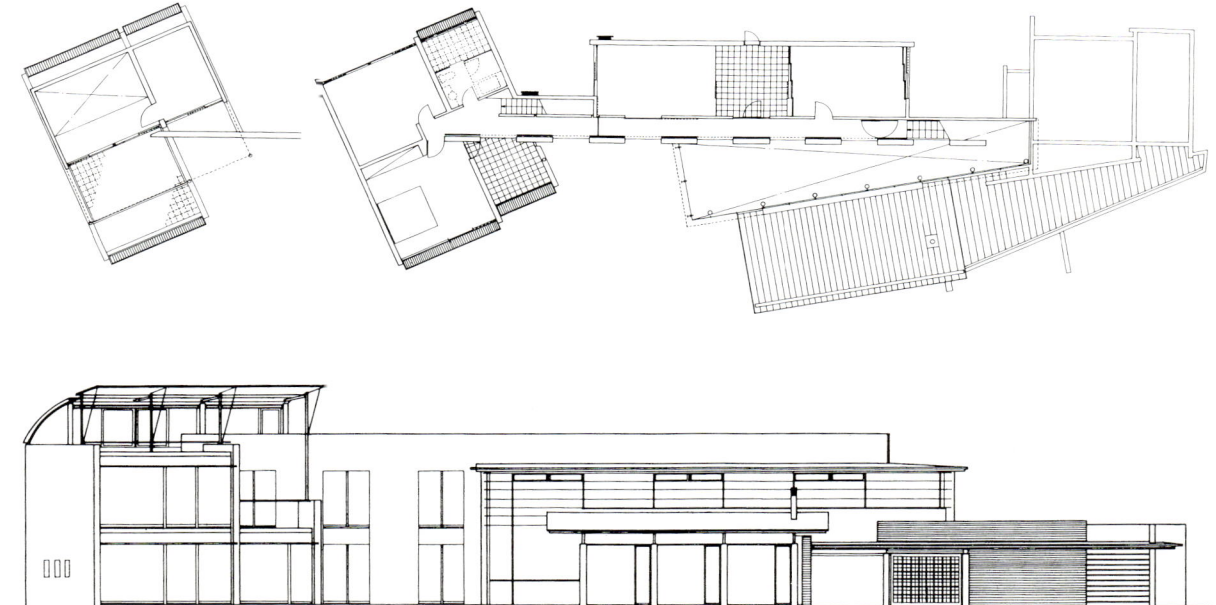

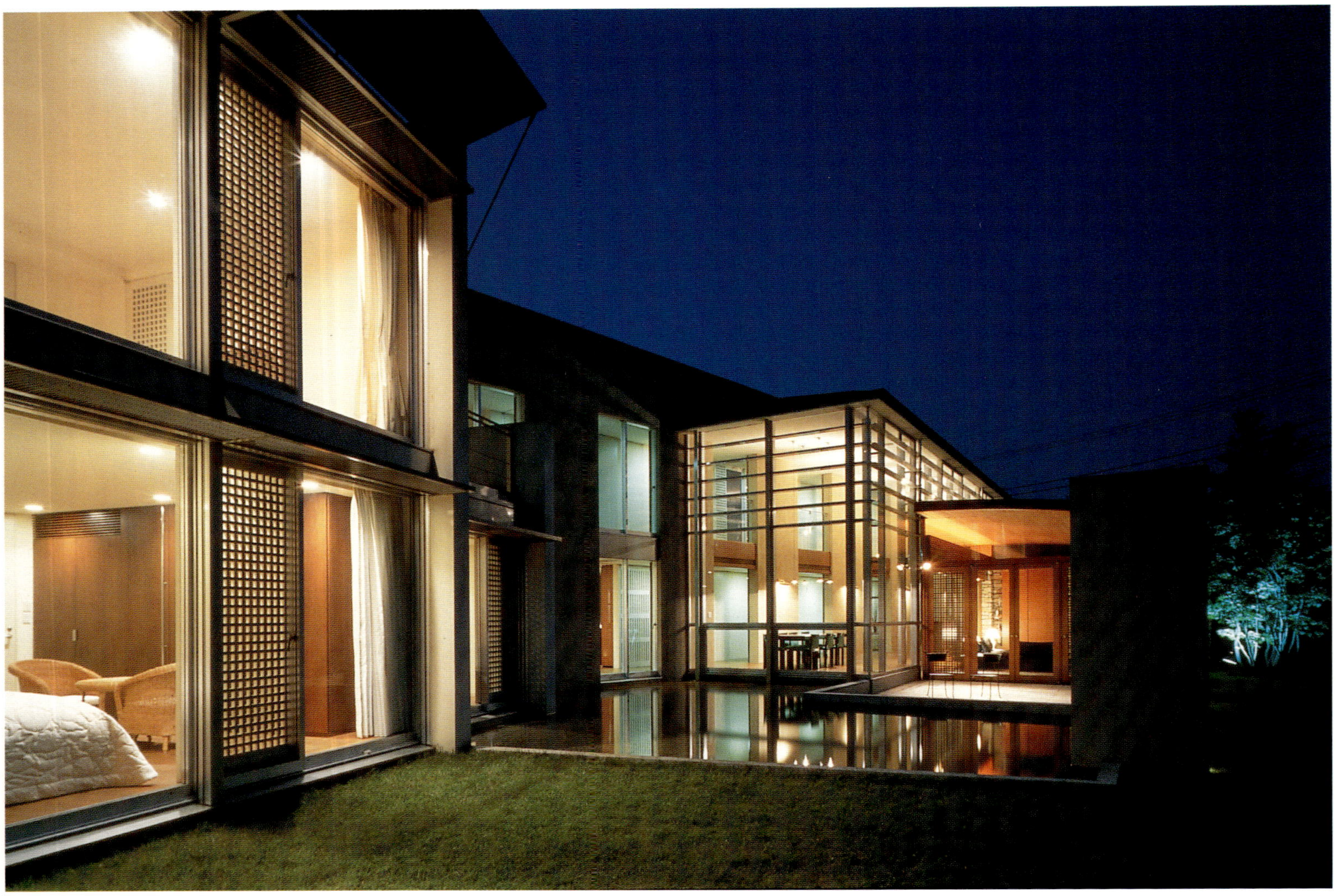

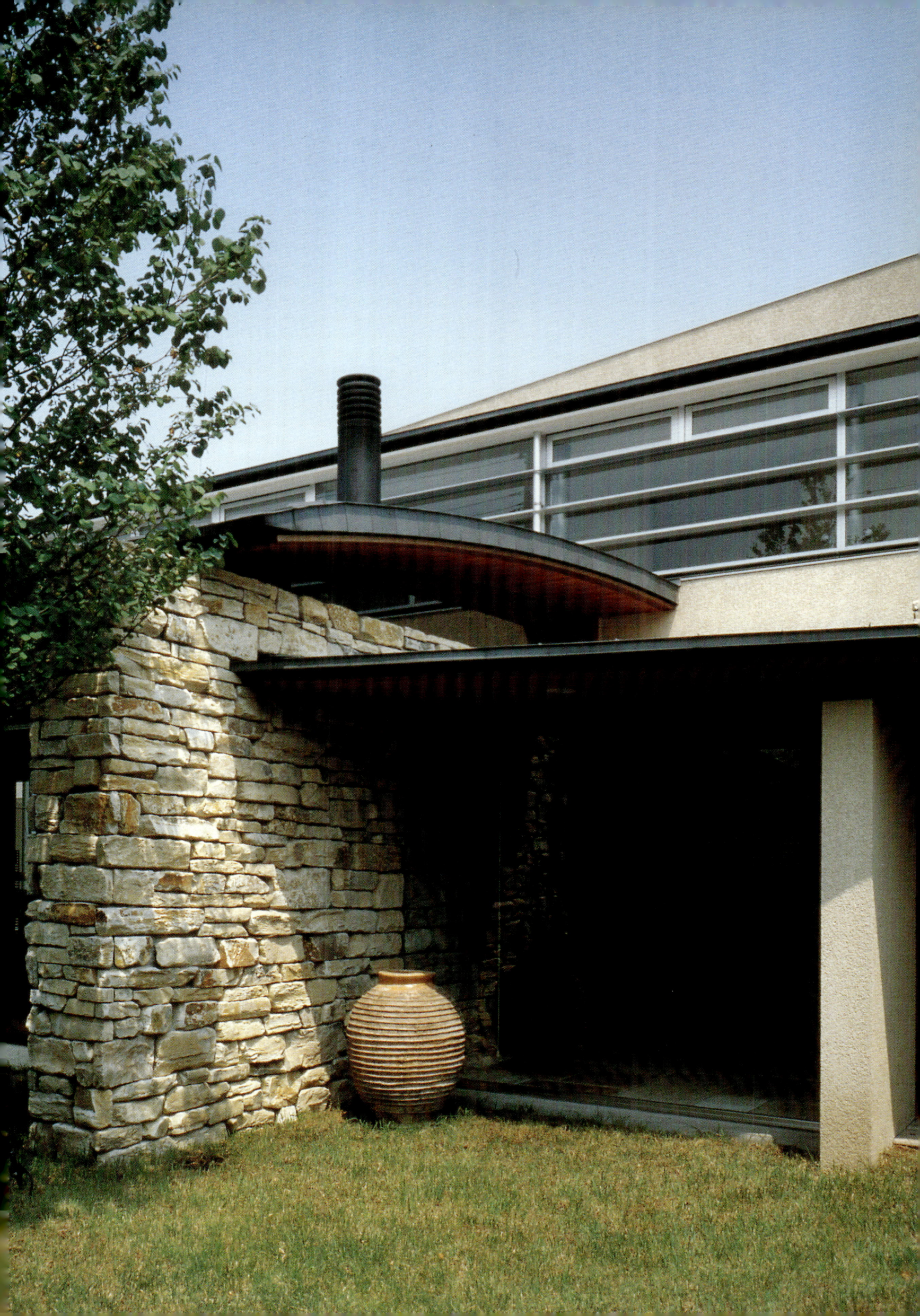

This page and previous page, these views underline the subtle architectural interactions between interior and exterior.

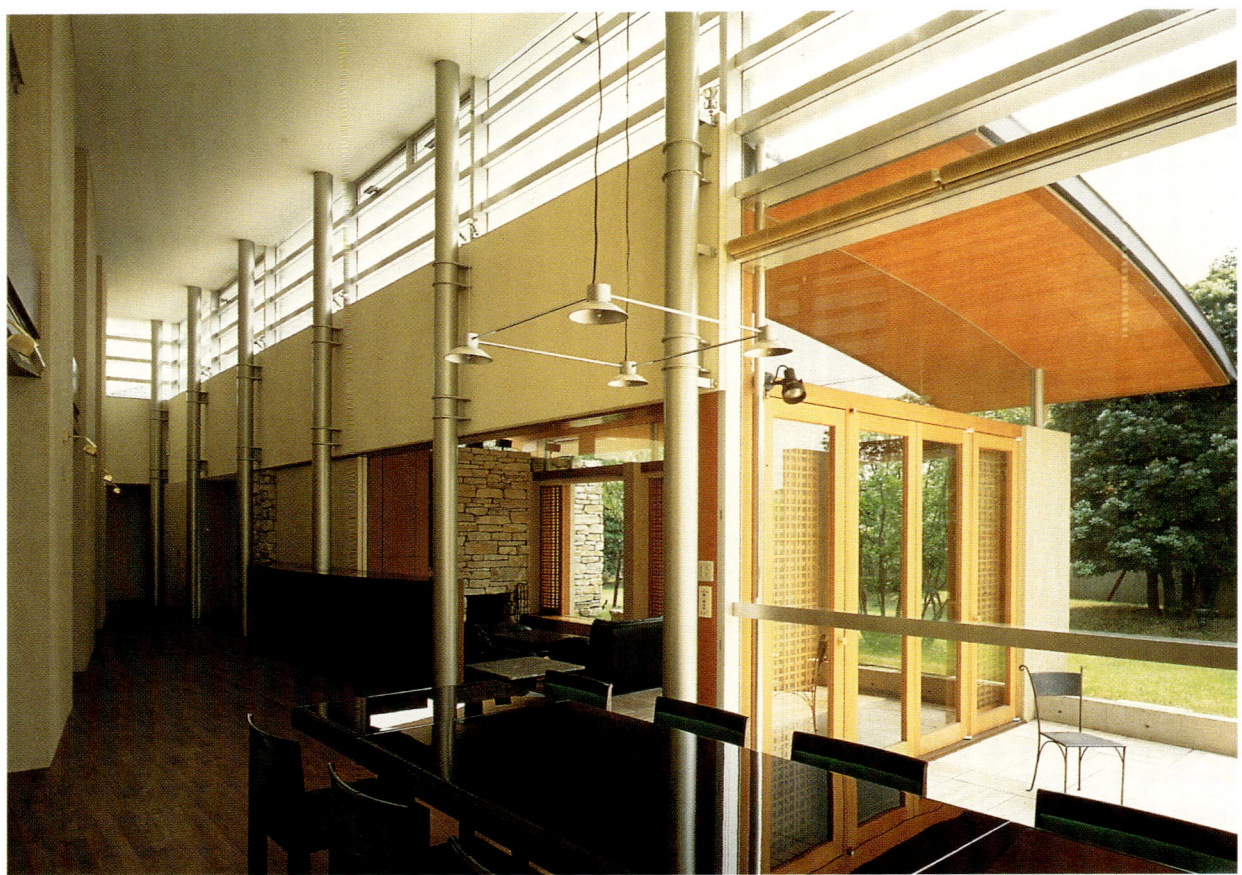

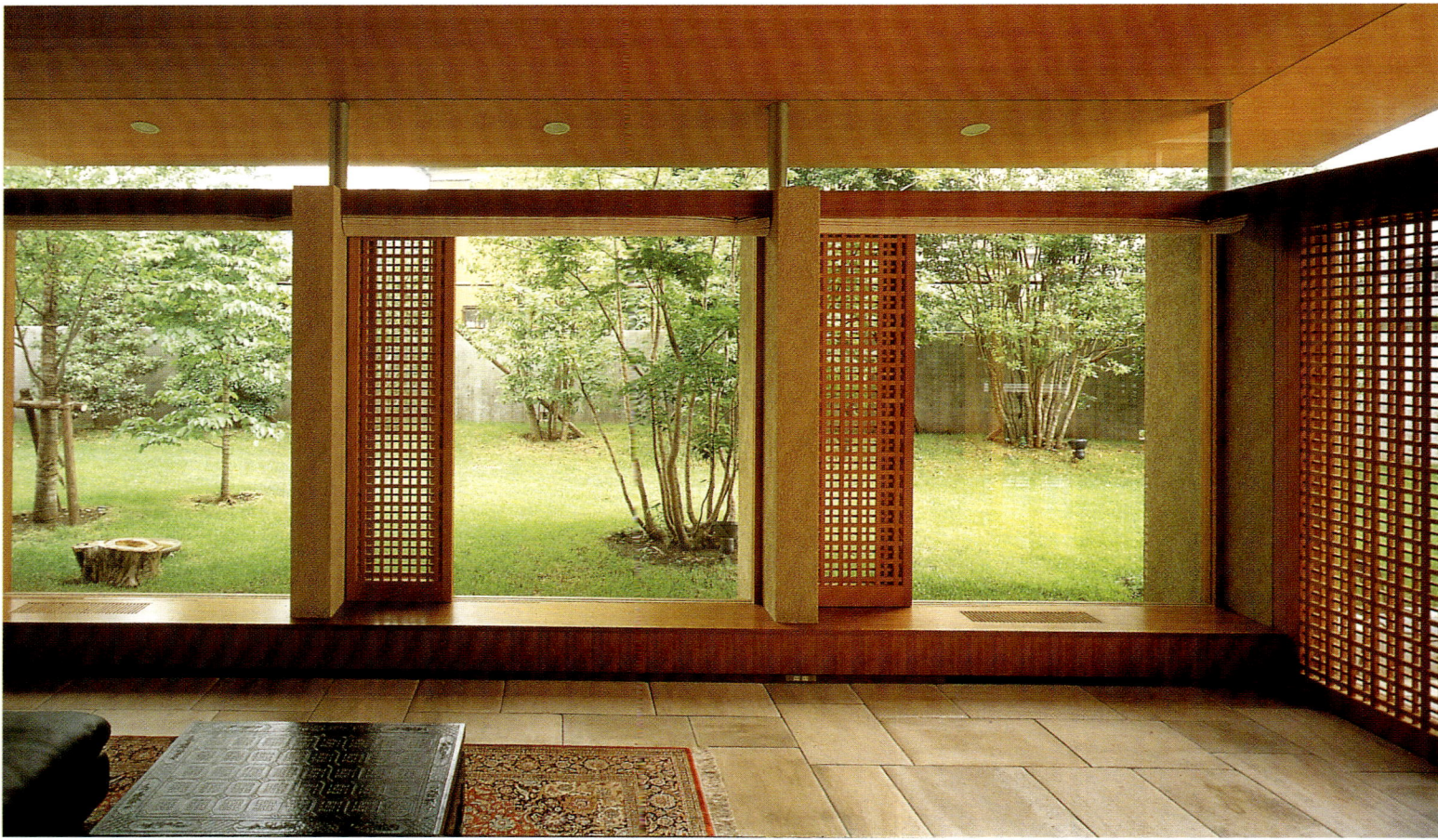

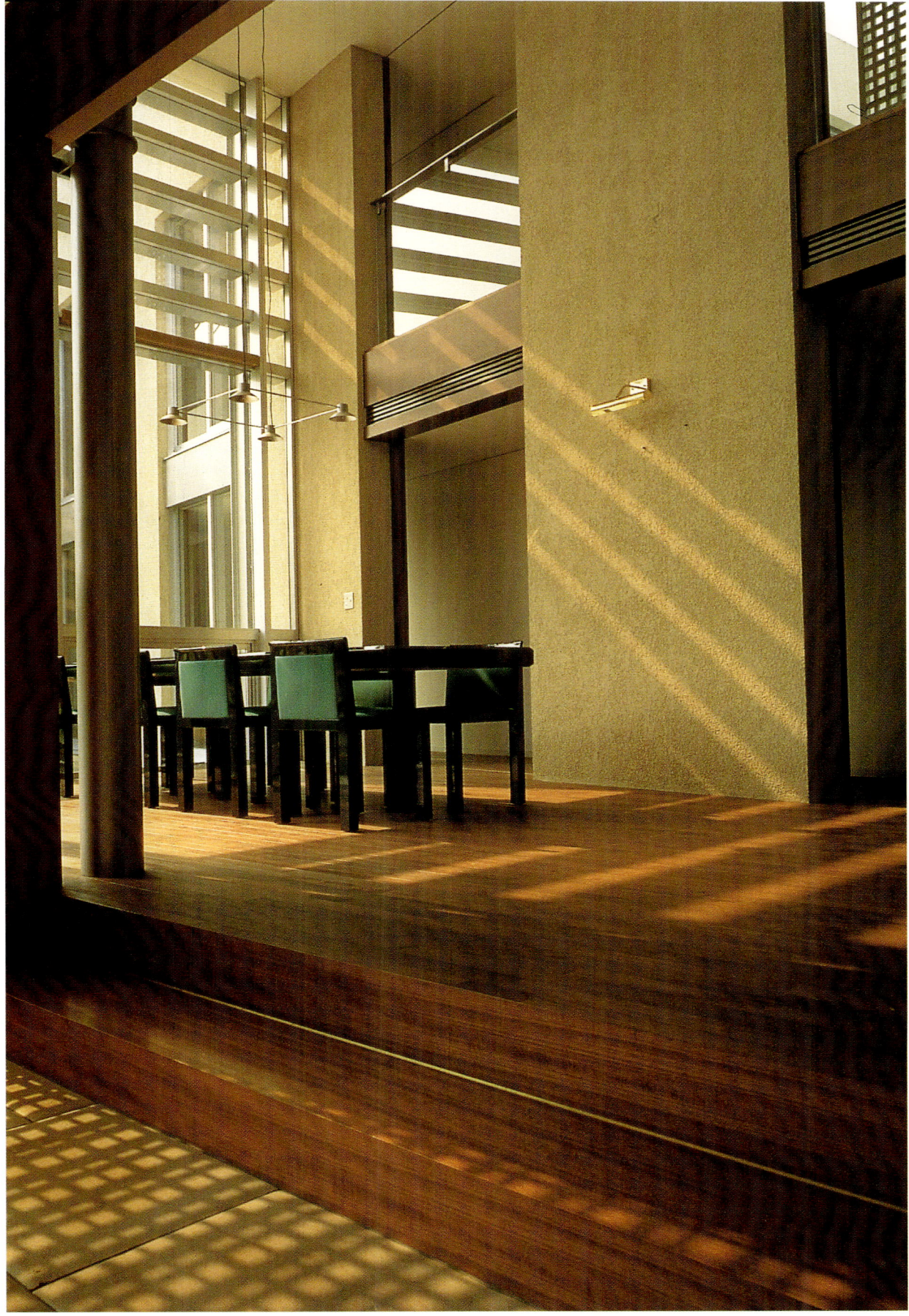

View of the interior courtyard between the kitchen and living room.

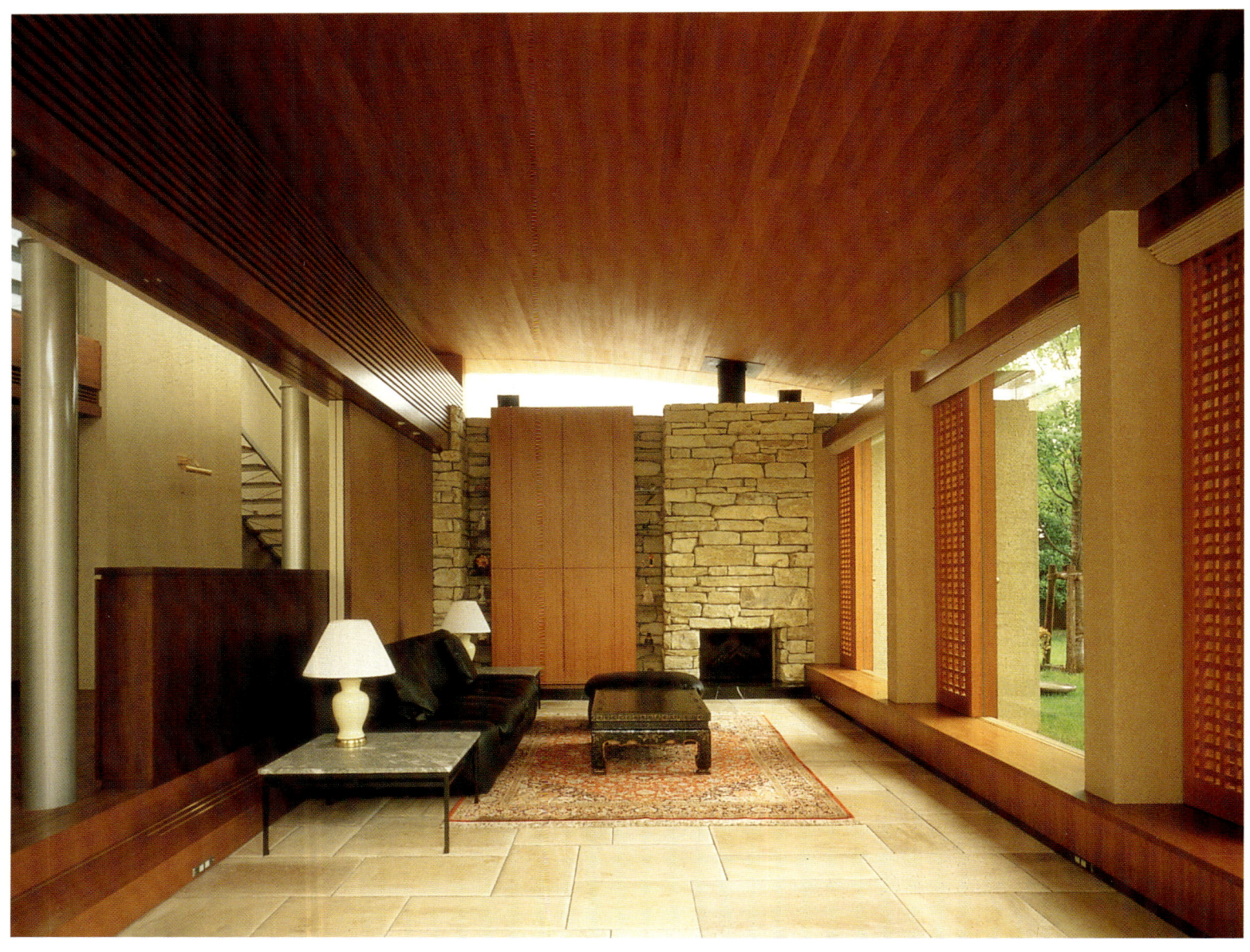

The living room opens onto the garden through sliding doors designed to recreate the typically Japanese concept of interaction between interior and exterior.

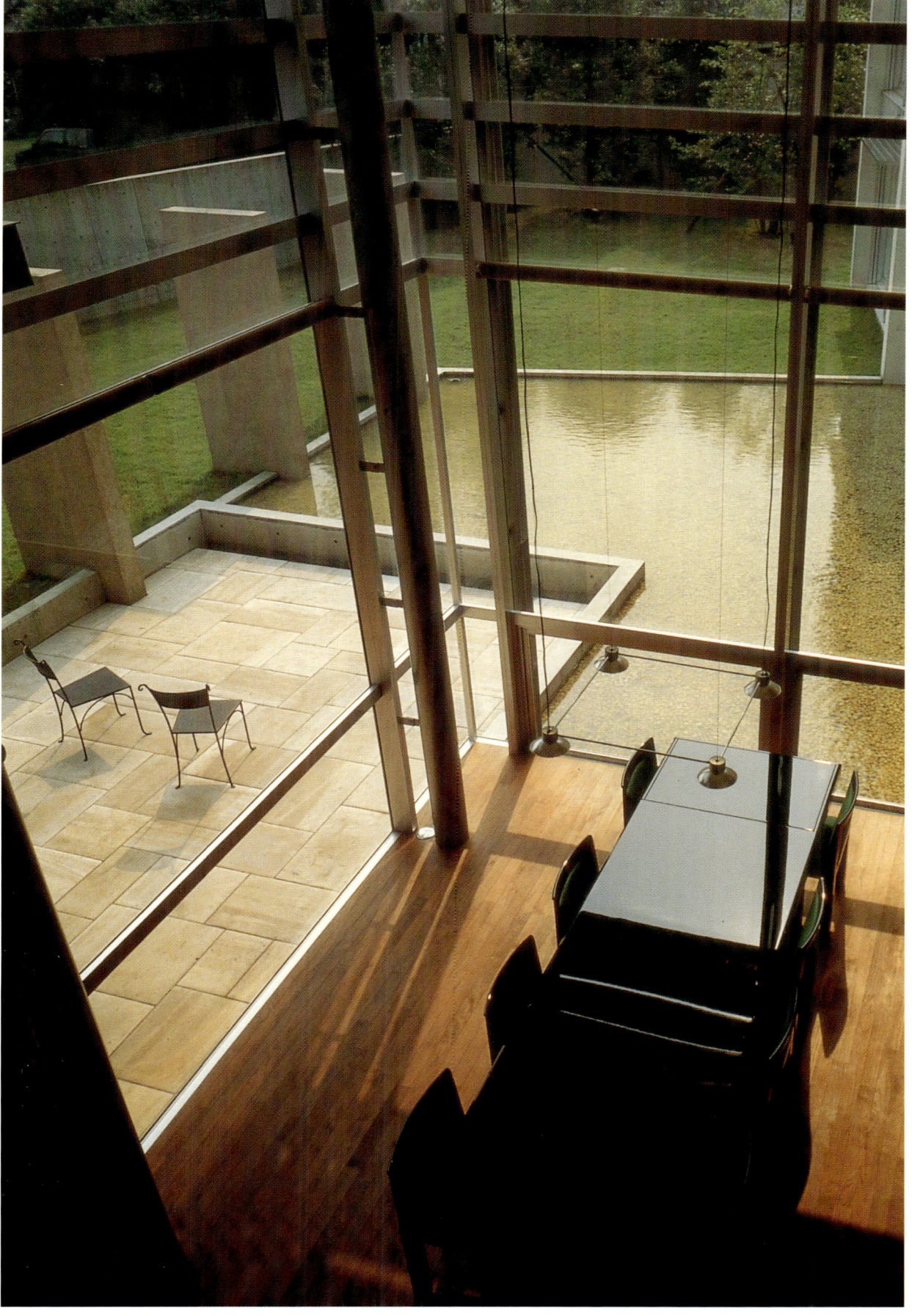

The dining room opening onto the garden and artificial pool.

Shiroishi N°2 Primary School

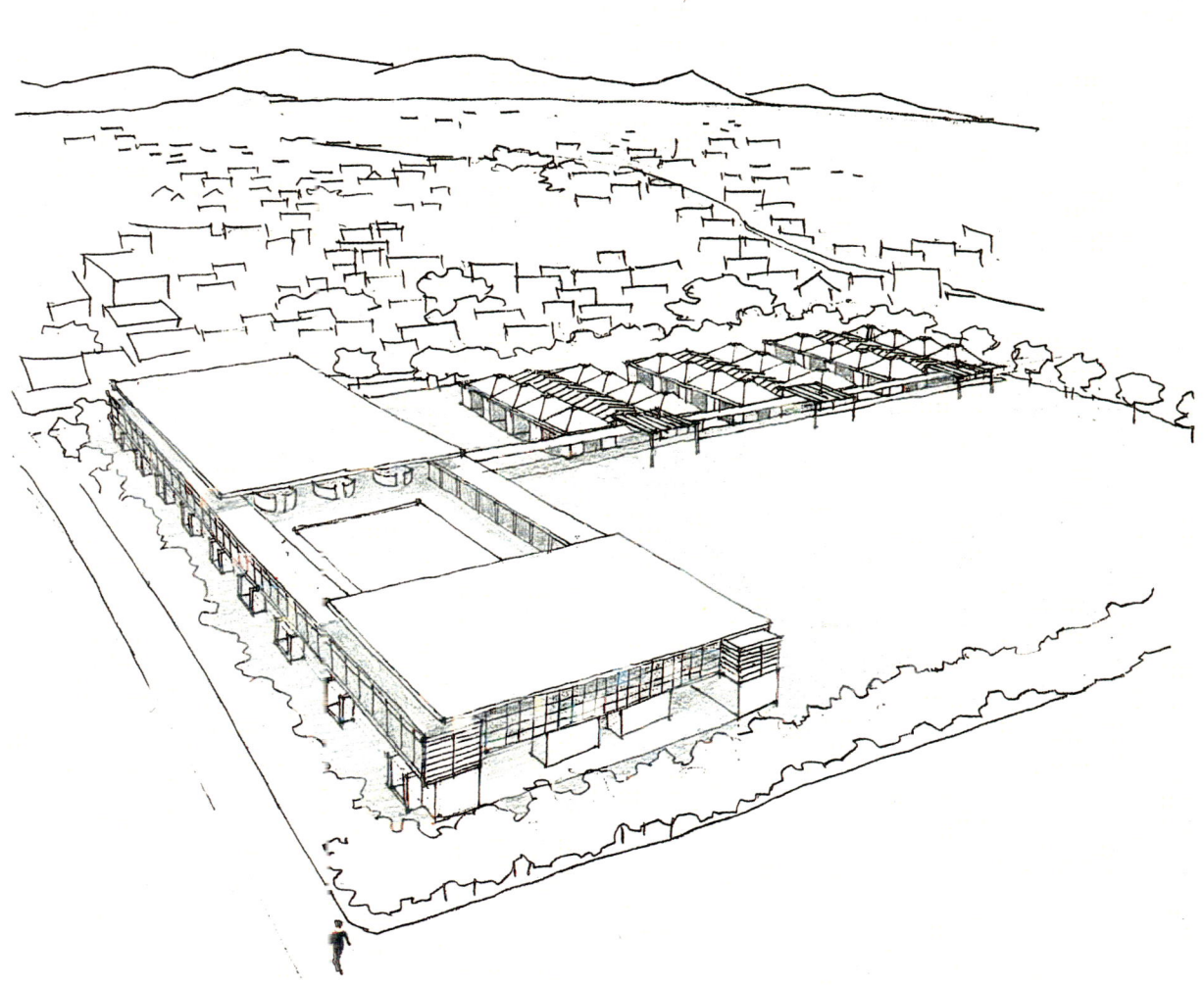

This primary school was designed as part of the town planning of Shiroishi City. As Shiroishi City was itself in the middle of searching for a new town form, we suggested that the administration, specialists and citizens combine to form the 'Shiroishi Design Forum', with the aim of providing an open forum for the advancement of town planning, and set about the design as a pilot project. Here, we used the open design method known as a 'workshop'. The plans were developed while constantly providing feedback from the participation of the children, parents and educators.
The layout of the school includes the teaching wing, and a public wing (gym hall, pool, special rooms, meeting rooms, teachers' rooms) that also functions as a facility for communication with the area. The two wings are in an L-shaped configuration. The keynote of the whole structure is an ecological design that gives due consideration to natural ventilation and lighting. The teaching wing is a single storey construction that utilises the charms of the old style school yard, and is reminiscent of the 'Hiroma, Hiroen' terrace of traditional Japanese houses. The layout of the spatial system is alternate single blocks of four classrooms, and a large corridor-hall (multi-purpose space), and central court. In addition to these plans, sliding walls allow various teaching methods.

North and west elevations.

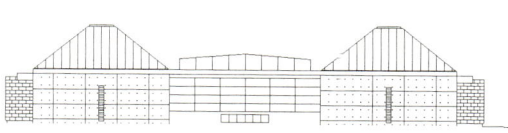
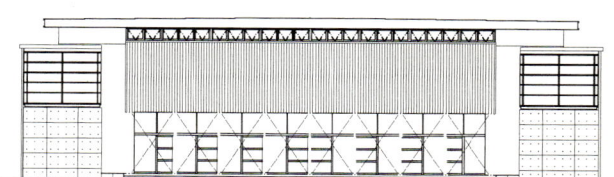

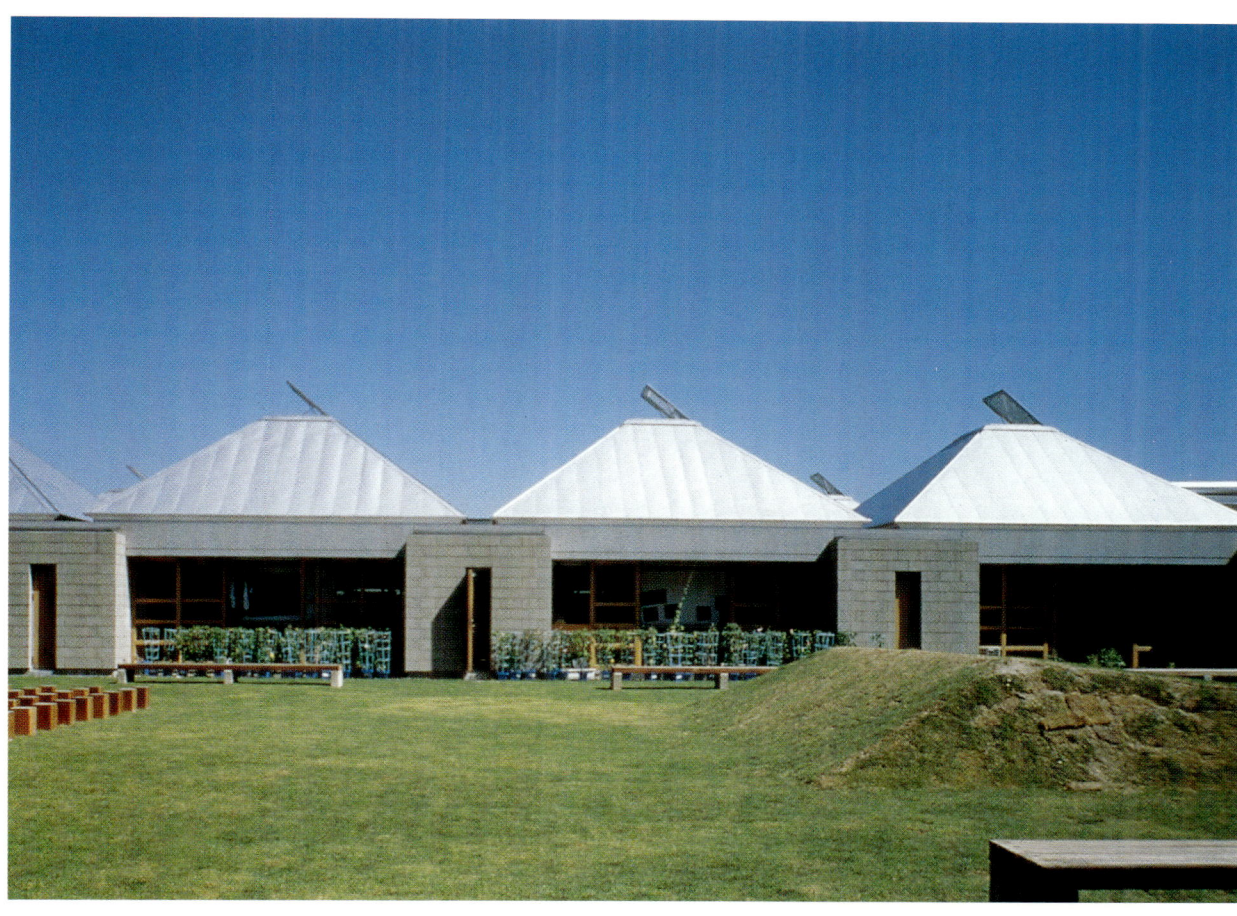

Two views of the classroom building. Following pages, the internal court.

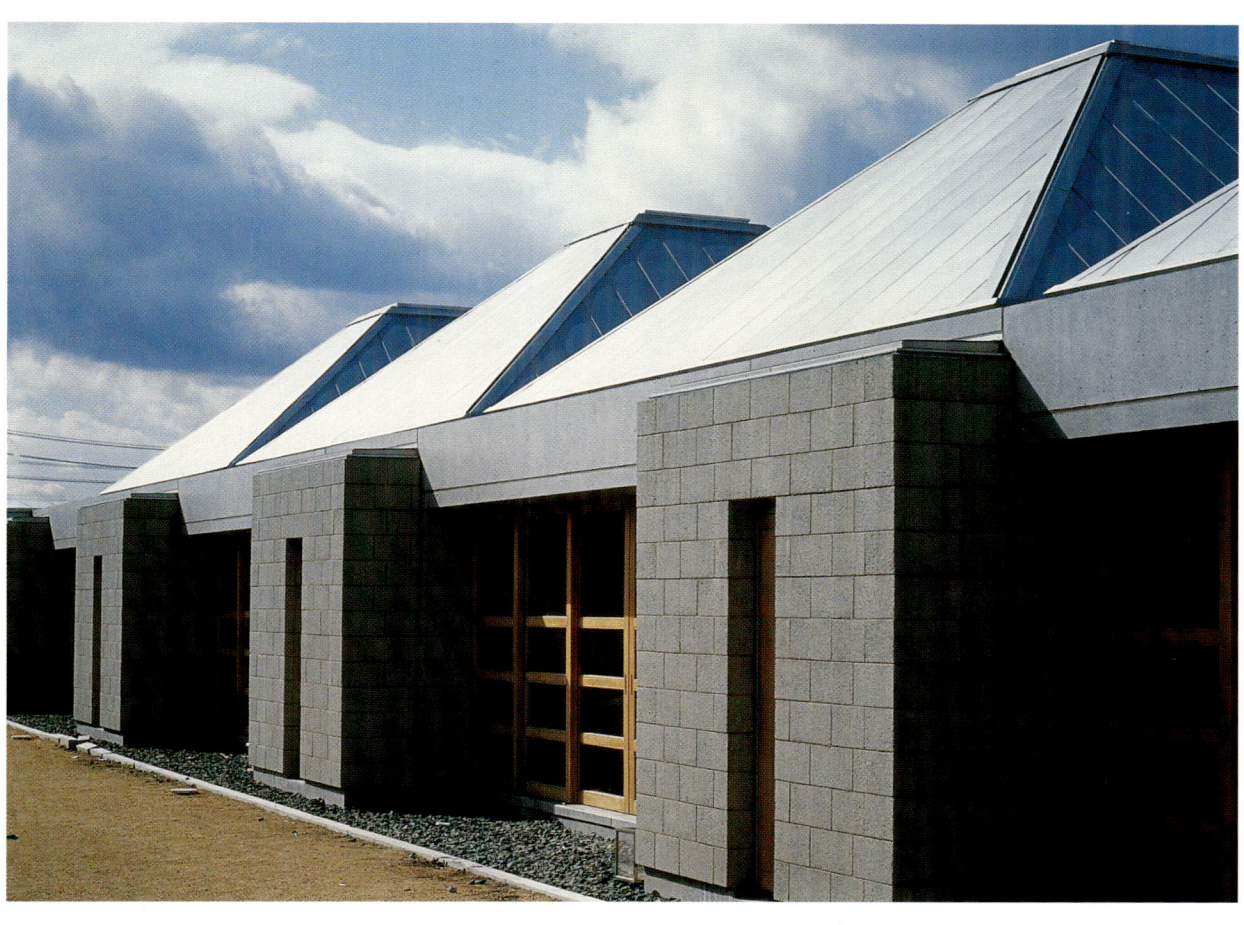

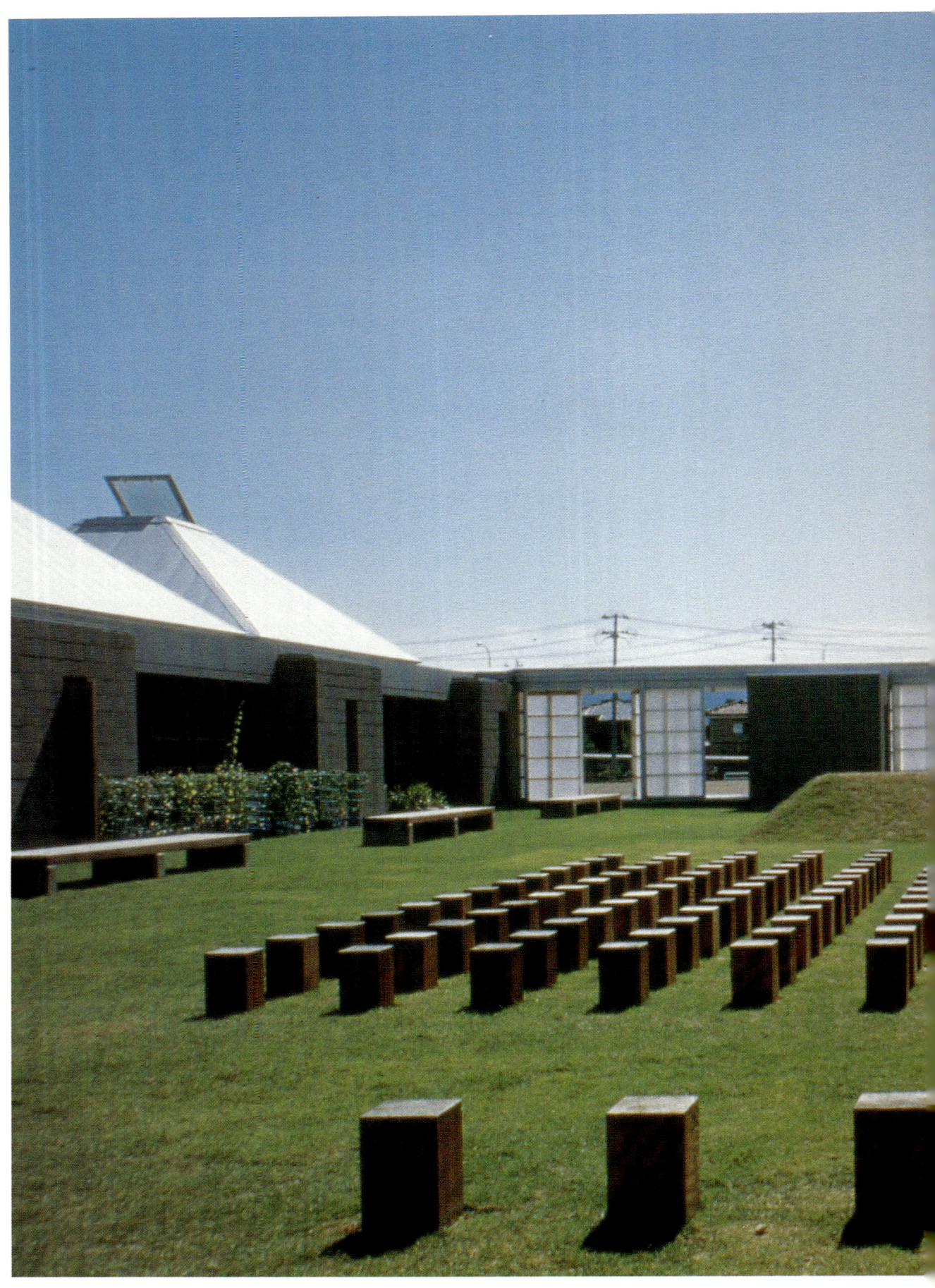

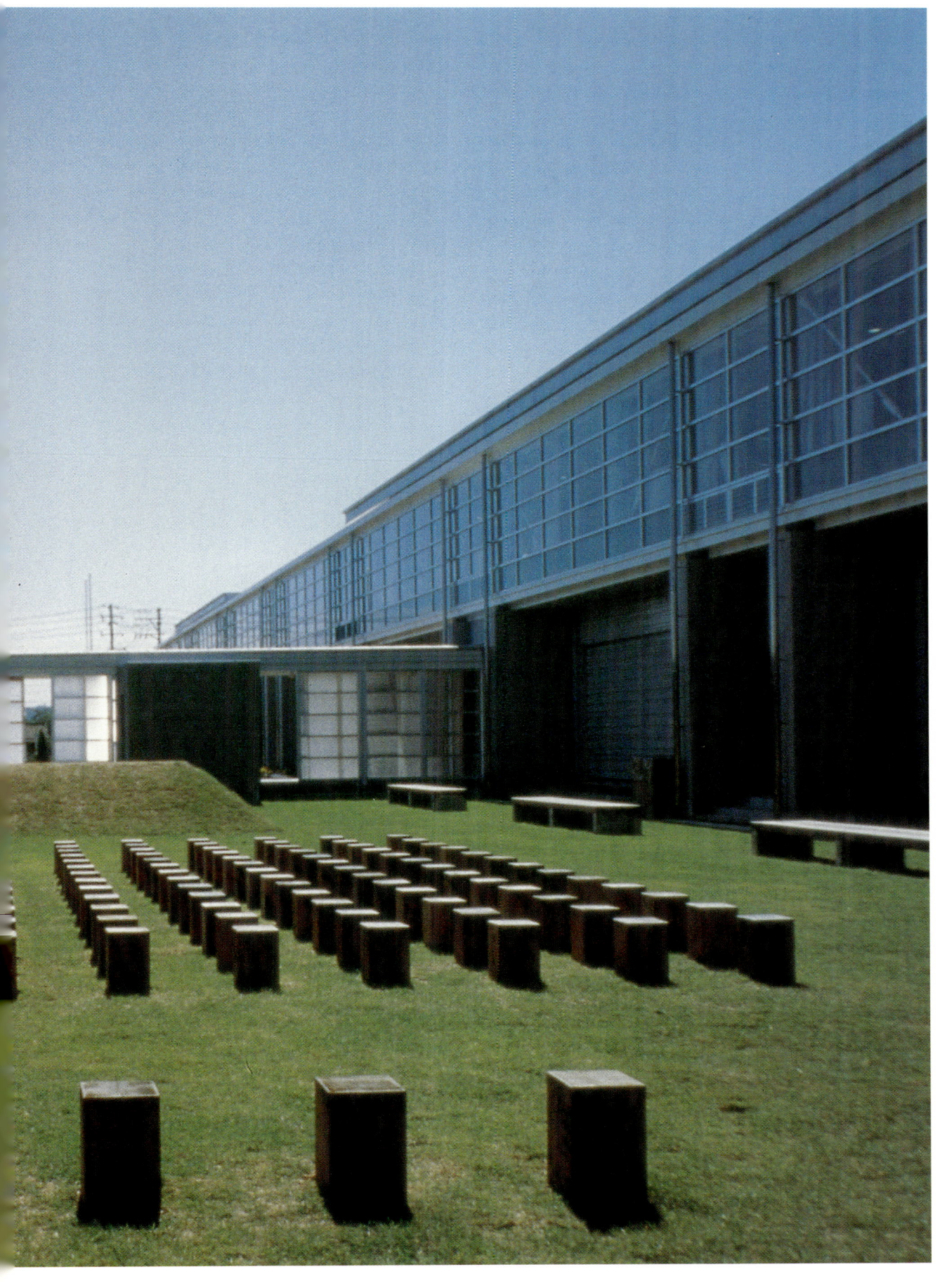

Plan of the second floor, picture of the model, and section of the multi-purpose building.
Opposite, an external valkway and, next pages, the main arena.

1. Entrance Hall
2. Arena
3. Grand Stairway
4. Principal's Room
5. Music Room
6. Cubicle
7. Multi-Purpose Space
8. Sub Entrance

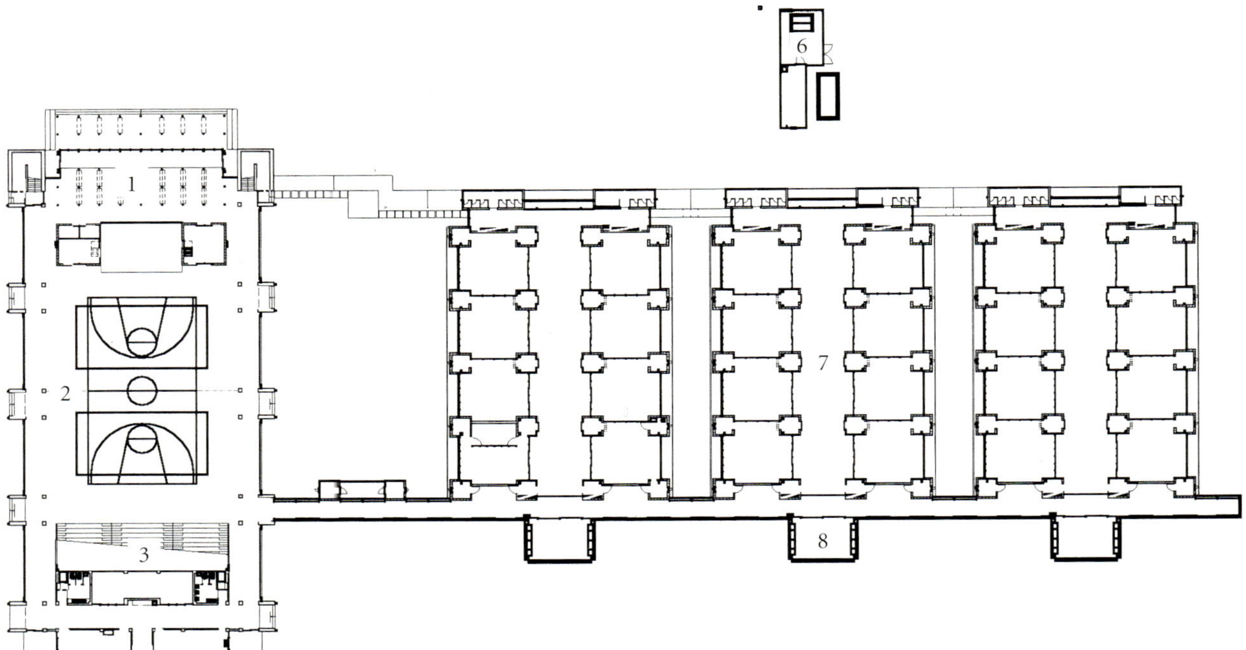

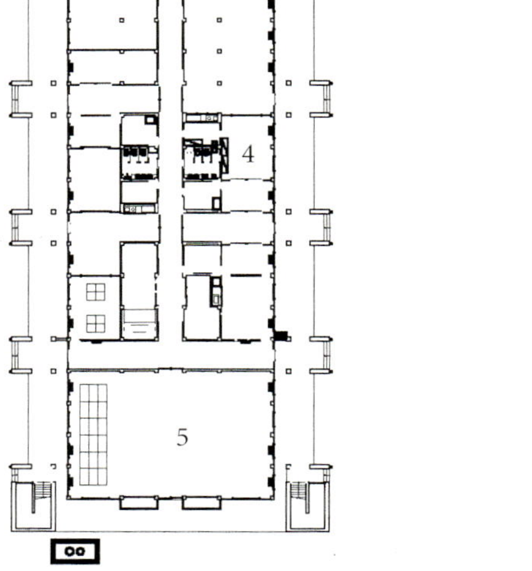

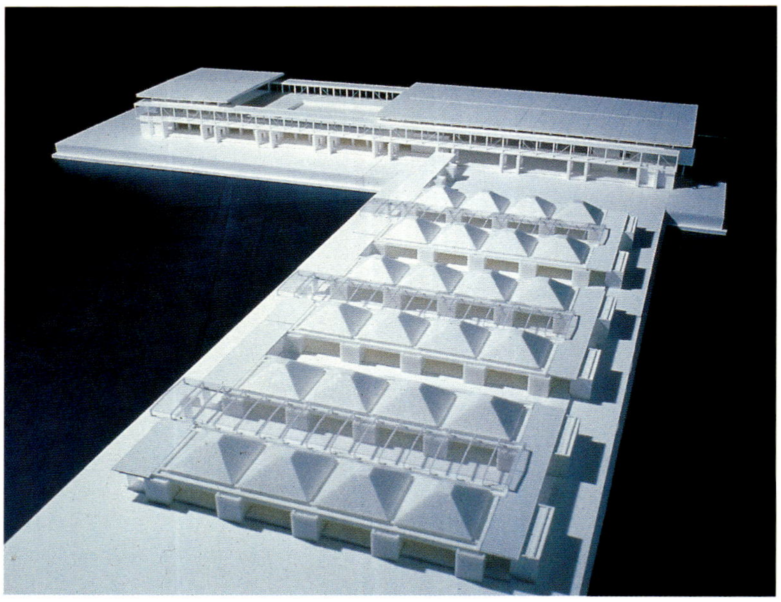

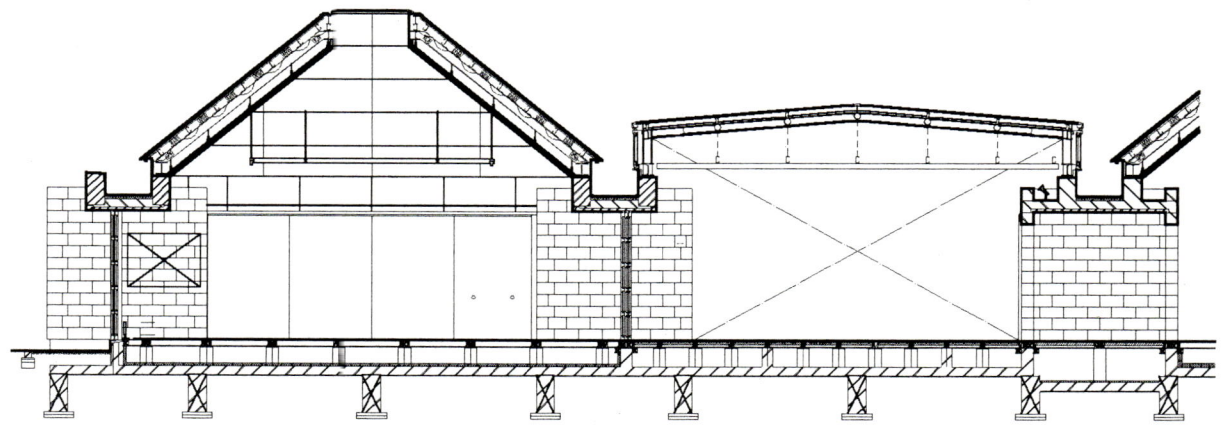

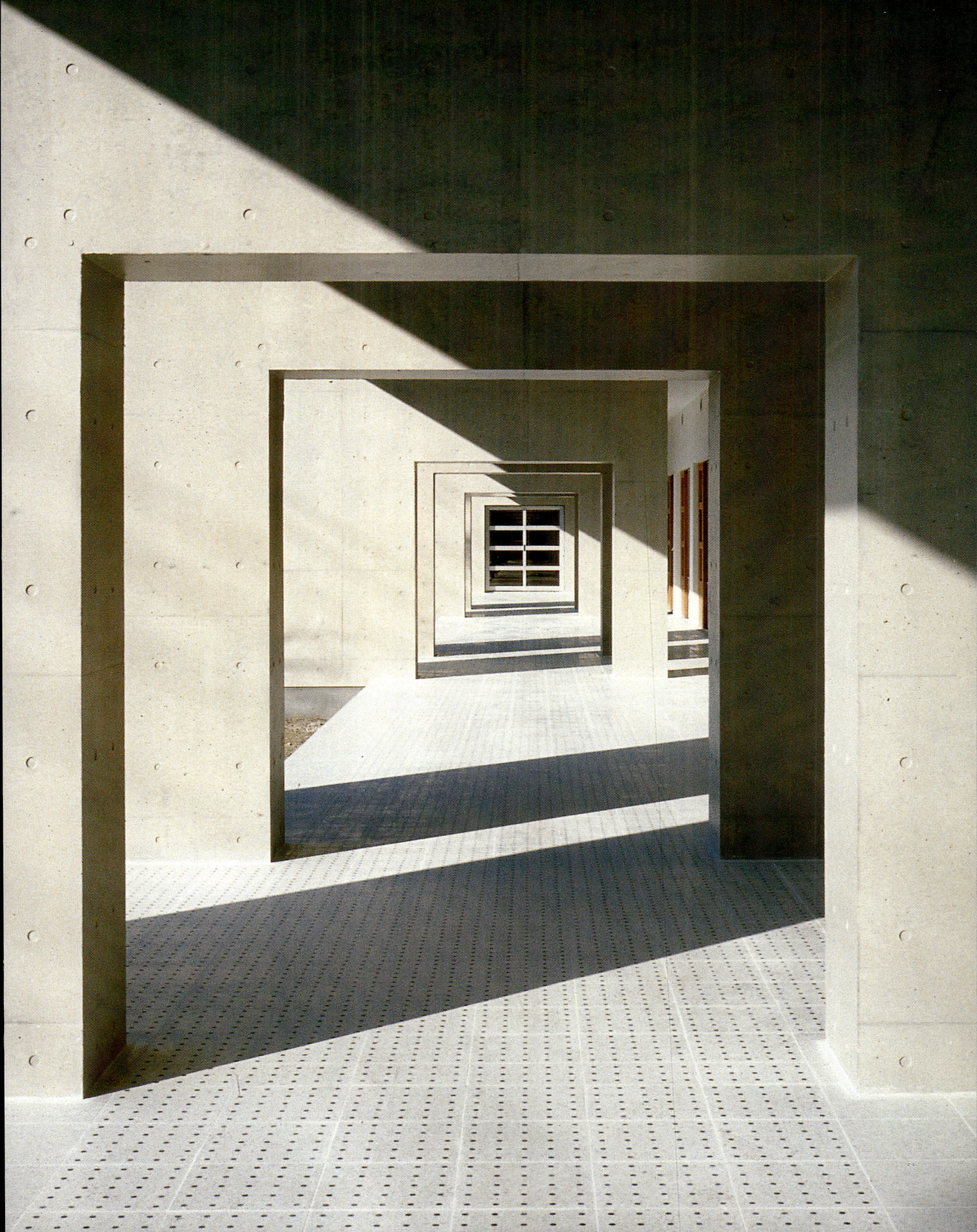

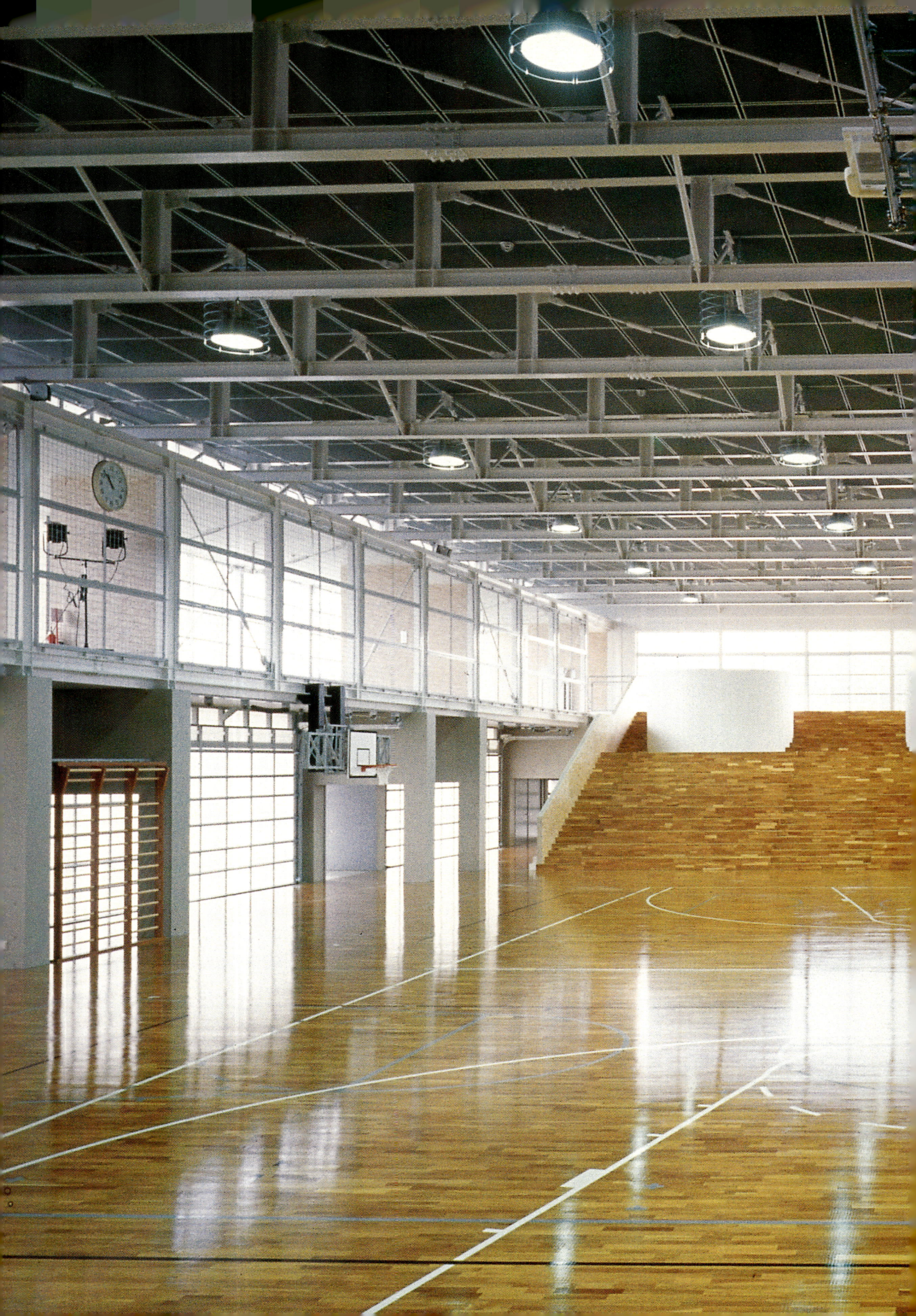

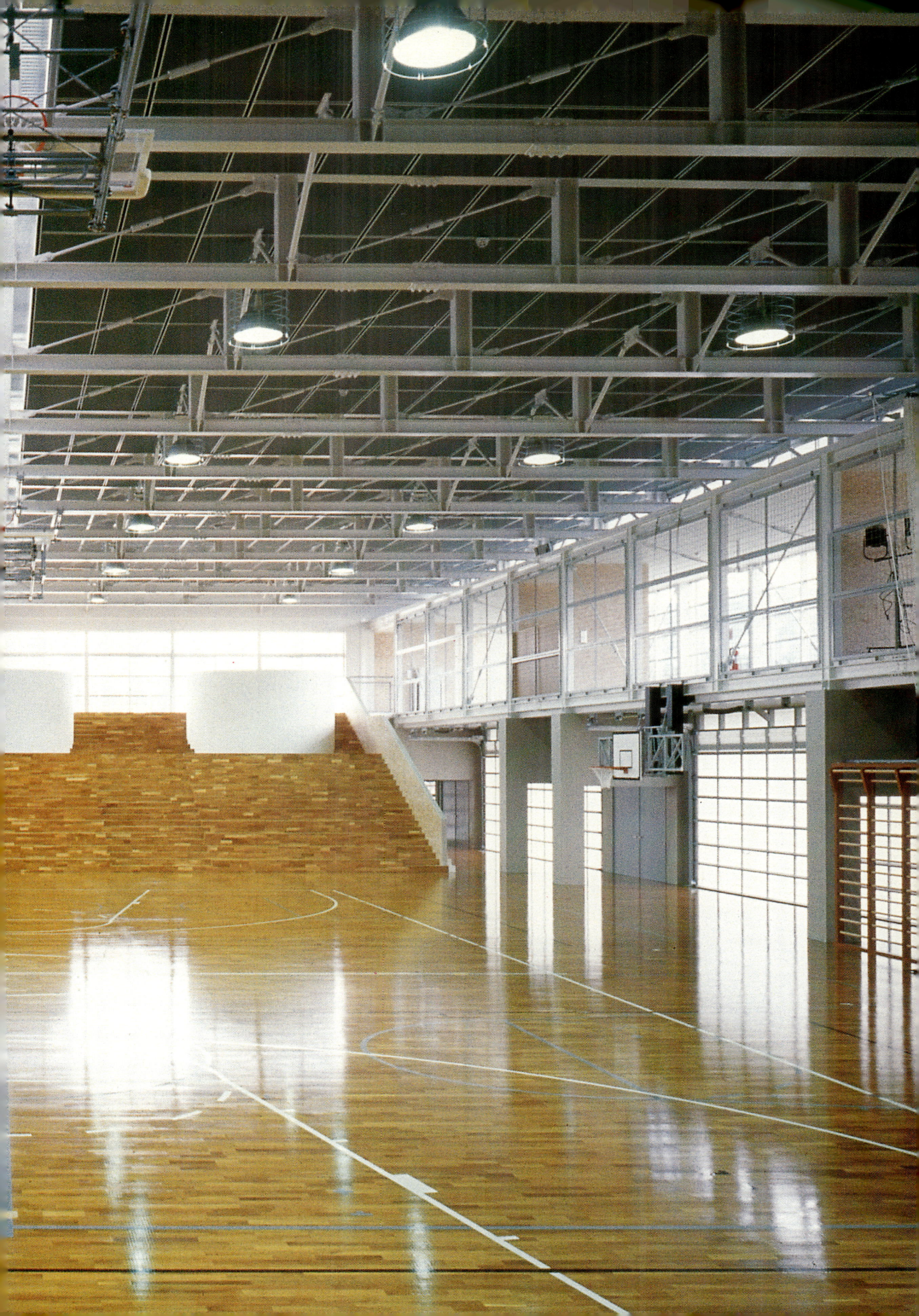

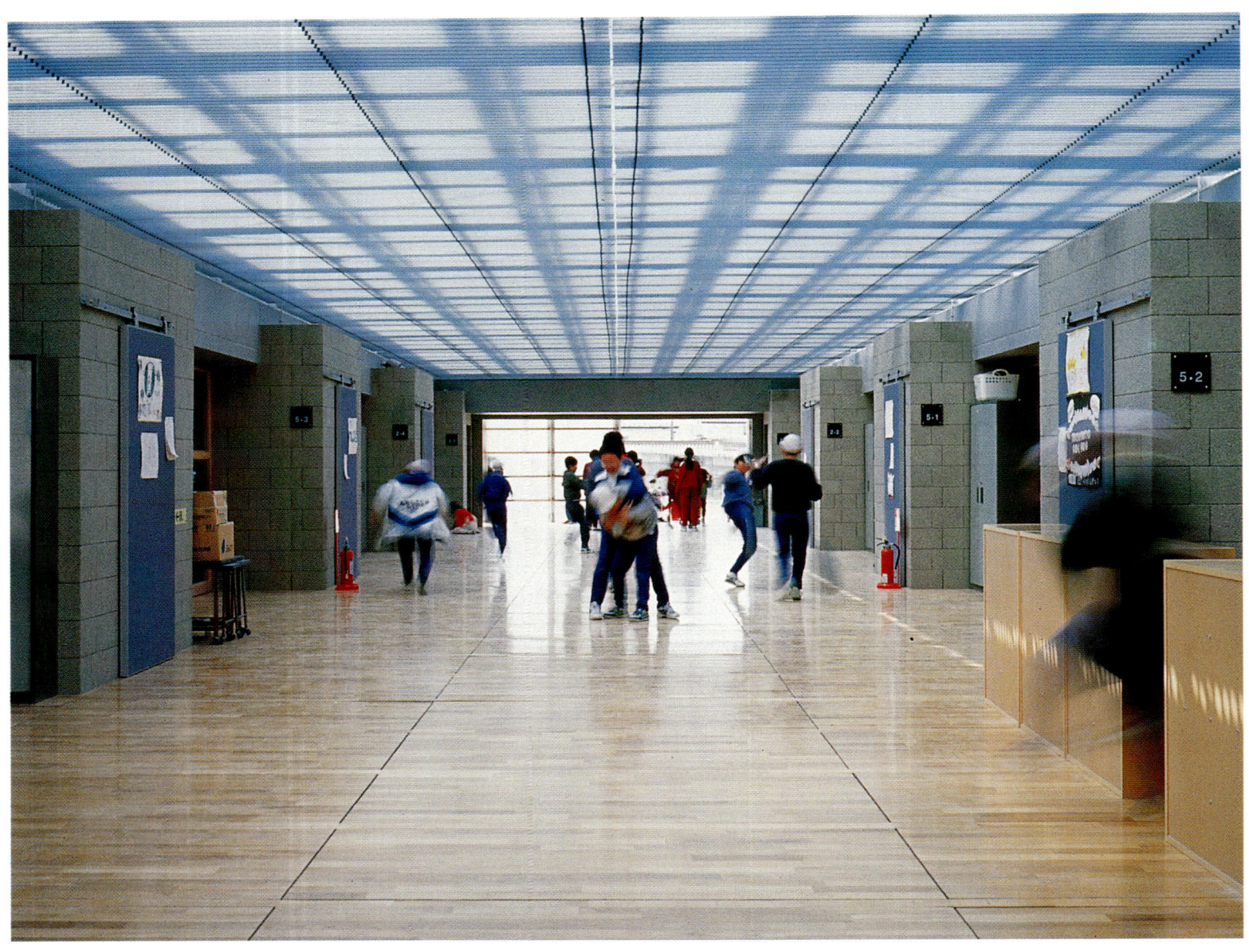

The multi-purpose space in the classroom wing.

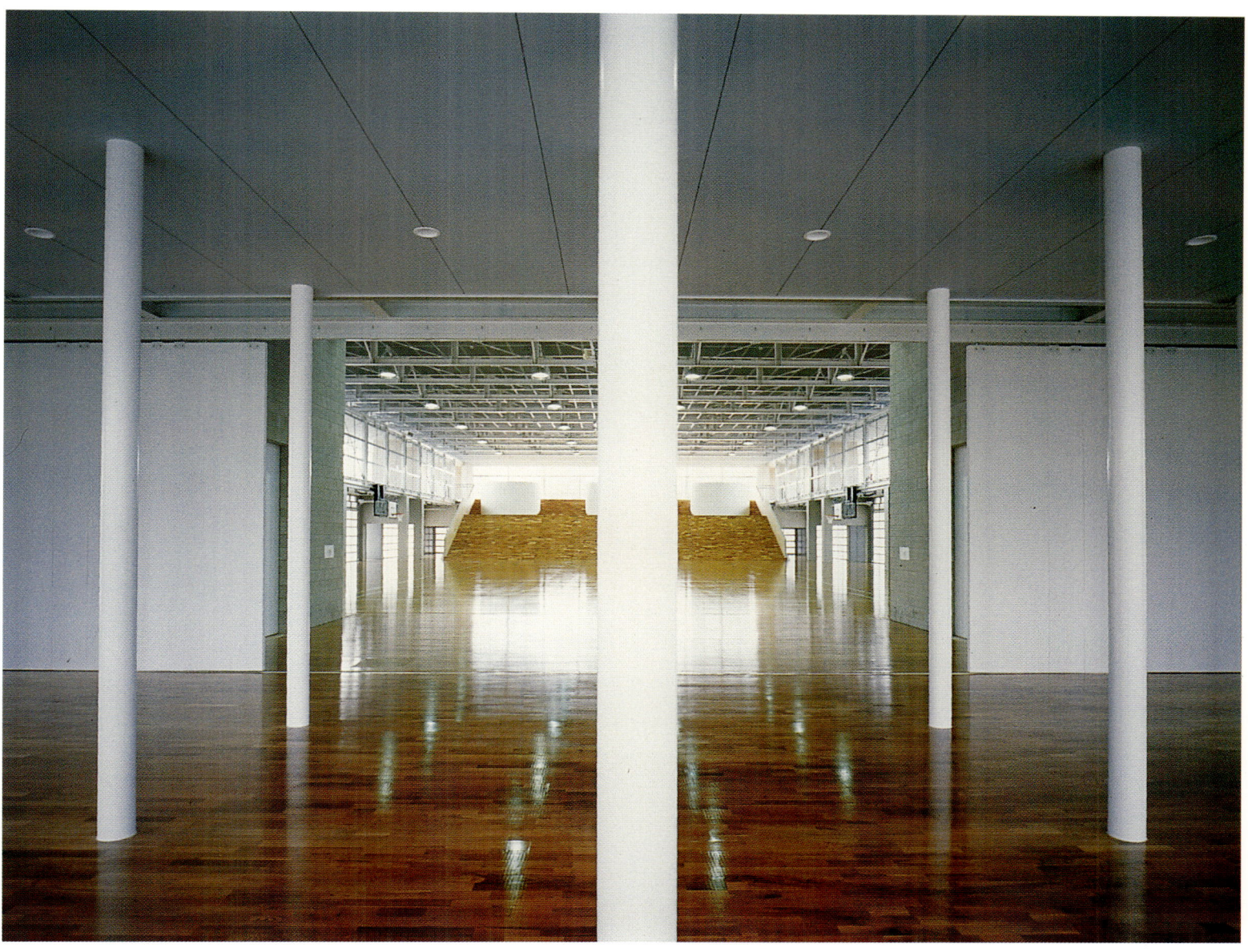
Main entrance.

The interiors are devised with an ecological design that gives due consideration to natural ventilation and lighting.

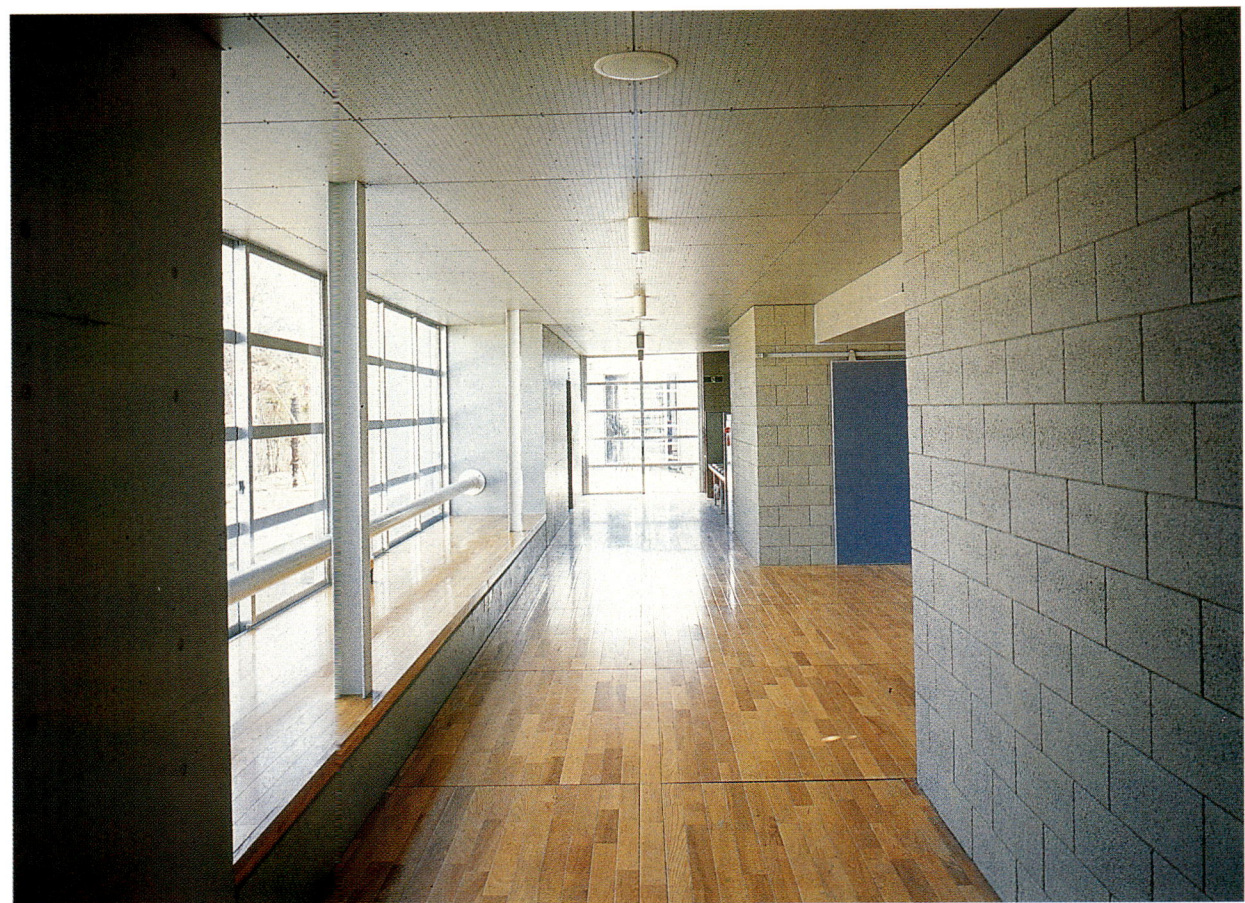

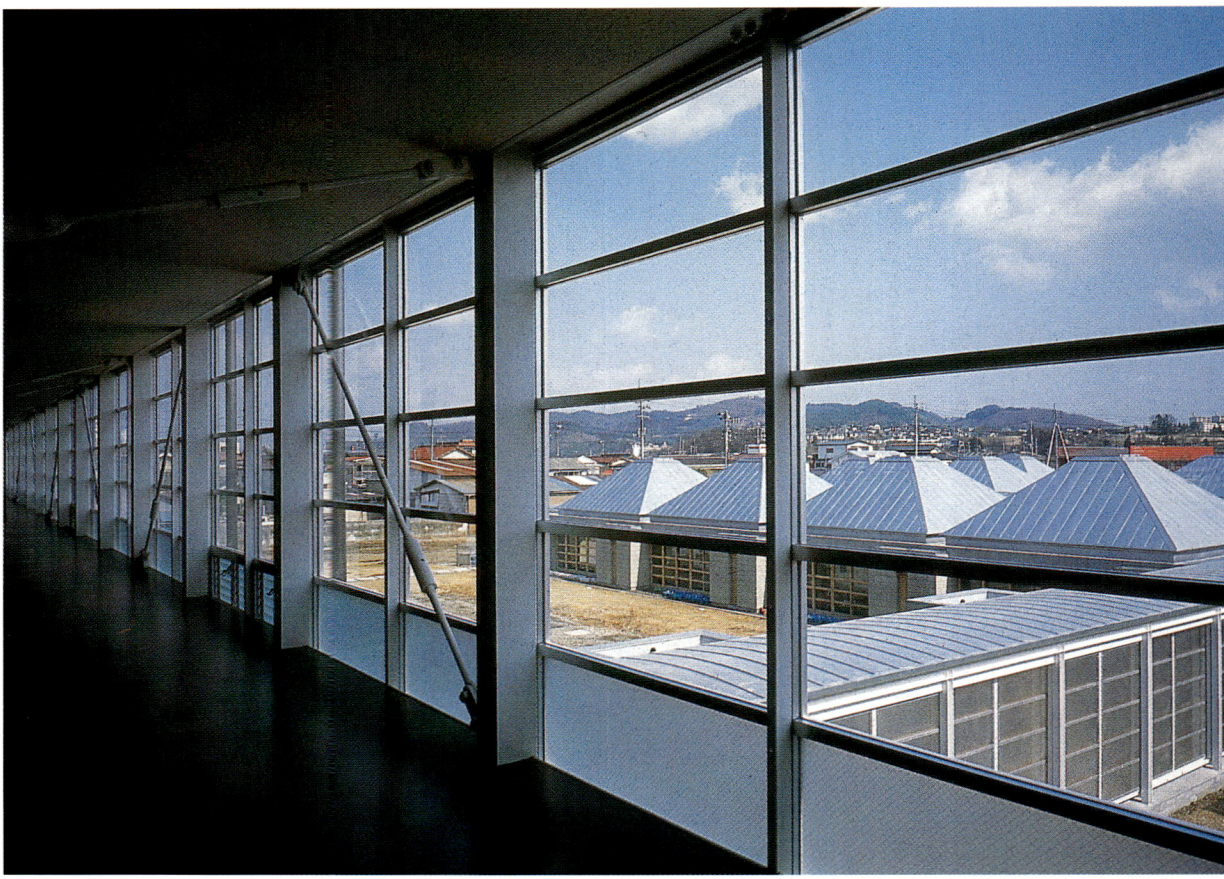

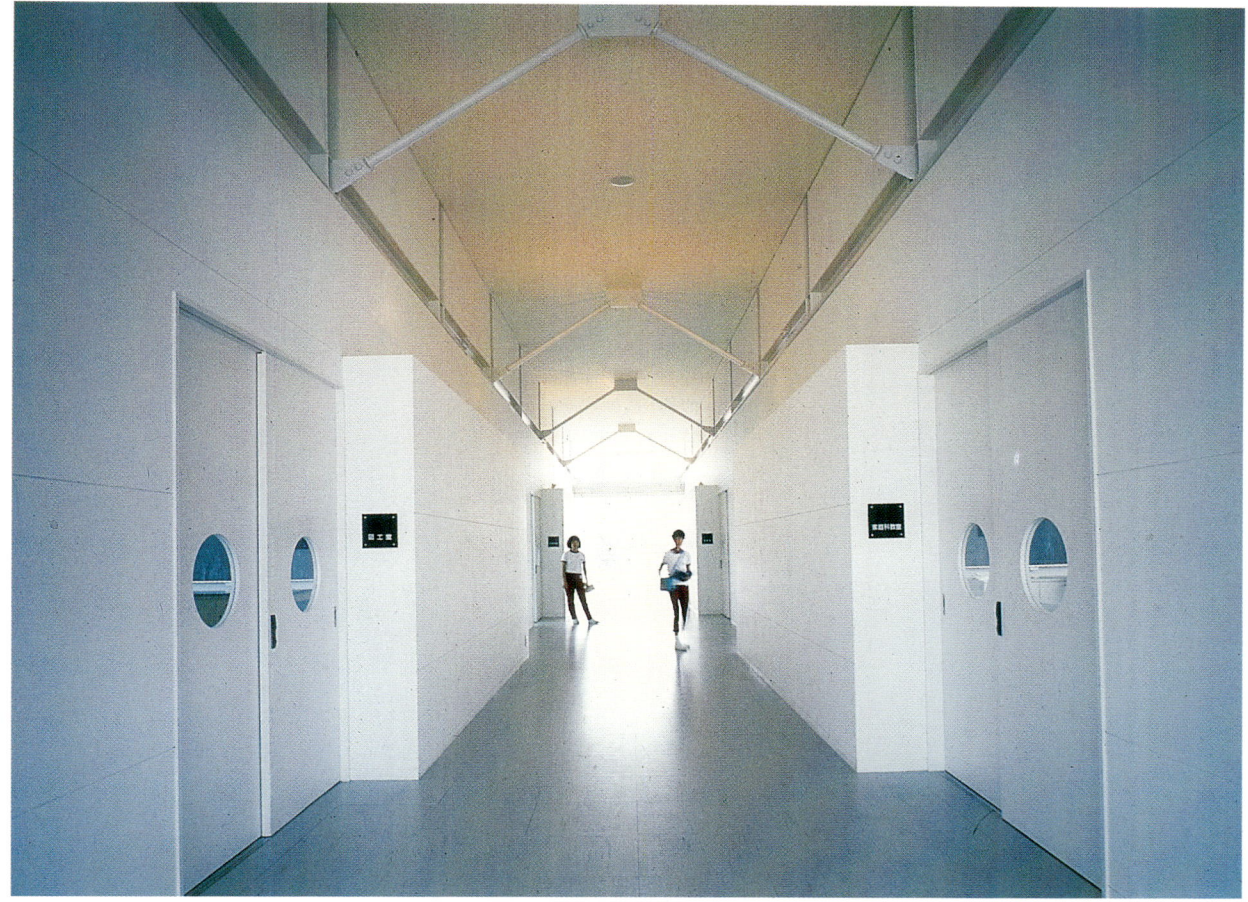

One of the corridors running between the classrooms and, below, the public lobby on the ground floor.

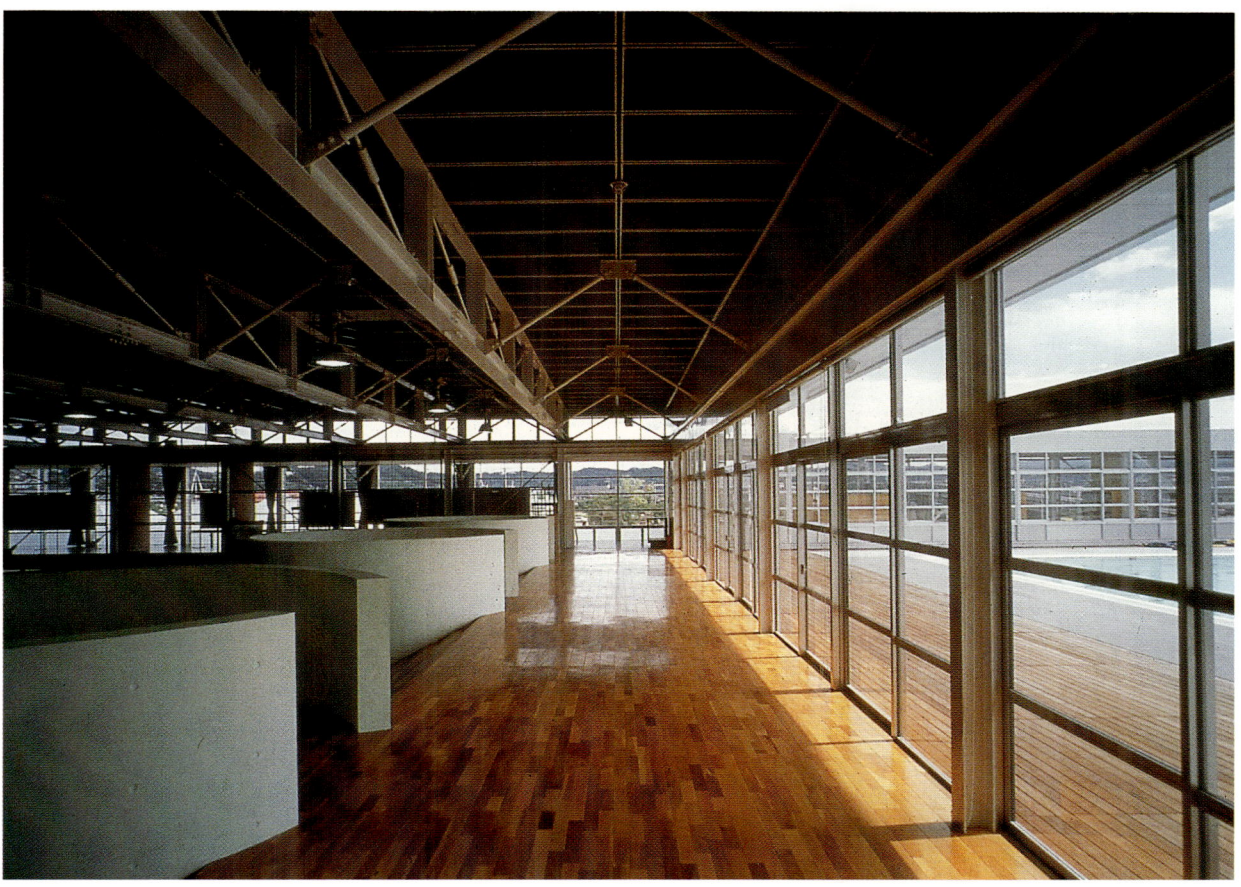

101

Hinomaru Driving School

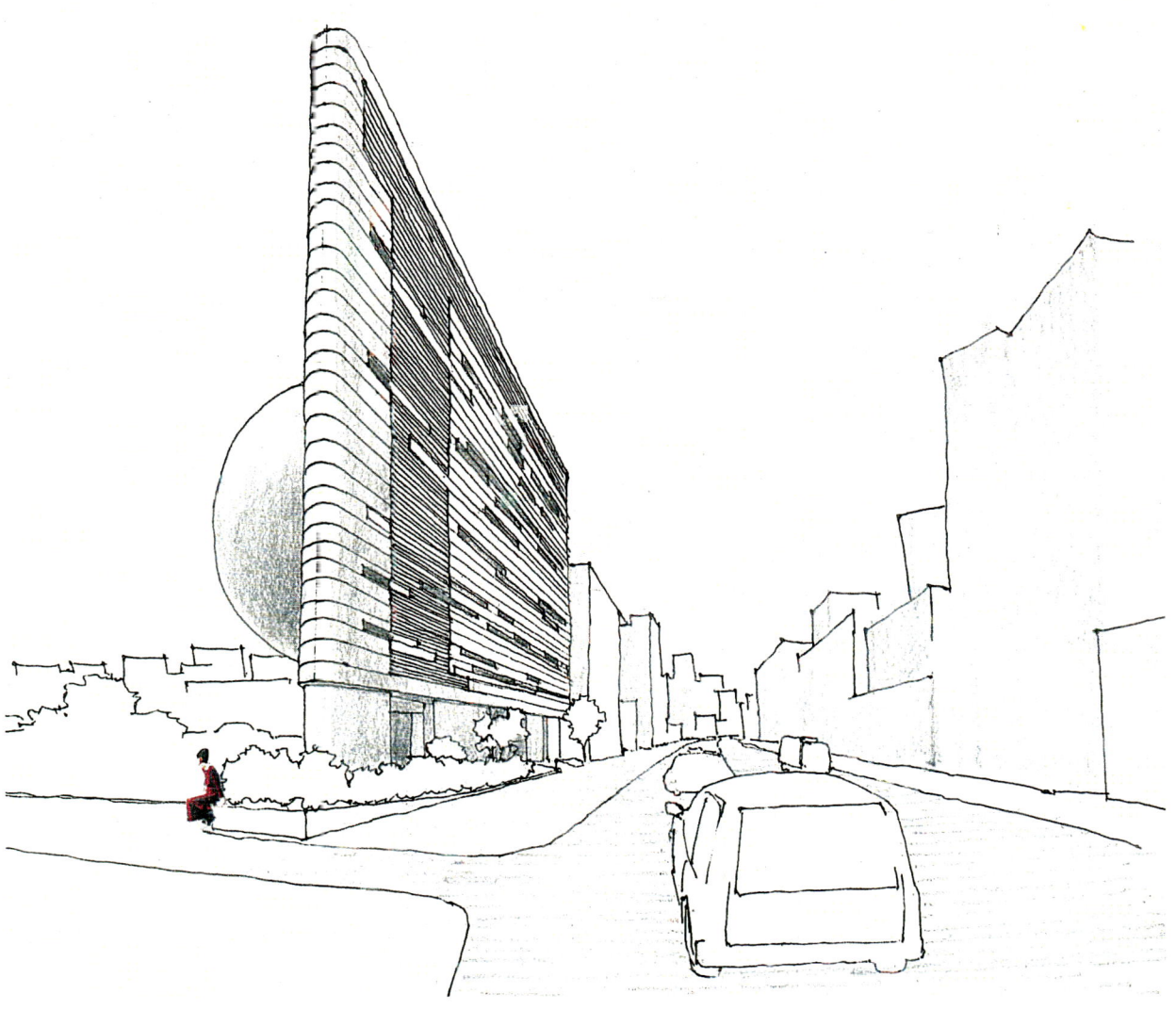

Tokyo is often described as a city of chaos, and this building also is surrounded by wooden residences, multy-storey apartment buildings, factories and a large redevelopment building, with a railroad running through the area. The encouragement of individual freedom is part of the dynamism of Tokyo, but is also a source of that same chaos.

The driving school looks onto a redeveloped building, through which several tens of thousands of commuters ride by train each day, and which has become a symbol of a new sight in Tokyo, and in order to promote the school, its own symbol, the sun, was chosen.

The 23-metre diameter sphere, made from welded iron plates, represents the company's CI, and broadcasts their strength to the outside world, and is also a source of vitality for those involved with the school. Inside, there is an annexed gallery, and an open space that functions as a large exhibition area, which is the base of the company's cultural activities.

West and north elevations.

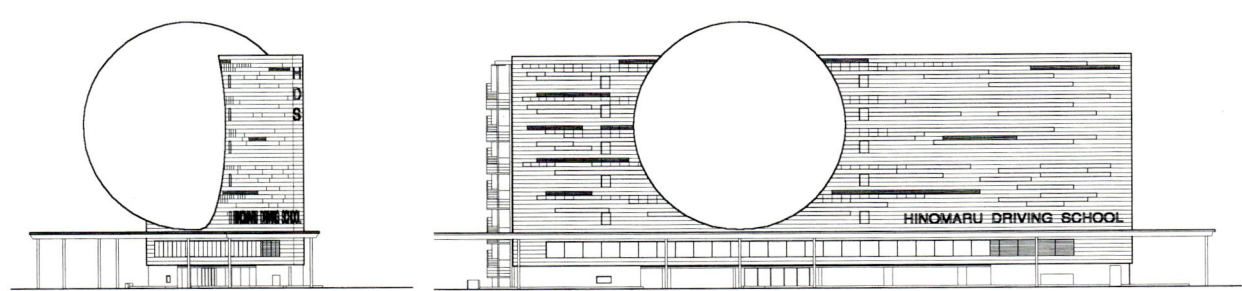

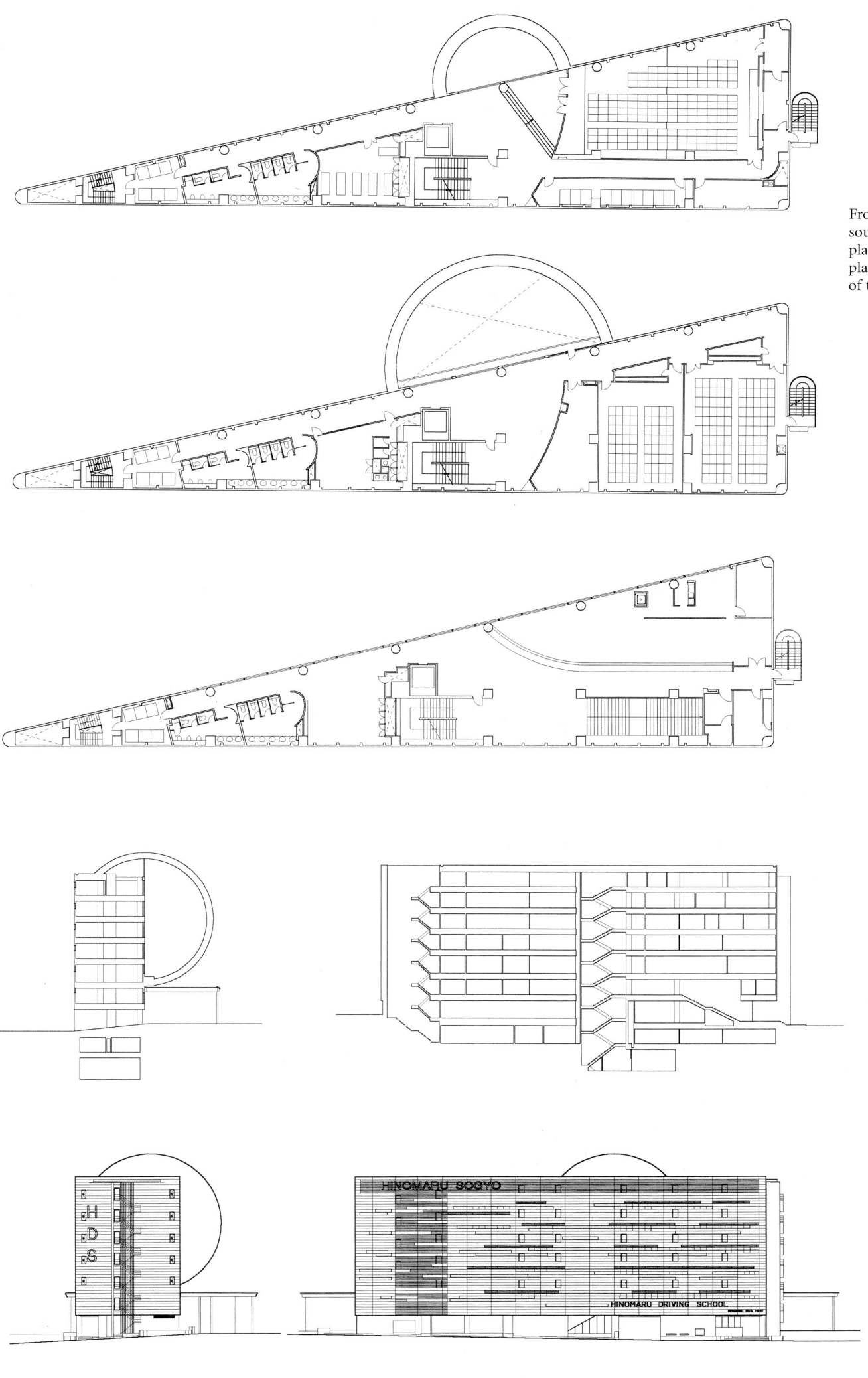

From bottom: east and south elevations; sections; plan of the second floor; plan of the third floor; plan of the fourth floor.

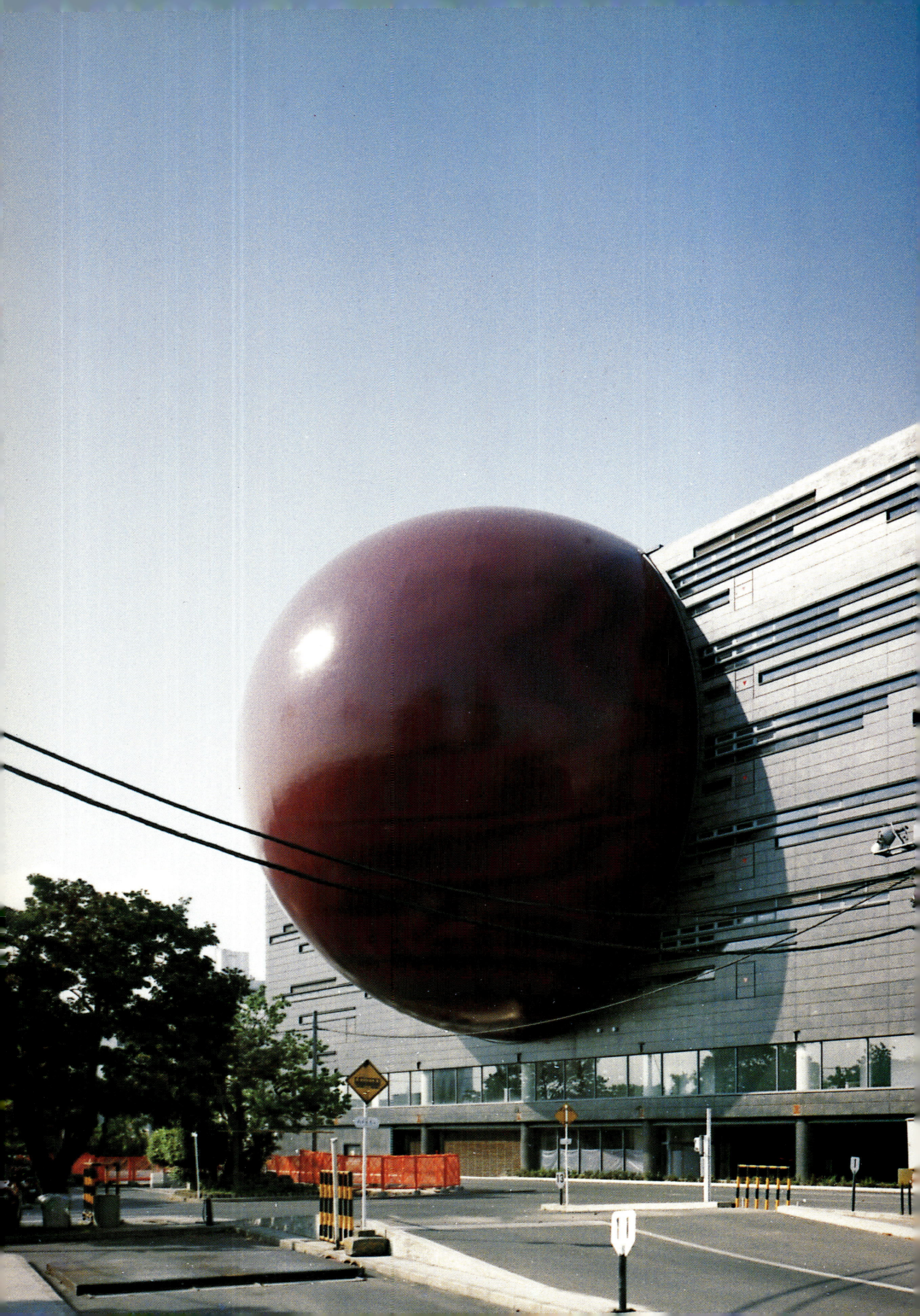

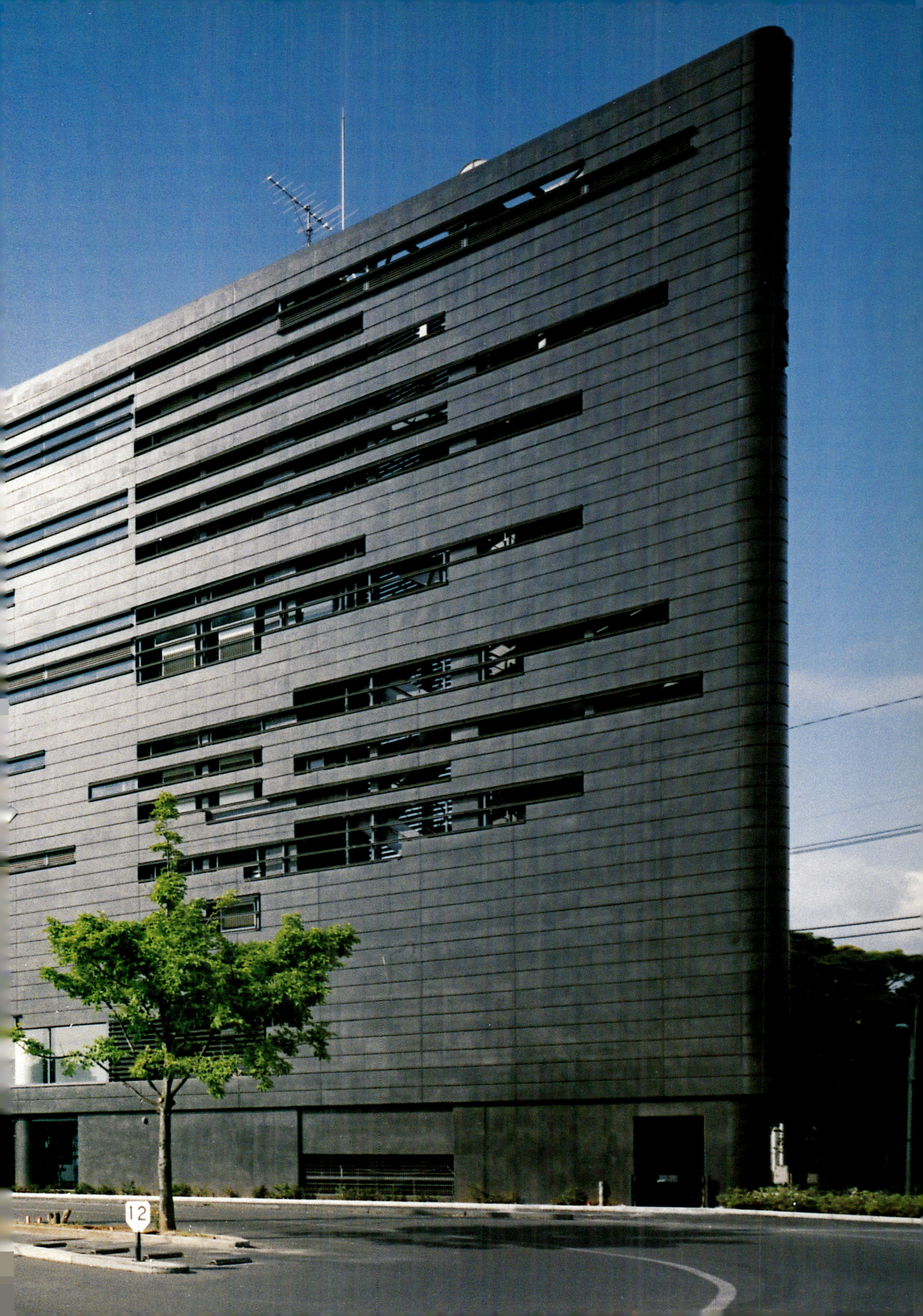

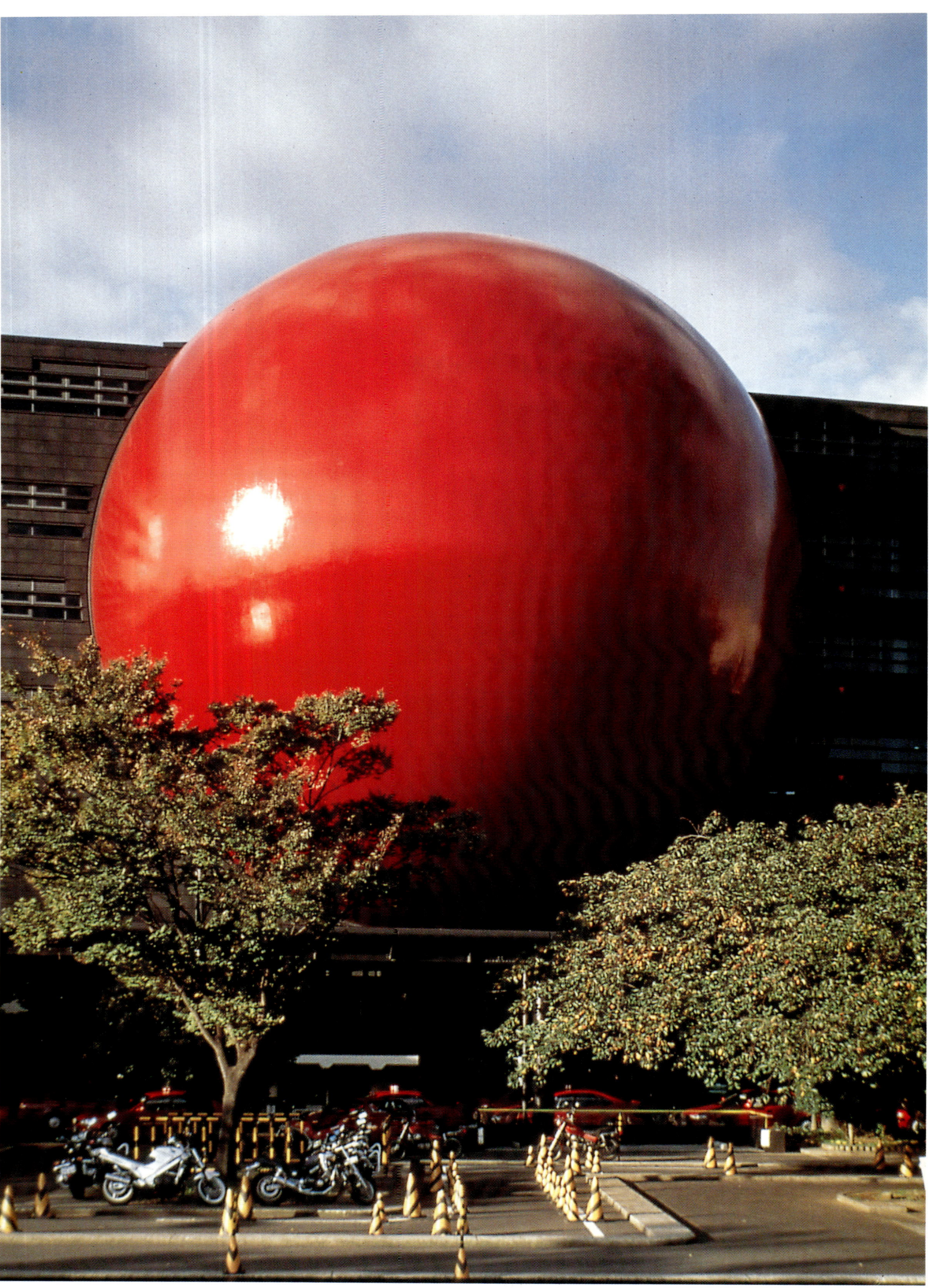

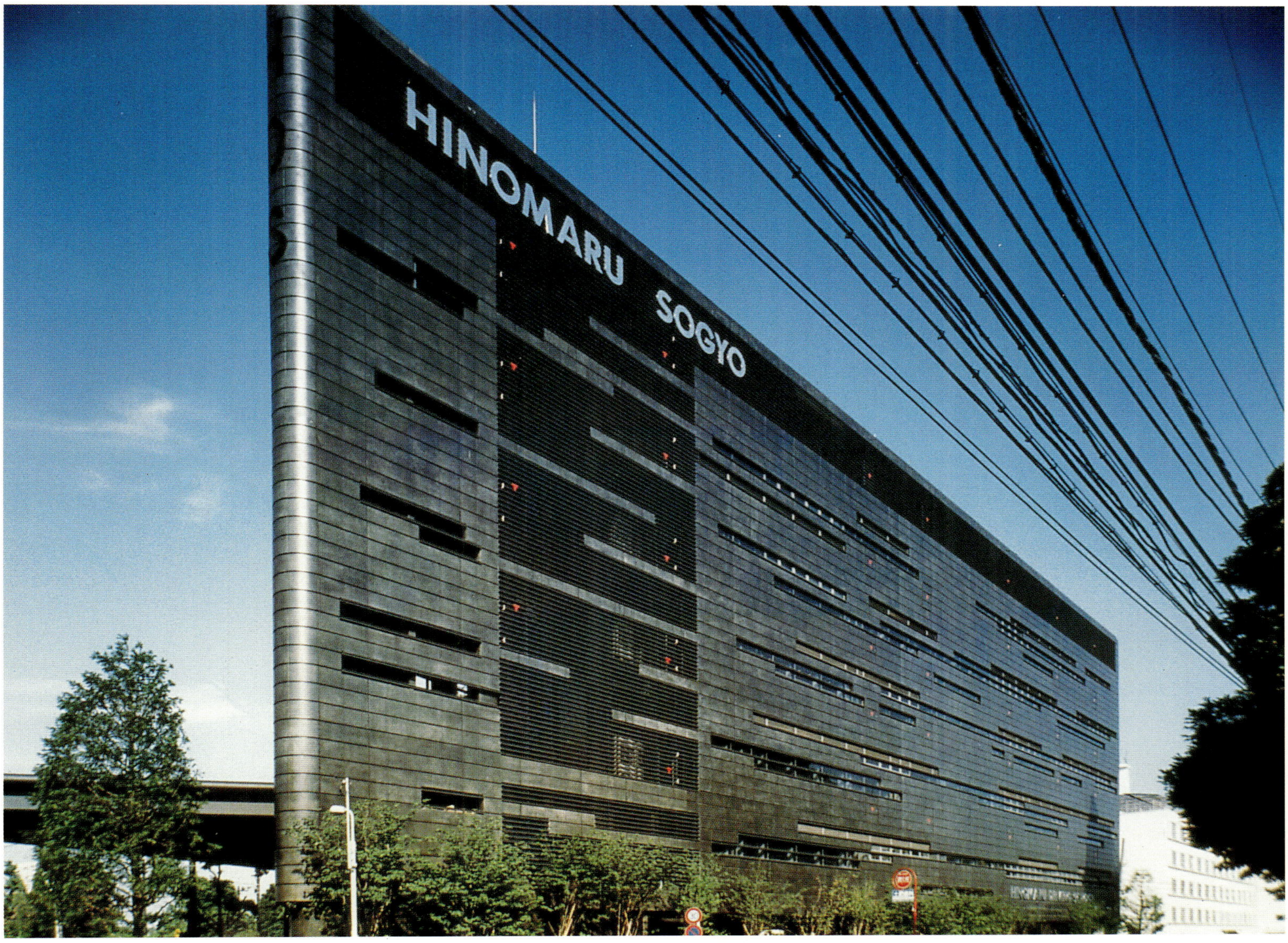

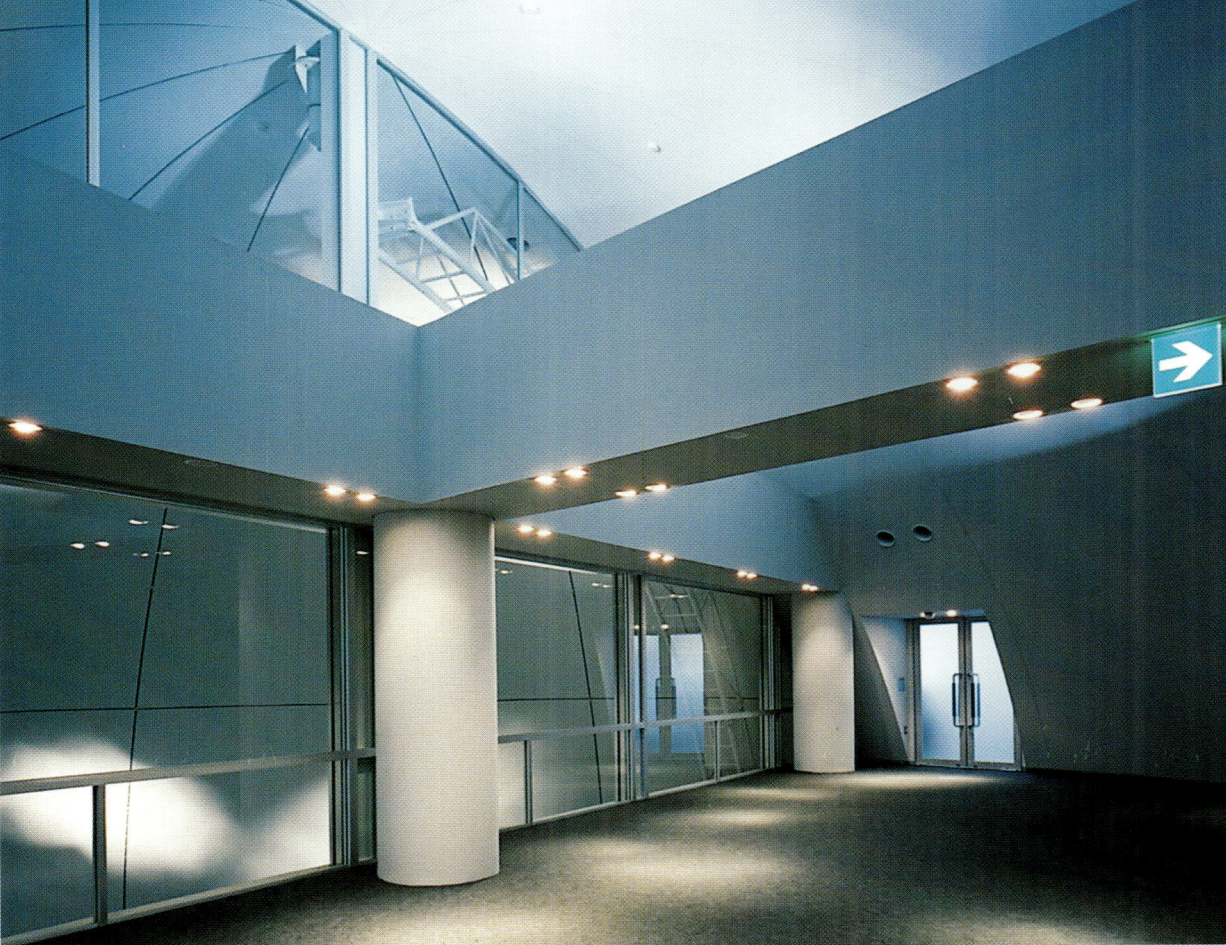

The south facade and, left, the hall.

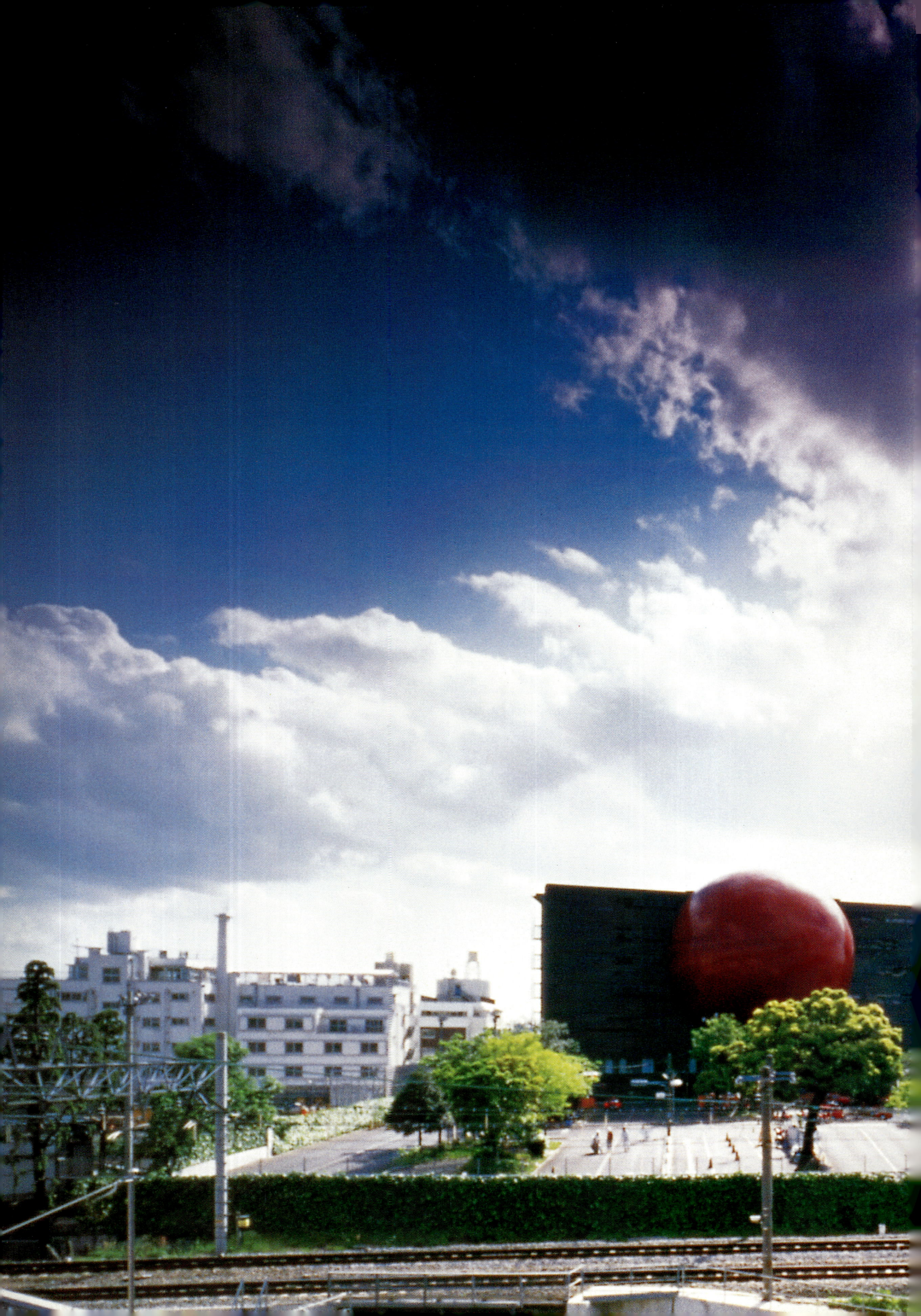

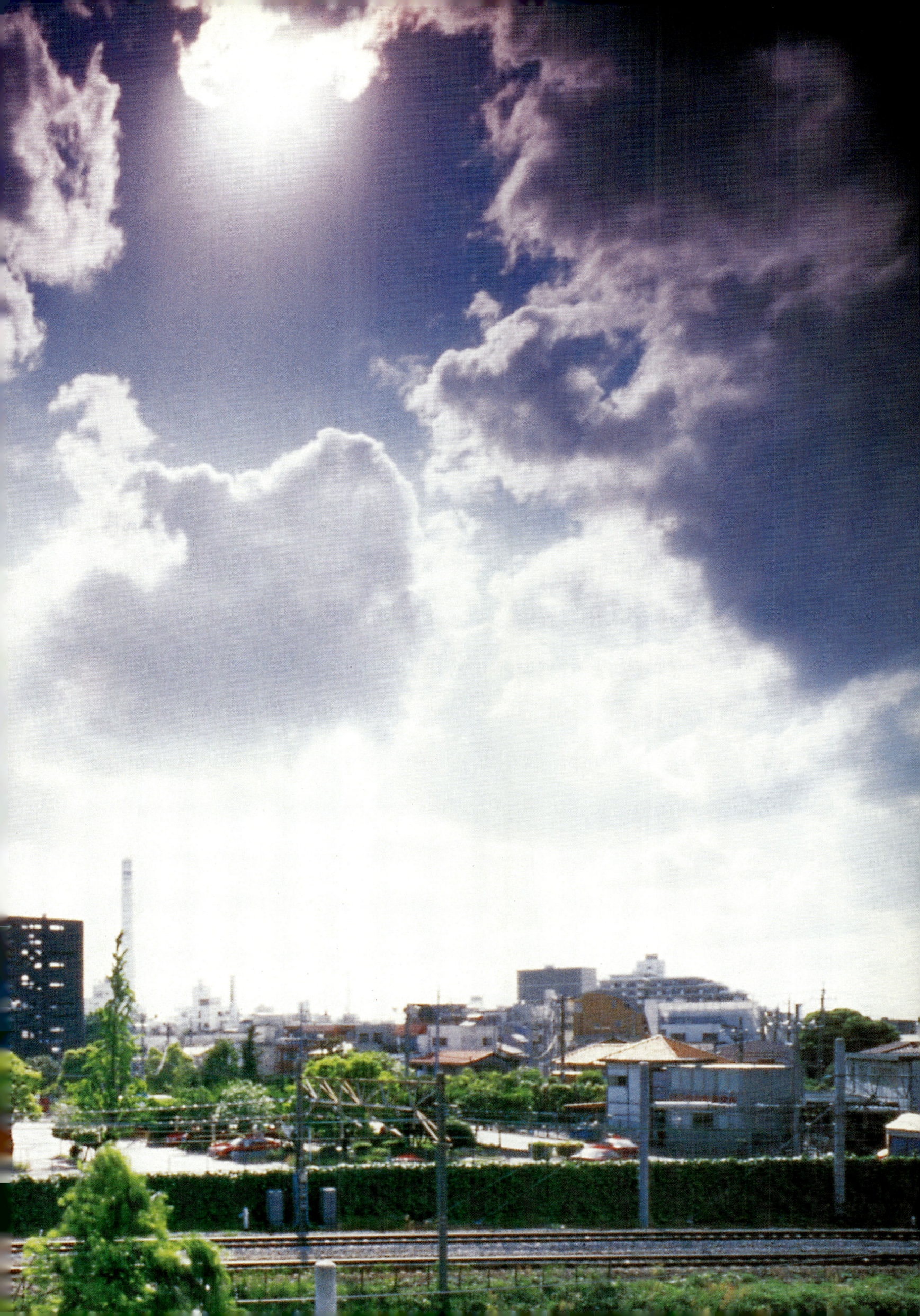

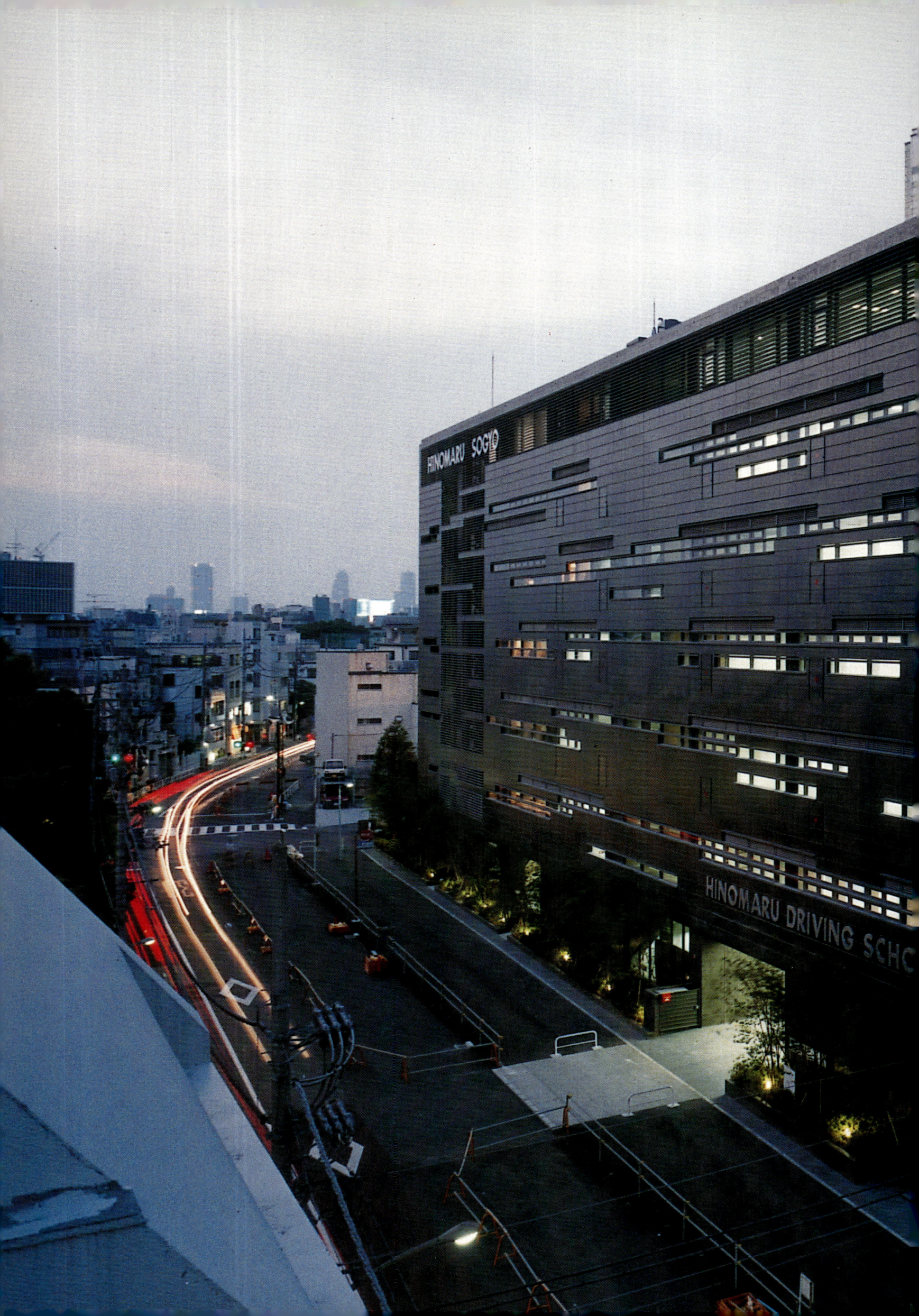

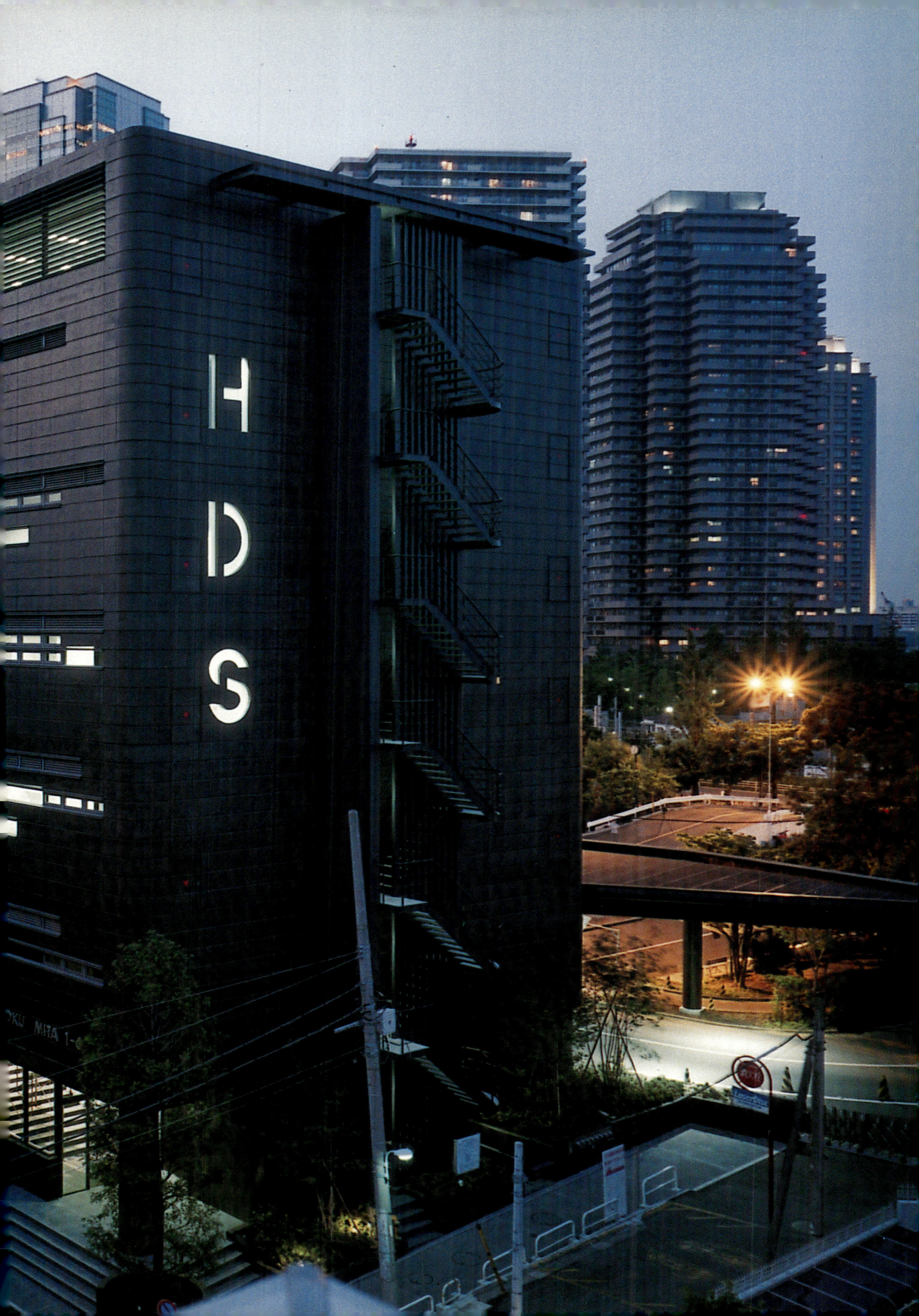

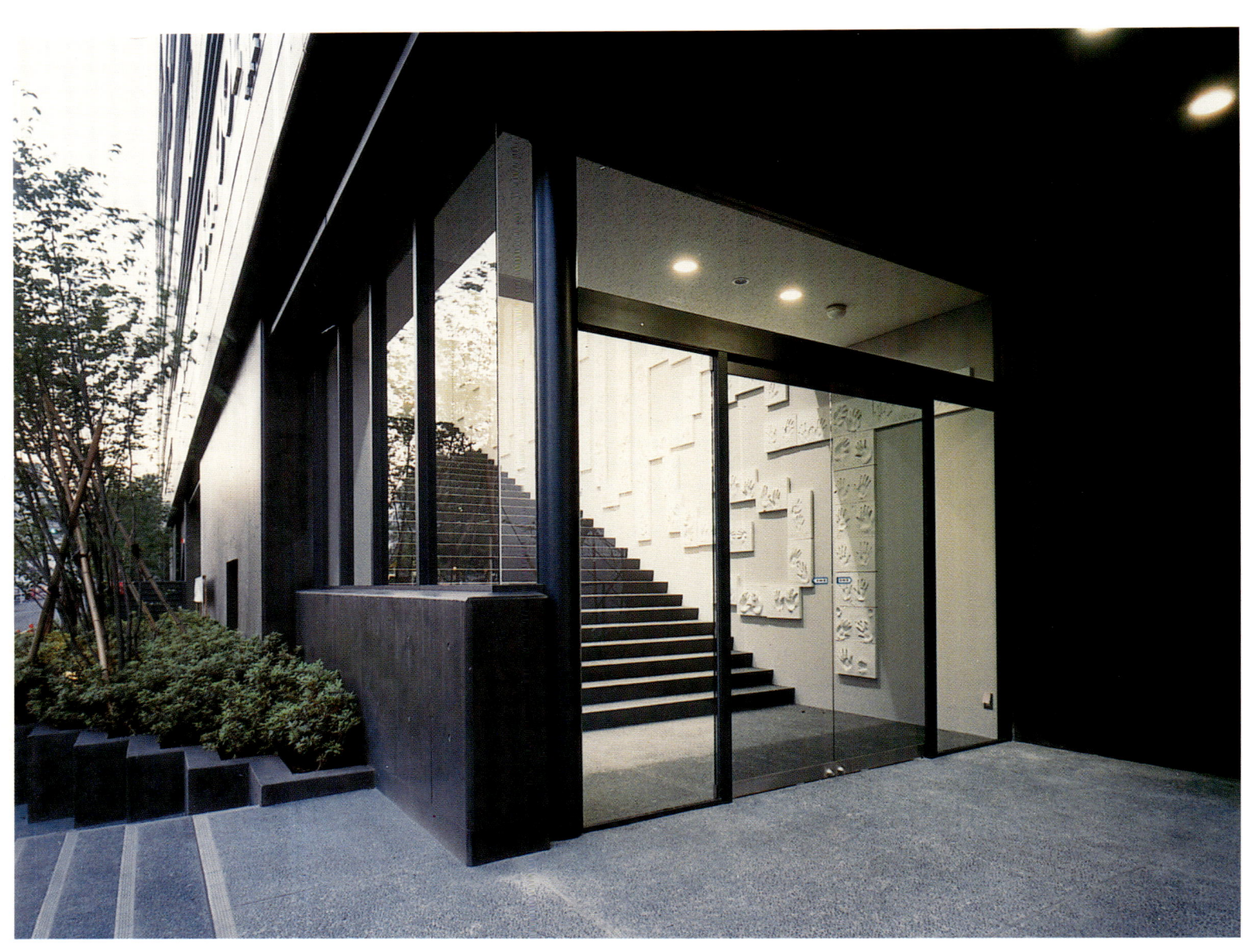

Side entrance to the building.

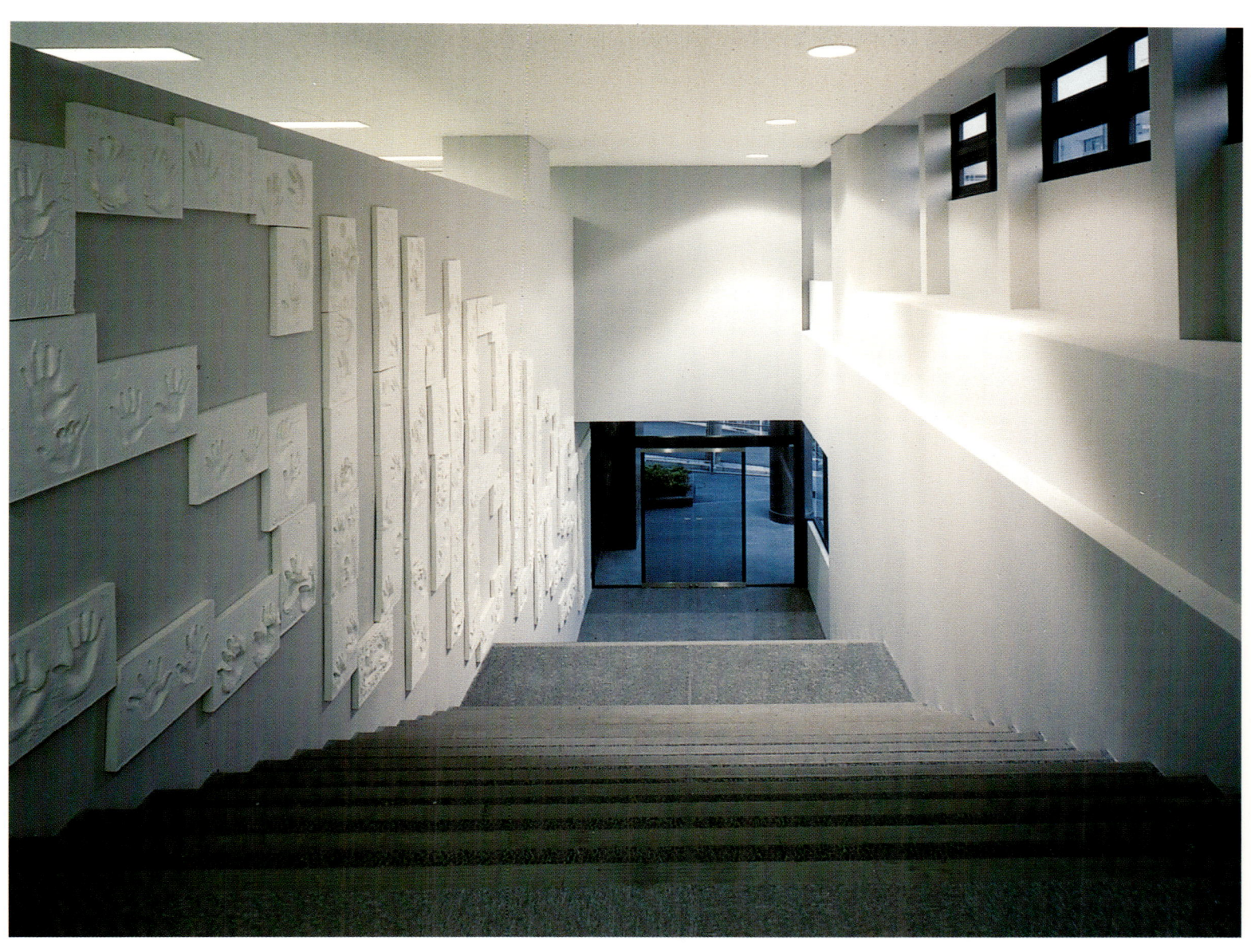

The inside stairway at the side entrance.

Johnson Products
Kakegawa New Factory

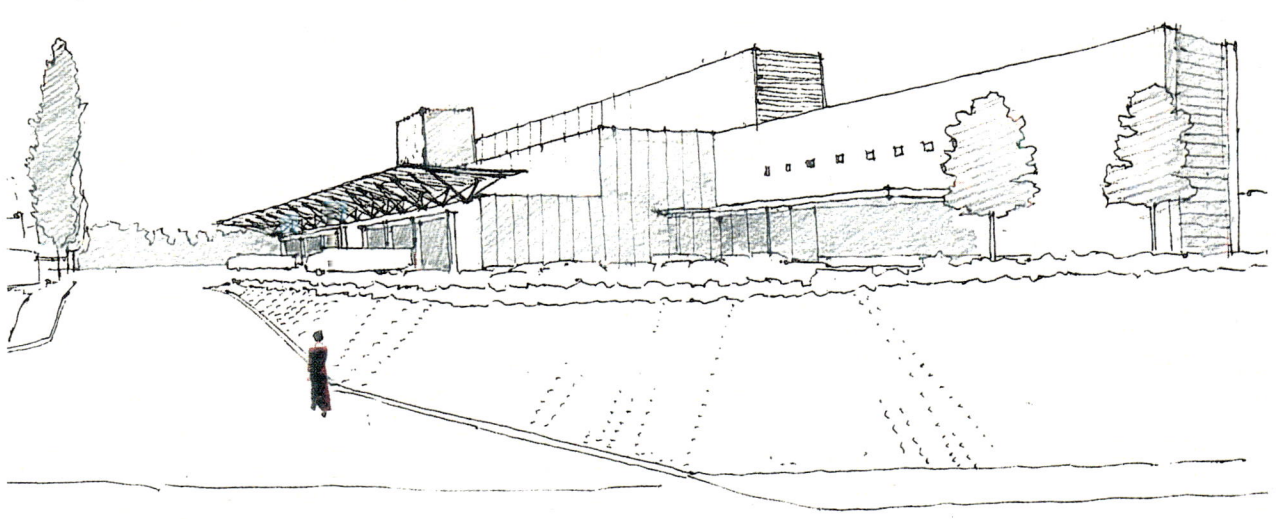

A business wax factory, erected in an industrial site in Shizuoka prefecture. The company's headquarters in Racine, USA, were designed by Frank Lloyd Wright and are known throughout the world. The construction project was the result of collaboration between the American management company and the Japanese engineering company. In Japan, the first consideration was the cost performance of the factory. The form was fixed, and there was little if any possibility for artistic expression on the part of the architect.

However, the demand for a new shape for the factory came out of the need to consider swift responses to the ever changing needs of society, and the environment of the people working there, as well as that of the area and of the earth itself. This factory, comprised of a central spine running through the middle, and an inorganic roofing system, is a new generation of factory that will be able to provide a flexible response to constantly changing conditions.

General plan and, opposite page, day and night views of the main facade enhancing influence of light on the different planes.

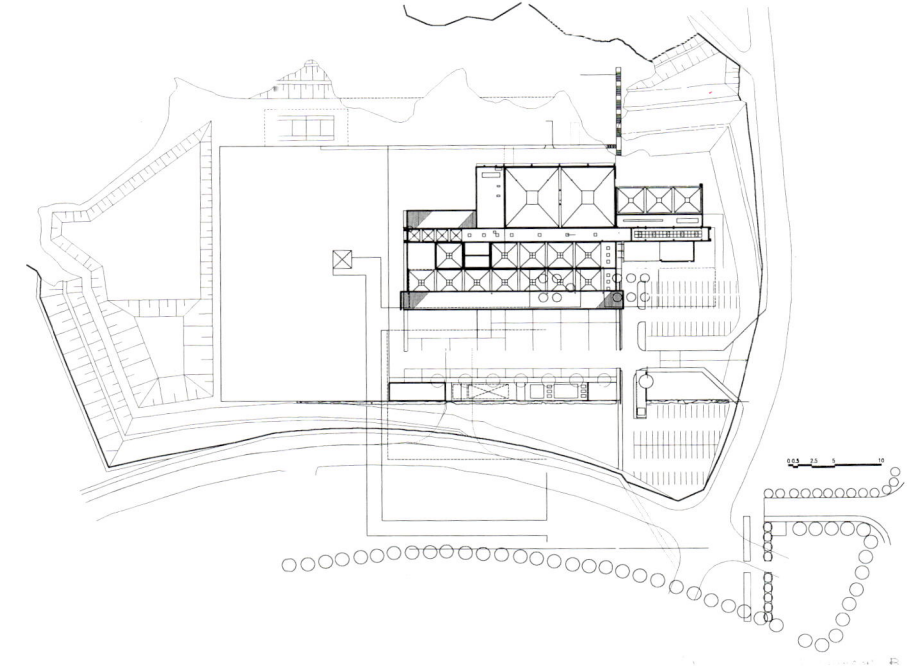

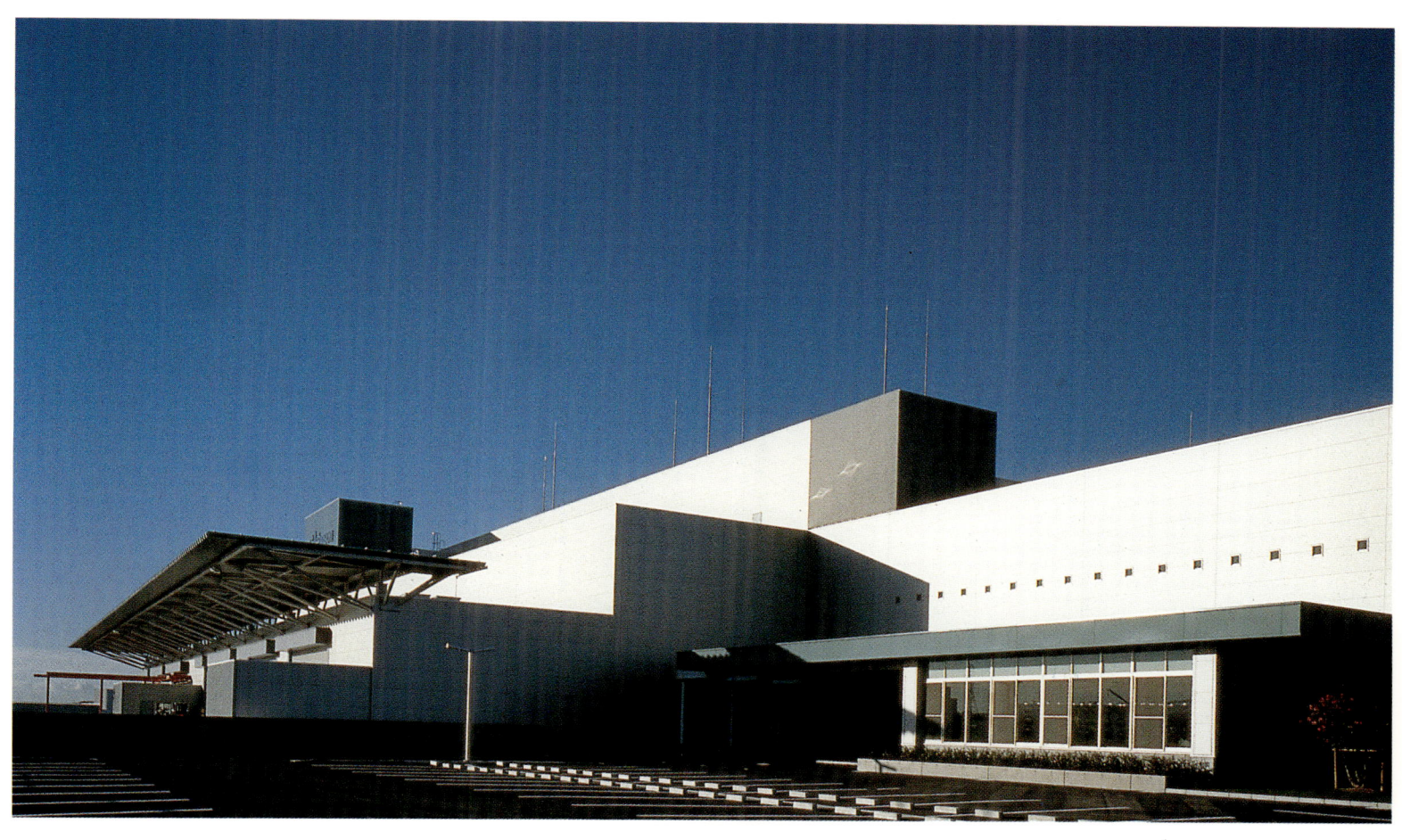
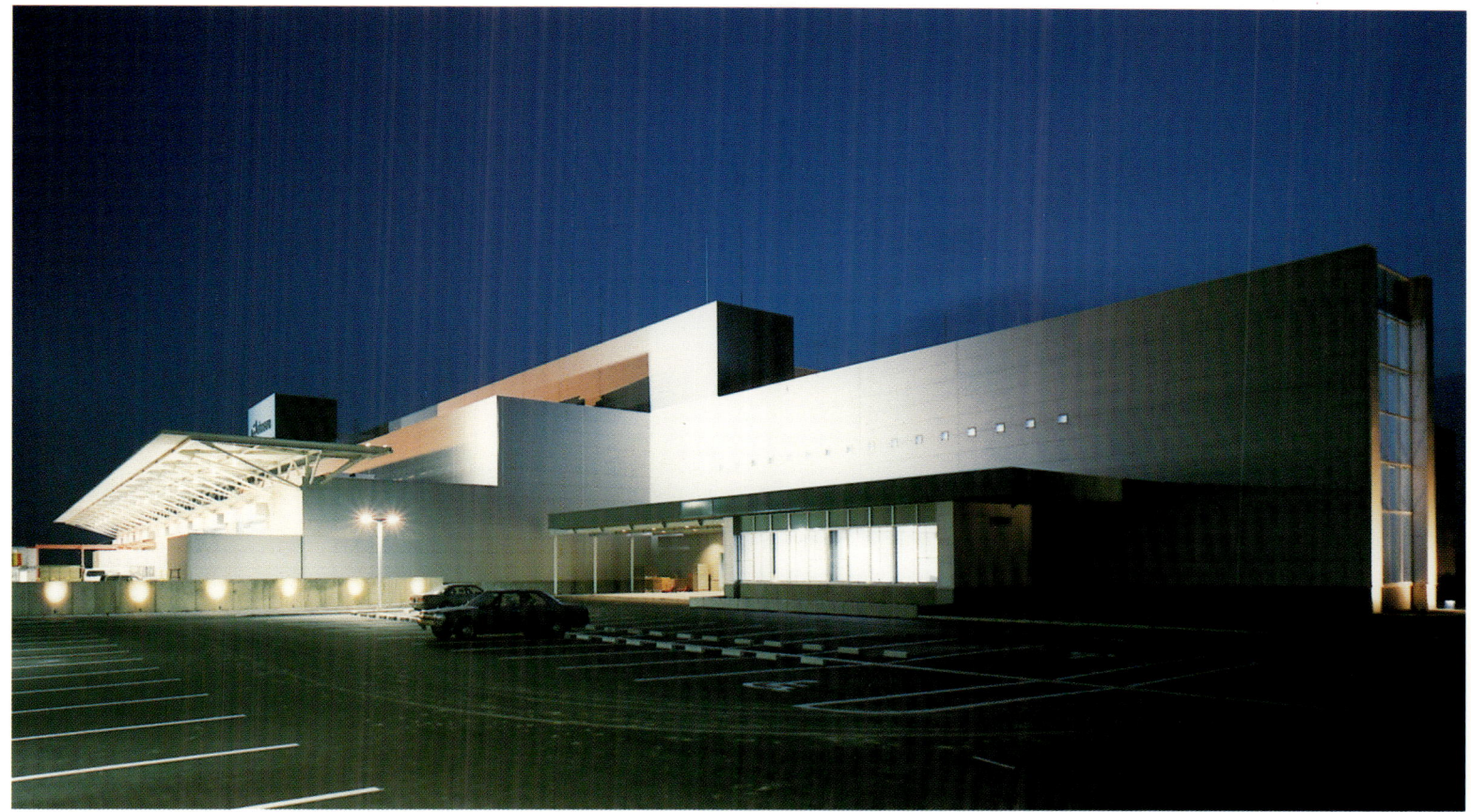

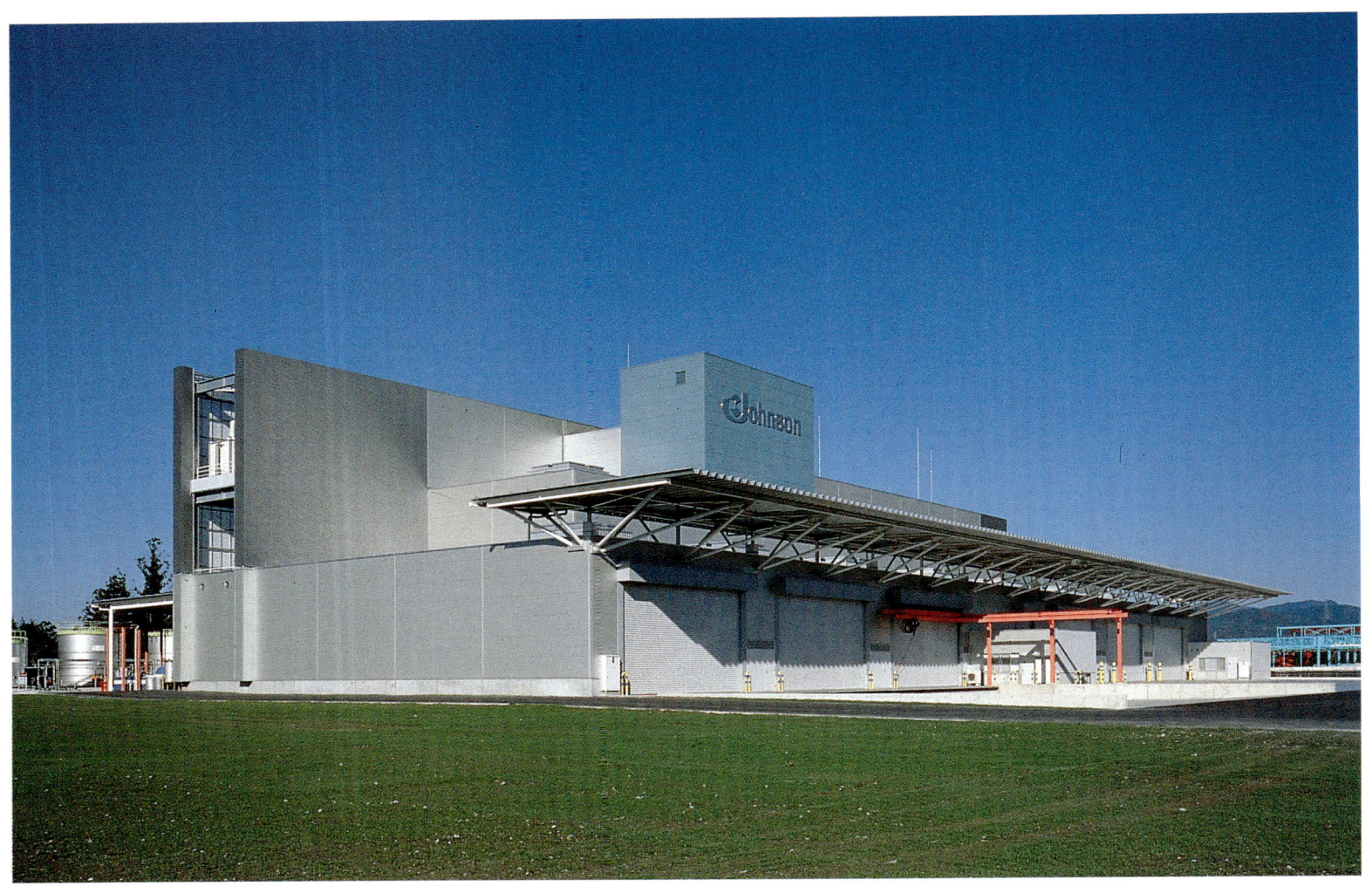

The cantilevered roof which covers the service entrances to the factory.

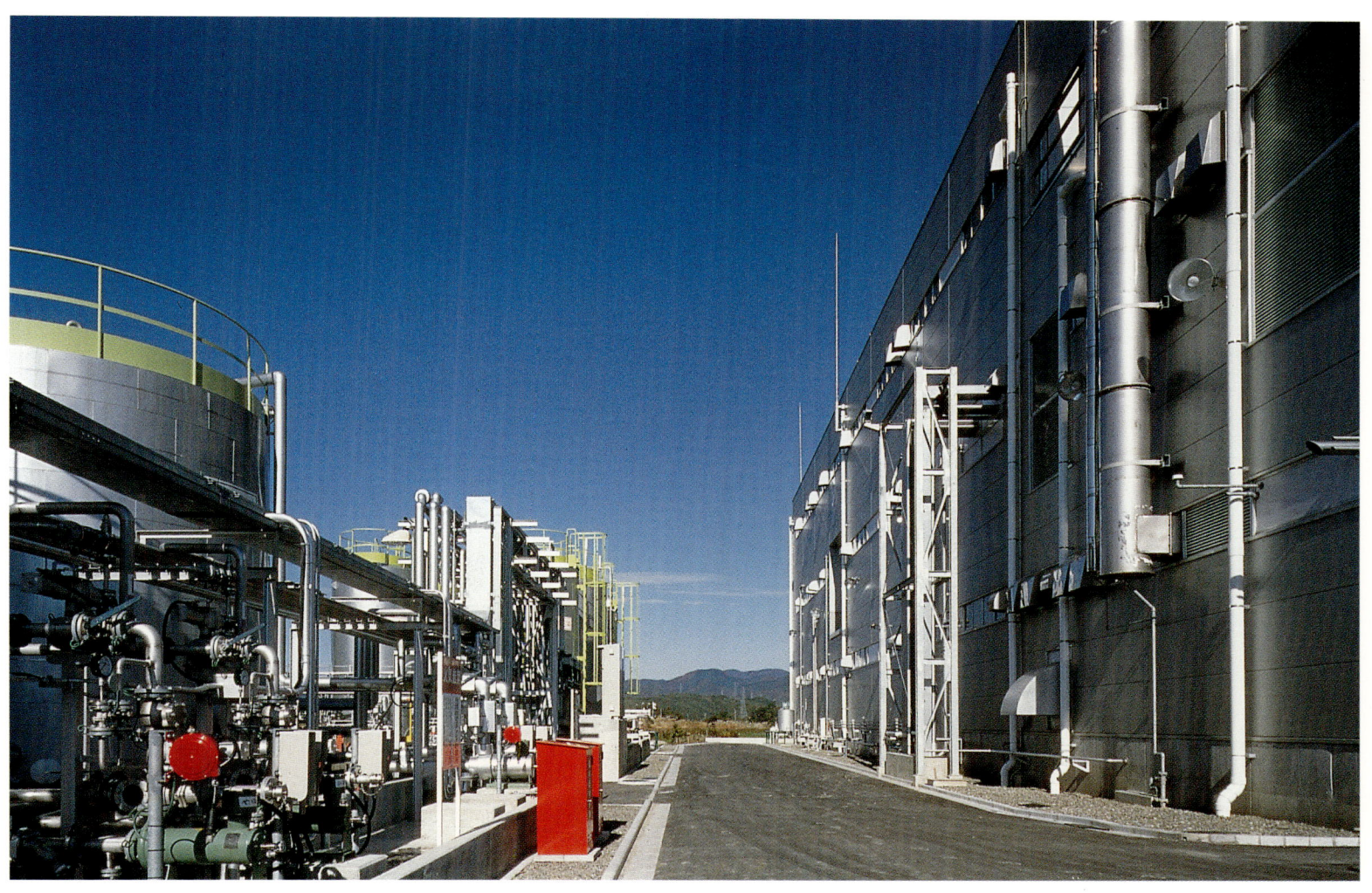

The open-air plants on the
back of the factory.

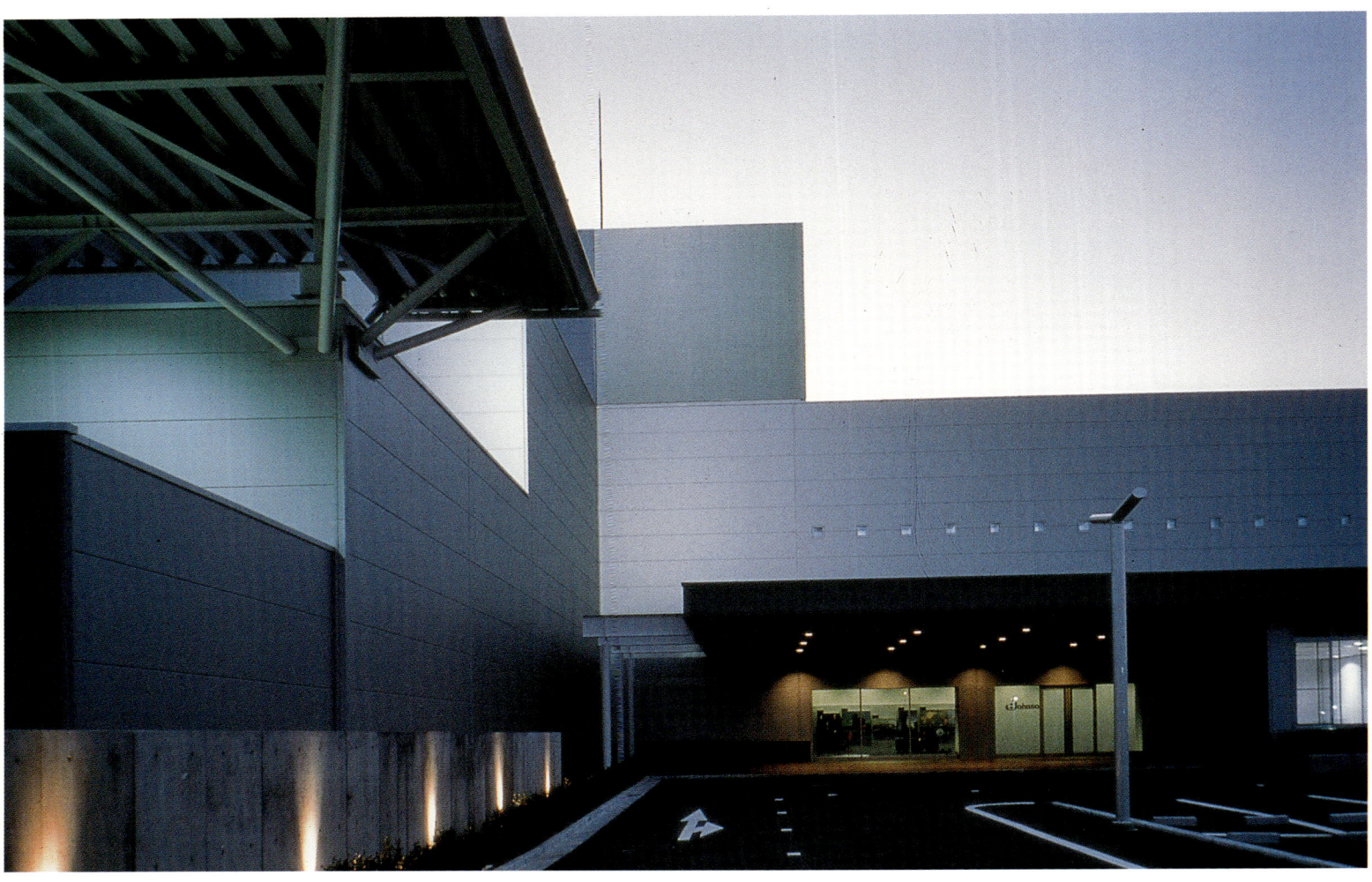

The road leading up to the facility.

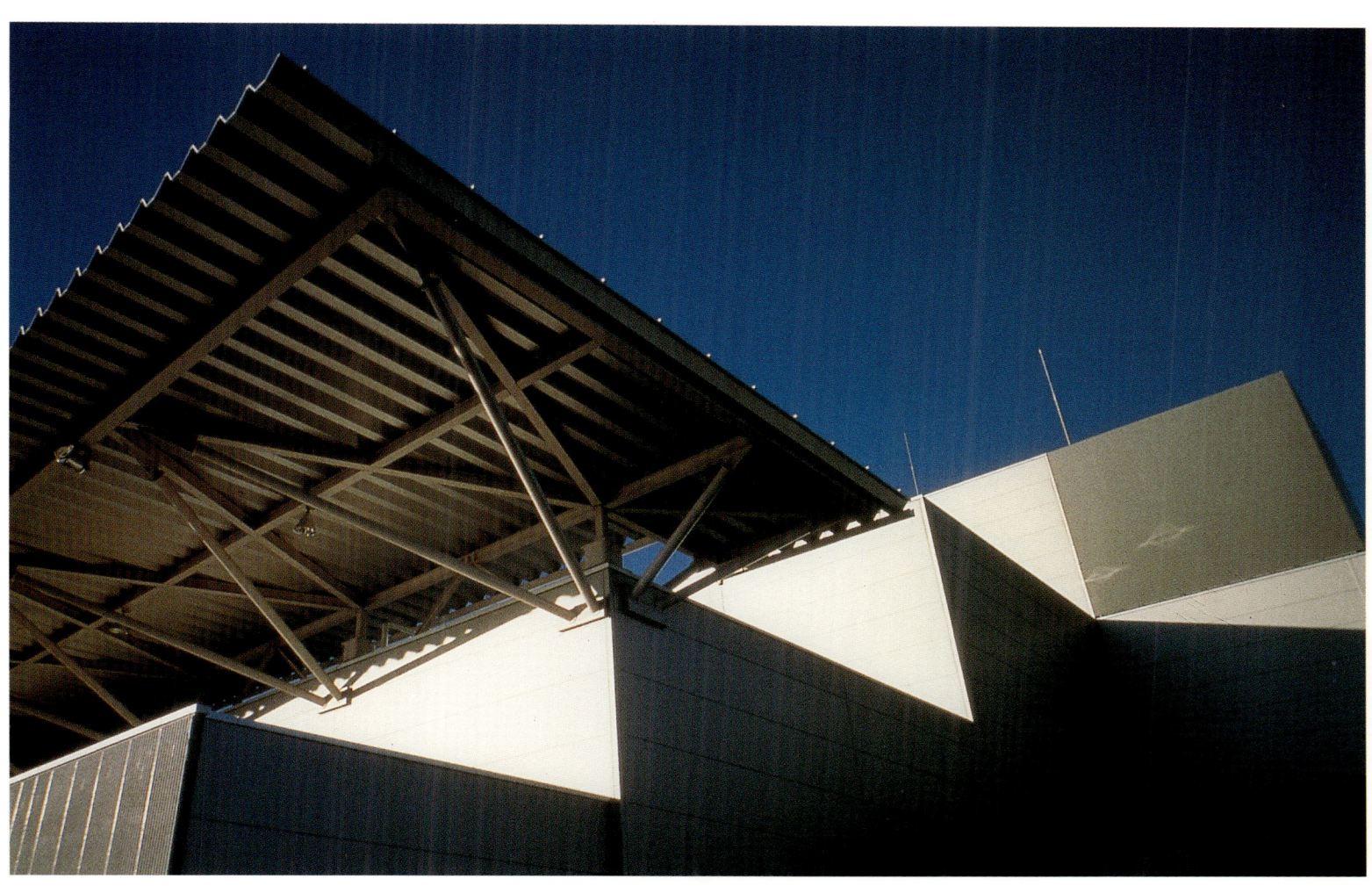

Detail of one of the roofs designed to protect the outside.

Two views of the interior, with the double-height distribution corridor.

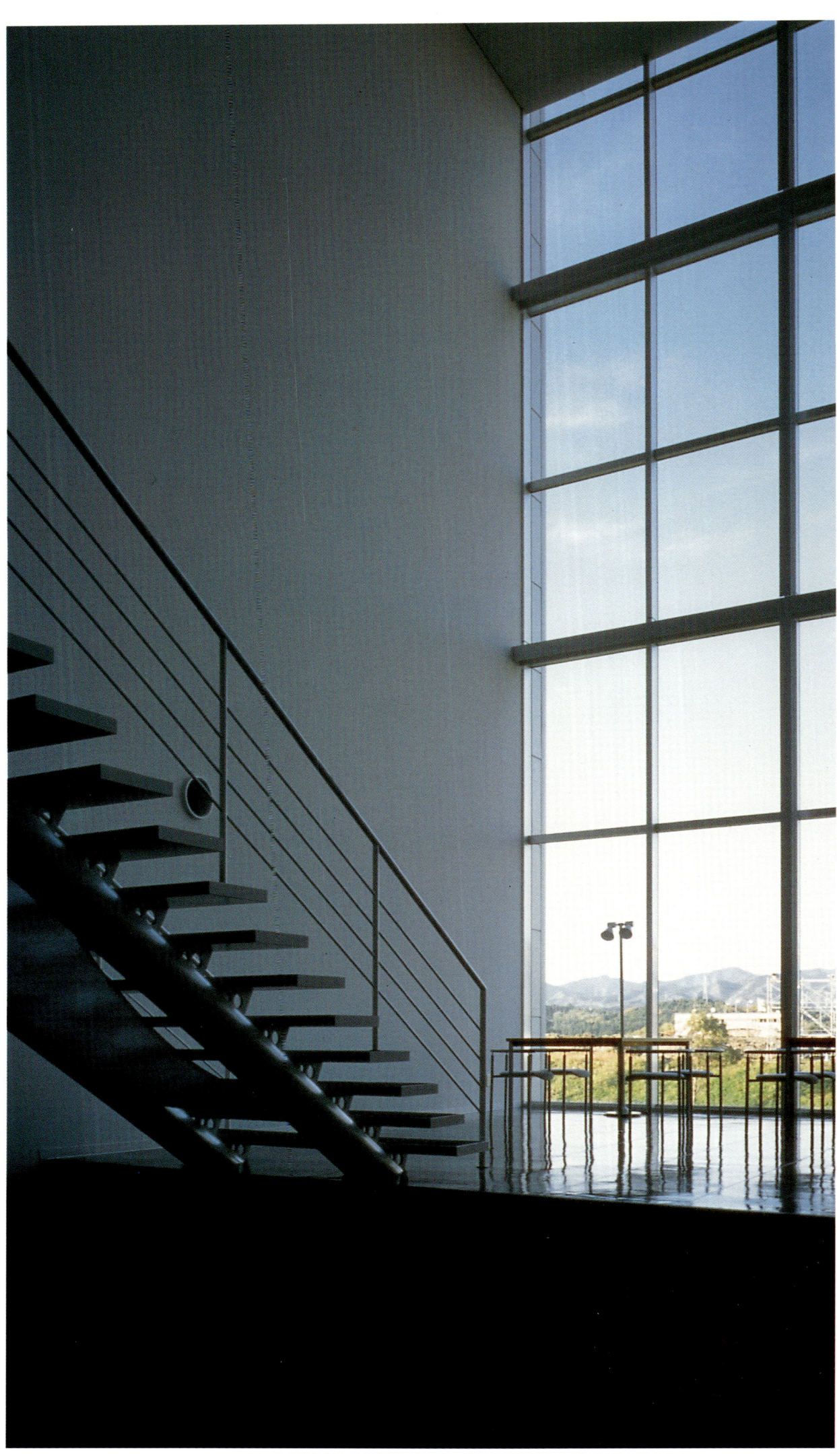

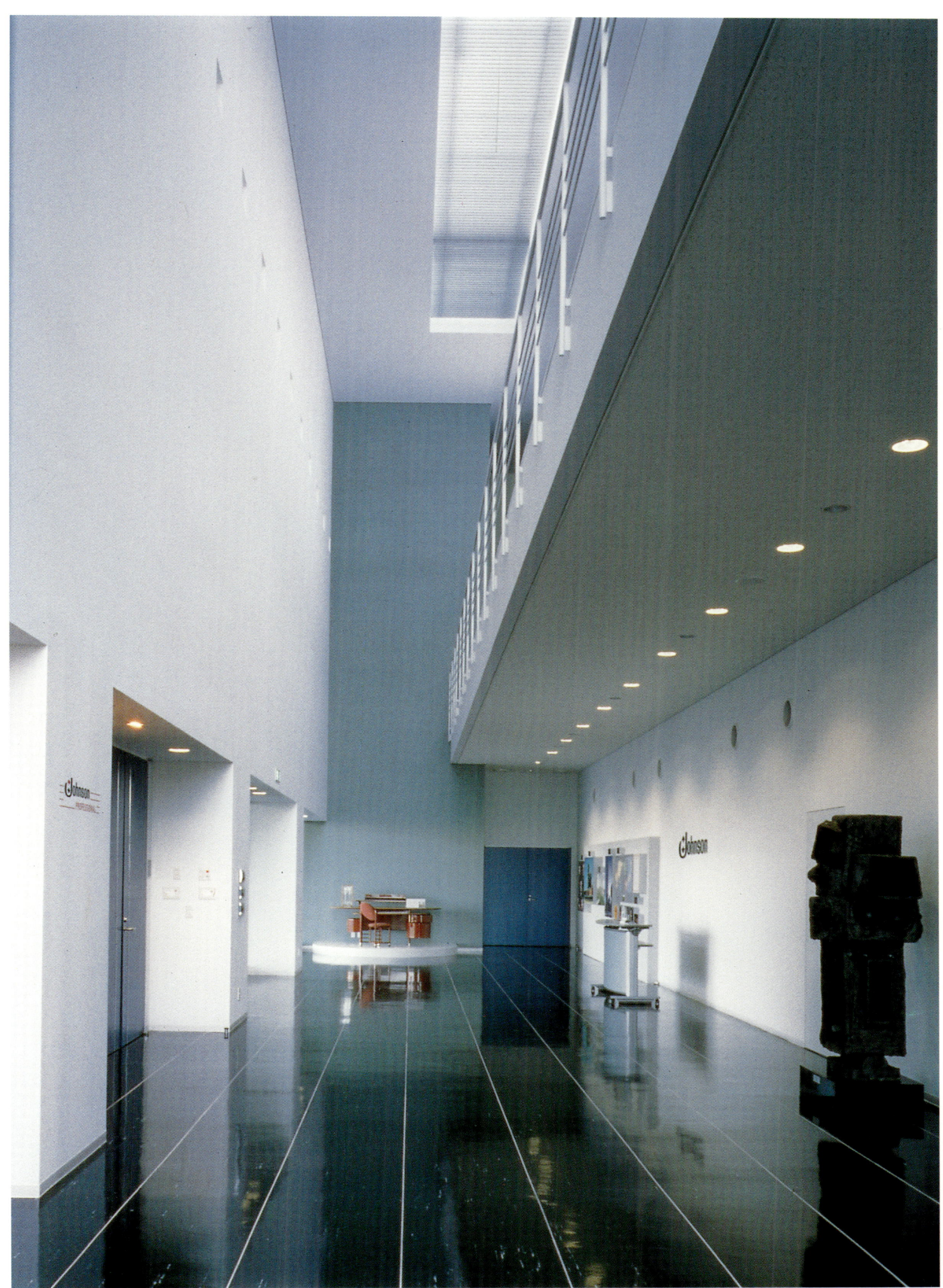

The building interiors are designed to foster productivity and flexibility in the organisation of labour.

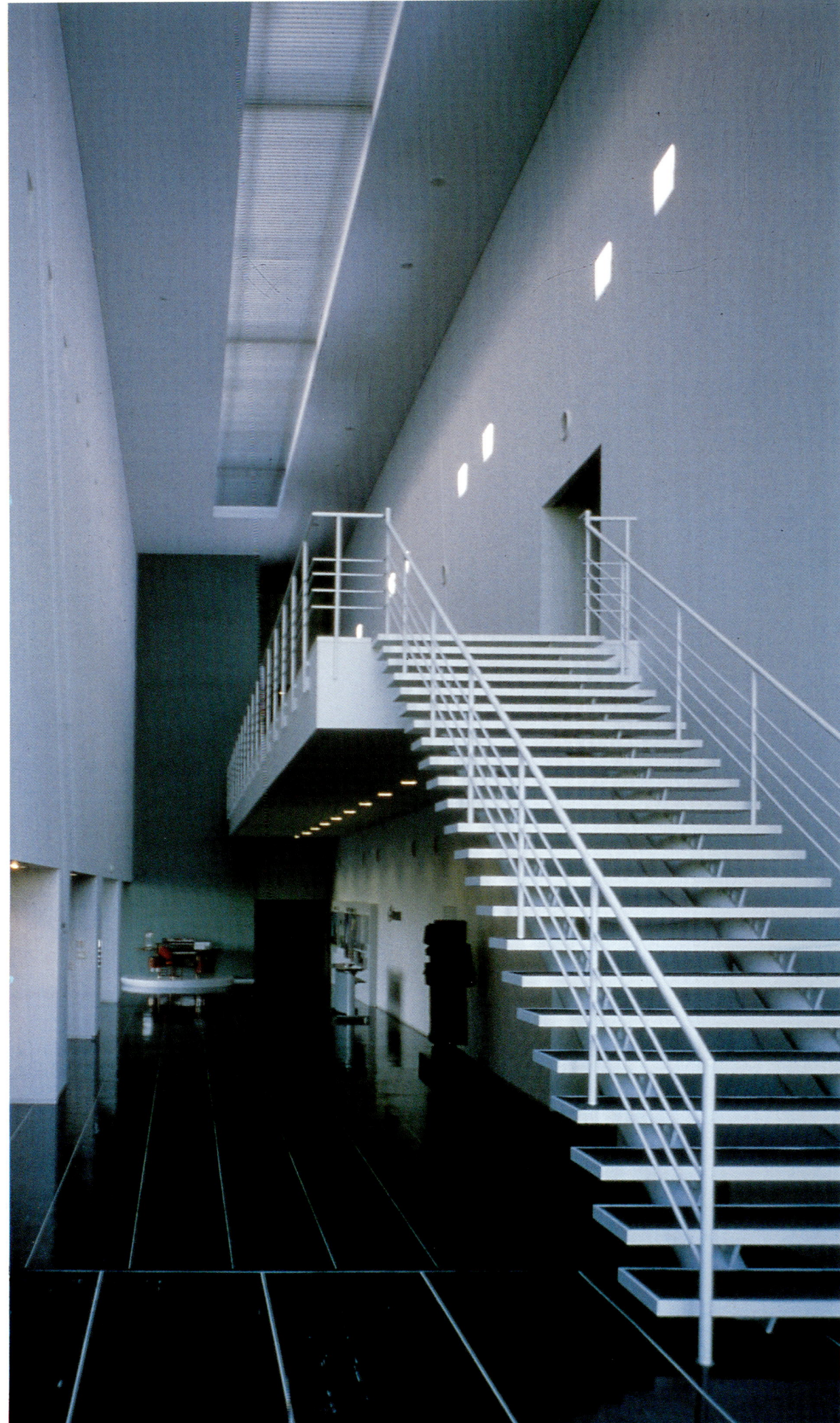

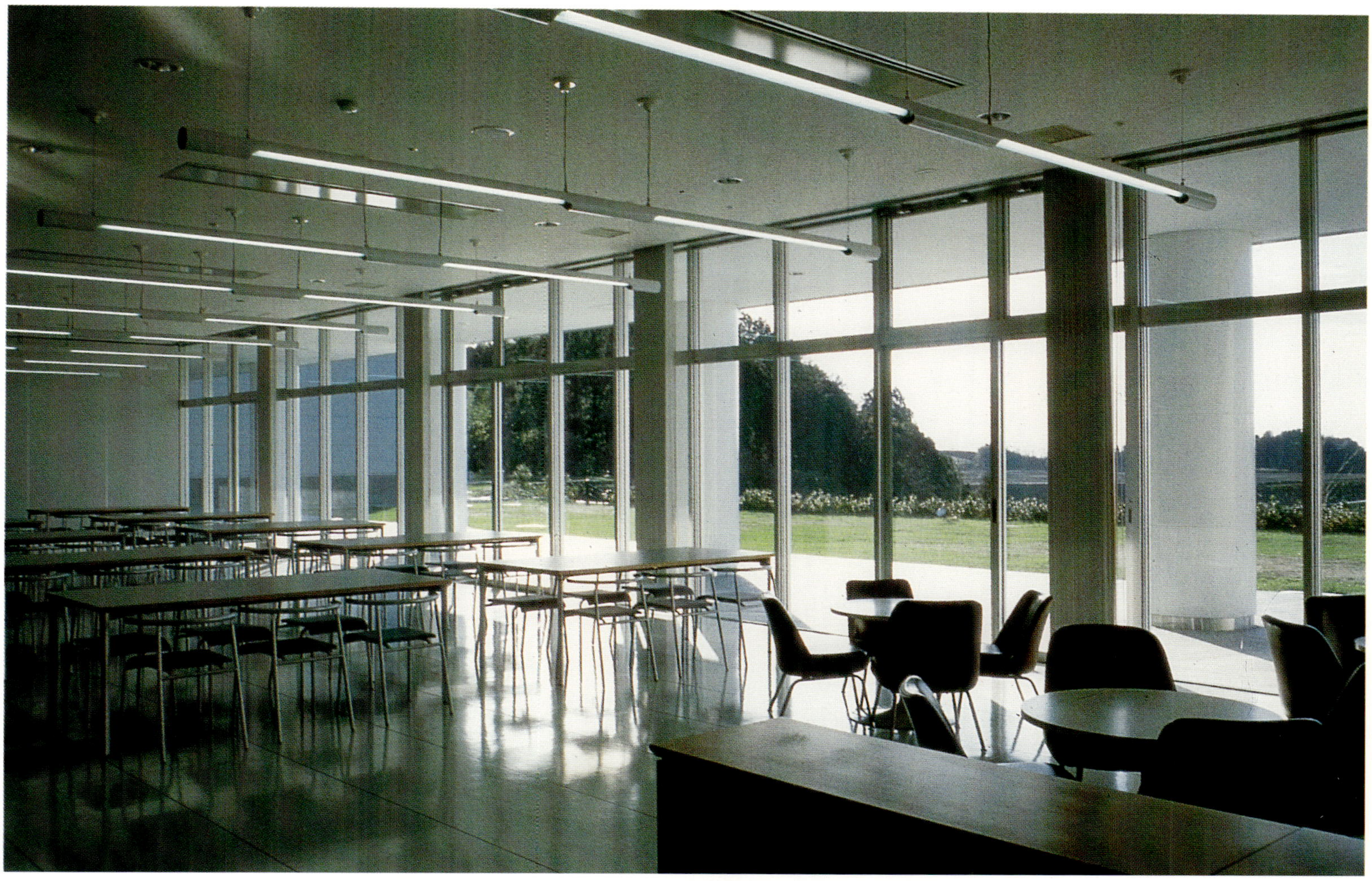

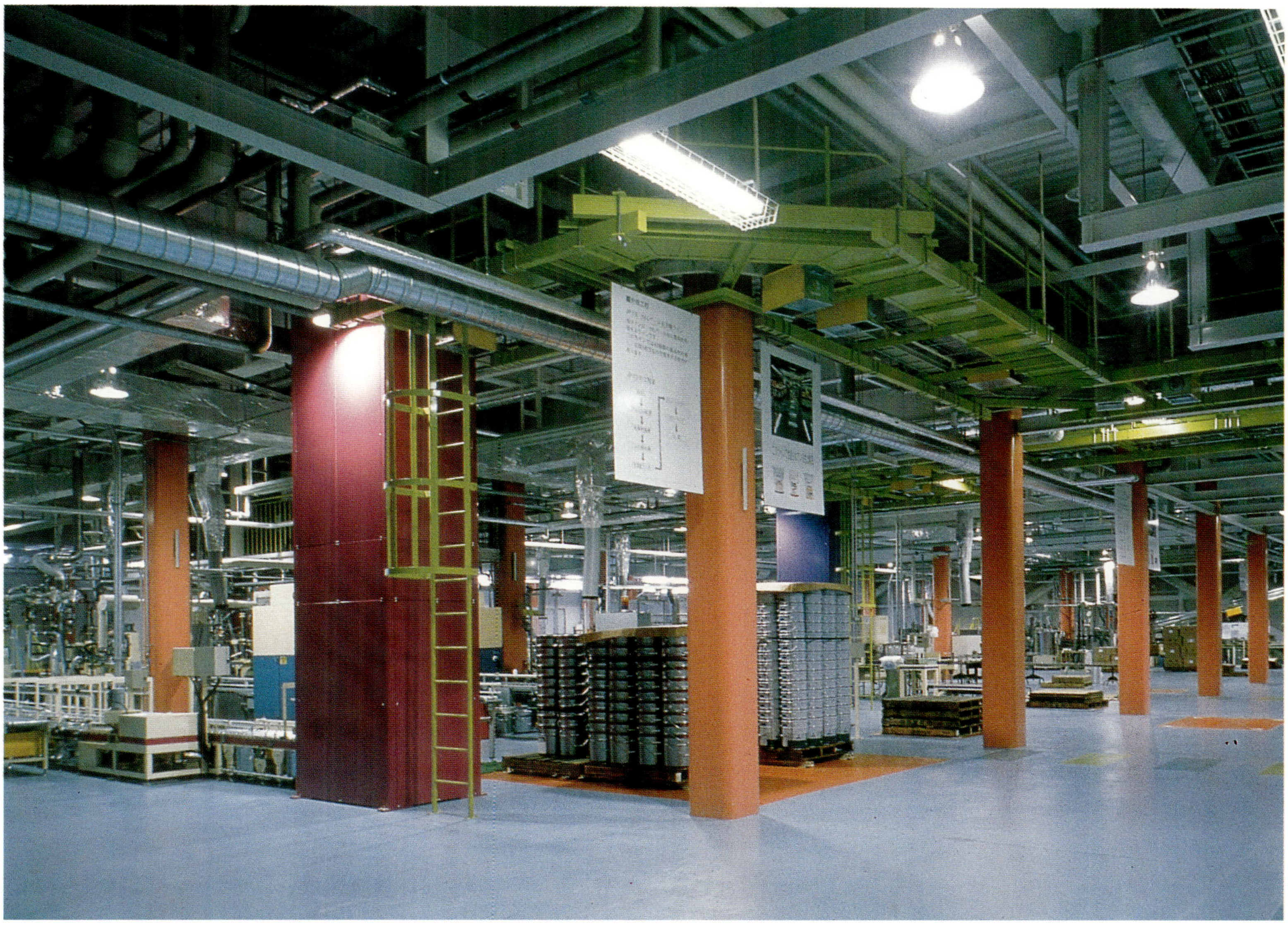

Mizushima Salon

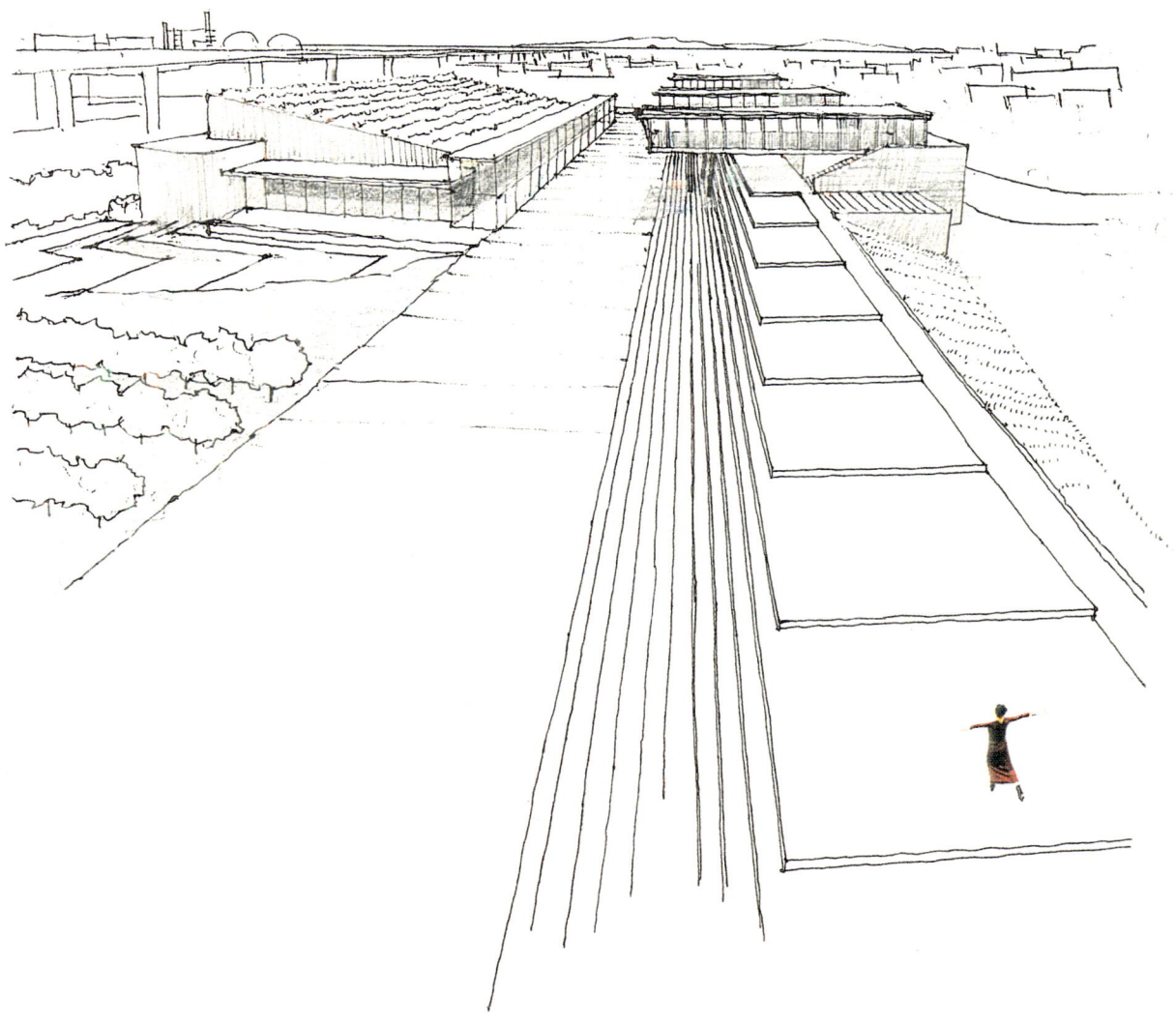

Mizushima Salon was proposed, based on 'Creative Town Okayama's concept of foster a city environment with an identity built over a long period of time, with the aim of building a new city as a settled residential environment'. It is a place for cultural exchange, with a facility that represents a fusion of art, culture and sports. It is laid out so as to provide a facility that is linked with surrounding facilities, and open to the area.

The plans called for a municipal park composed of three separate 'boxes', each with a different function, a green-roofed 'multi-purpose space', and an 'open space' comprising the Mizushima Steps, green square, green slopes, plaza and parking space.

The approach to the park from the neighbouring station can be seen from between the trees of the undulating green space, and from the gently extending stairway. The stairway provides an open, public space for people, and the framework of the facility functions as an approach to the buildings.

The roof of the multi-purpose space is covered with greenery, and acts as an extension to the green square. Then, the three 'boxes' appear to float from the top step of the stairs. The three glass boxes were designed with the nightscape in mind, and in addition to a visual message as the hub of the Mizushima area, as 'boxes' fulfilling a function as instruments open to the area, they also give the area its identity.

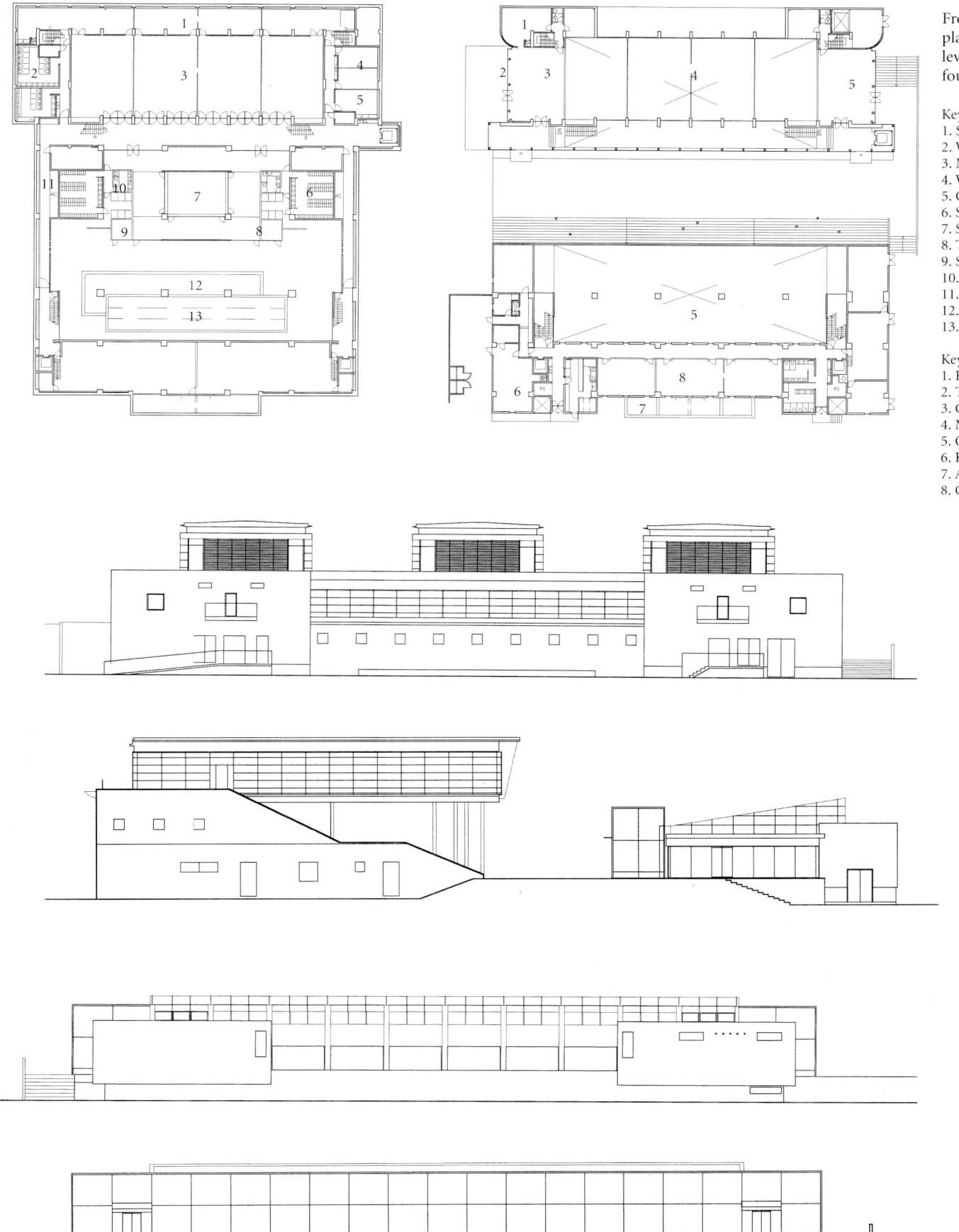

From top of page down, plans of the first and second levels of the complex and all four building elevations.

Key1 (left)
1. Storage
2. Women's Bathroom
3. Multi-Purpose Space
4. Waiting Room
5. Office
6. Shower Room
7. Studio
8. Training Space
9. Sauna
10. Shower Room
11. Men's Locker Room
12. Massage Room
13. Swimming Pool

Key2 (right)
1. Kitchen
2. Terrace
3. Cafeteria
4. Multi-Purpose Space
5. Open to Below
6. Kitchen
7. Areaway
8. Conference Room

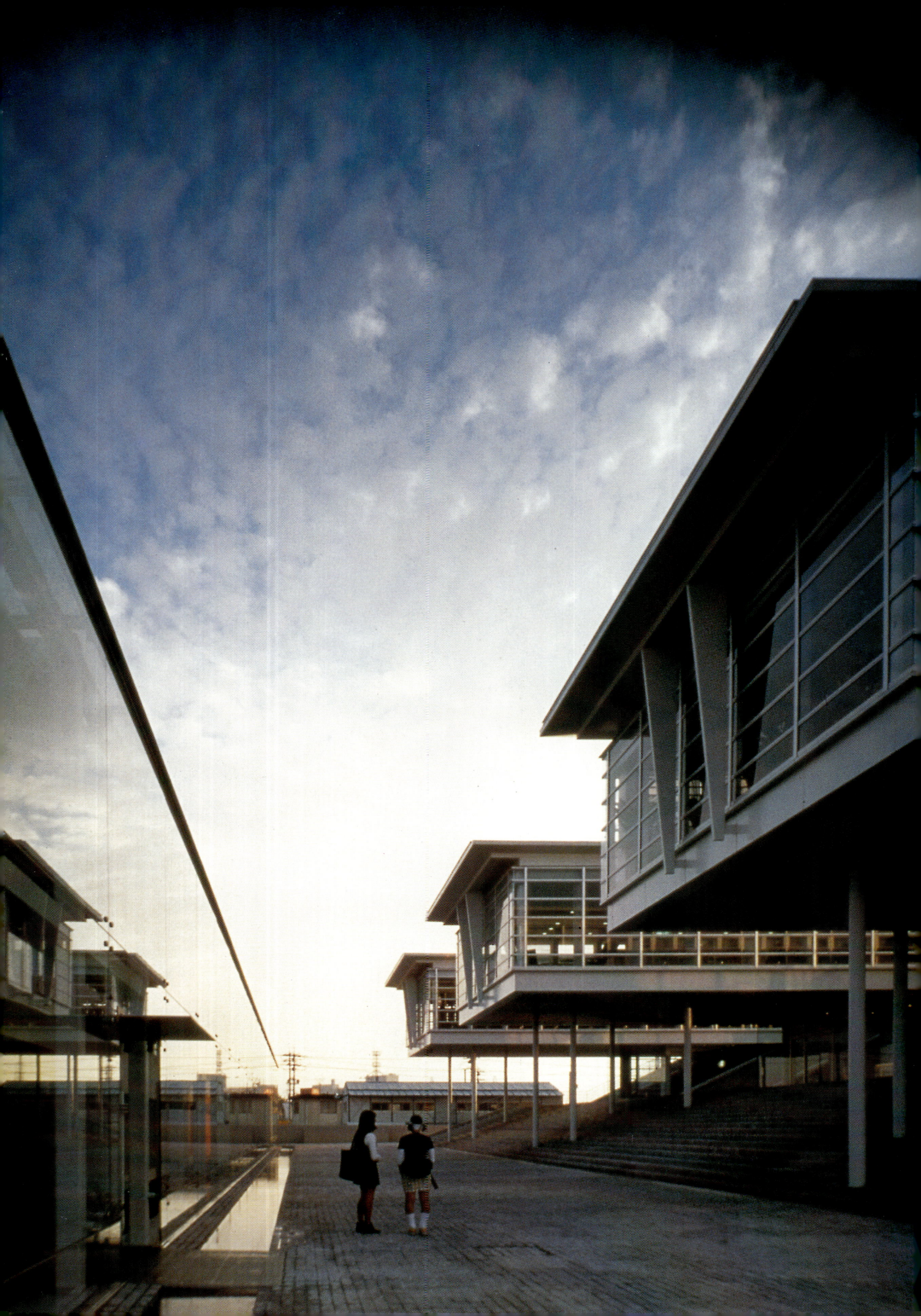

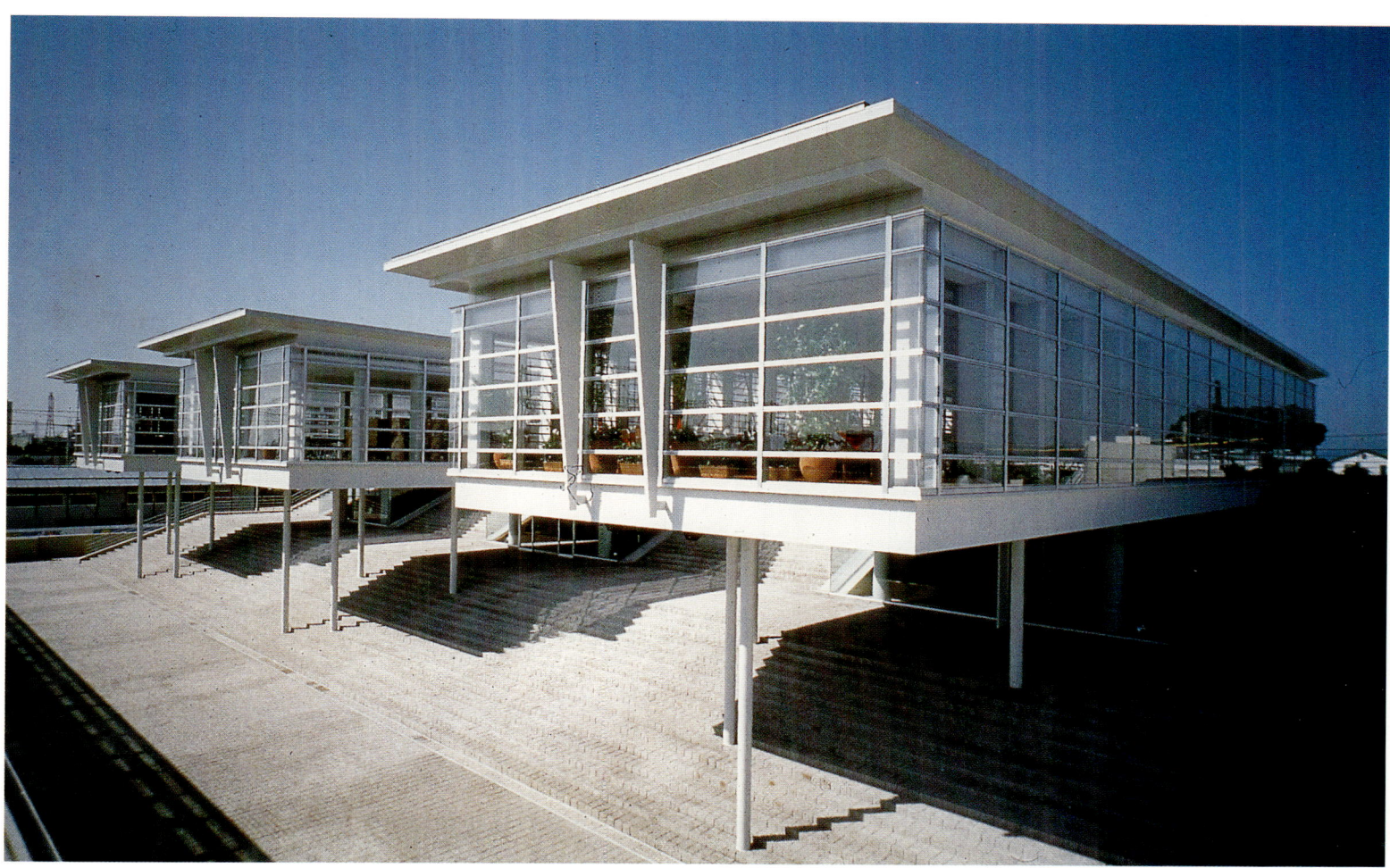

Views of the "boxes", each hosting a different function.

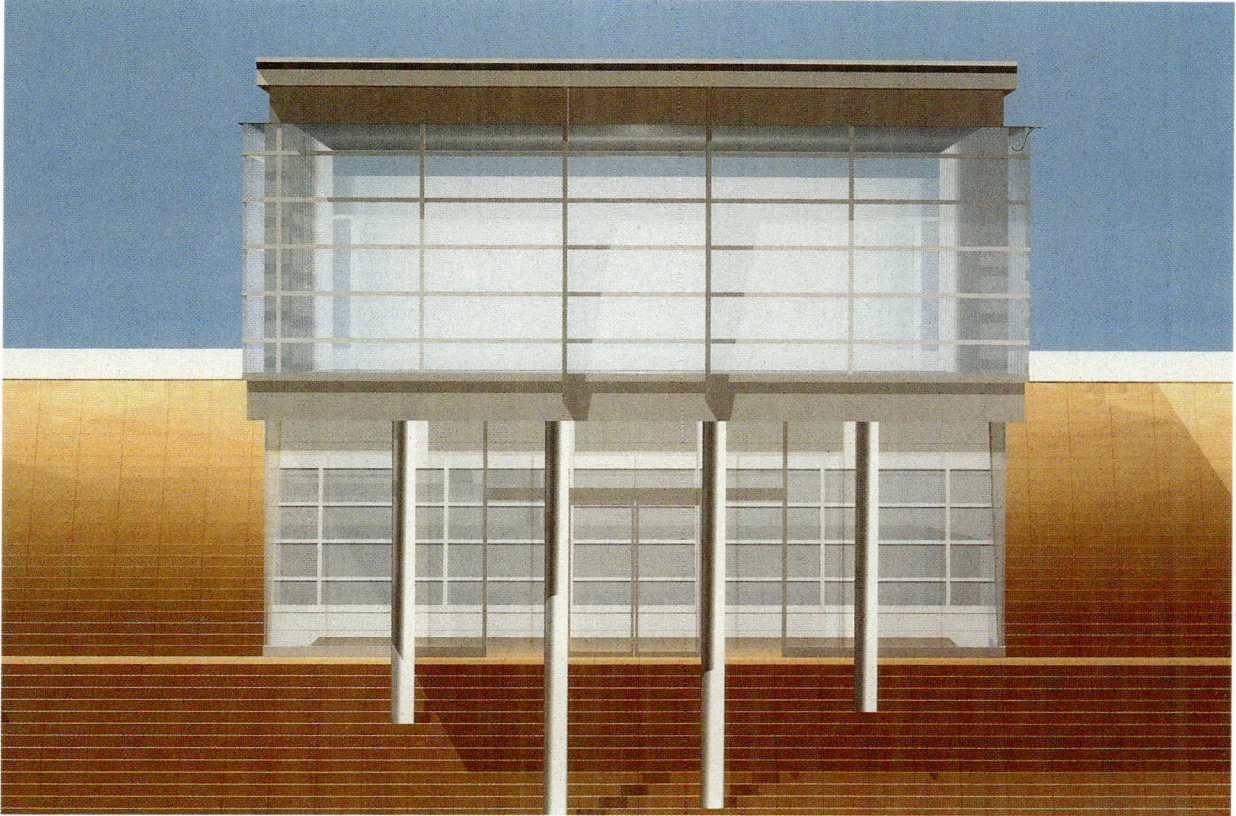

127

Diagram of the functional layout of space and rendering of the complex.

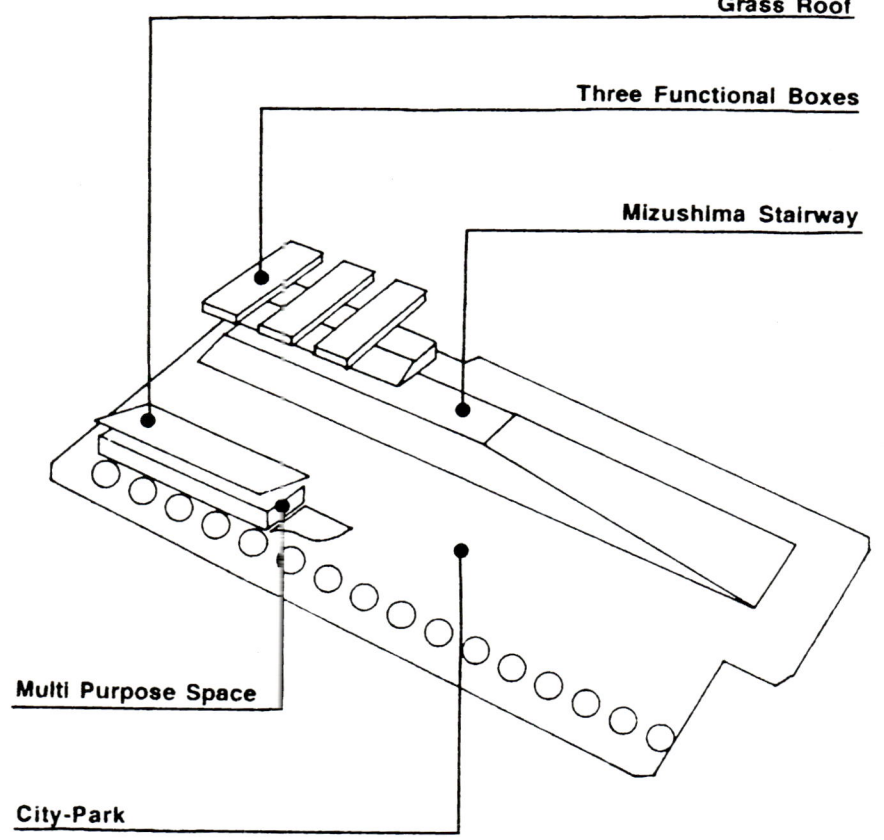

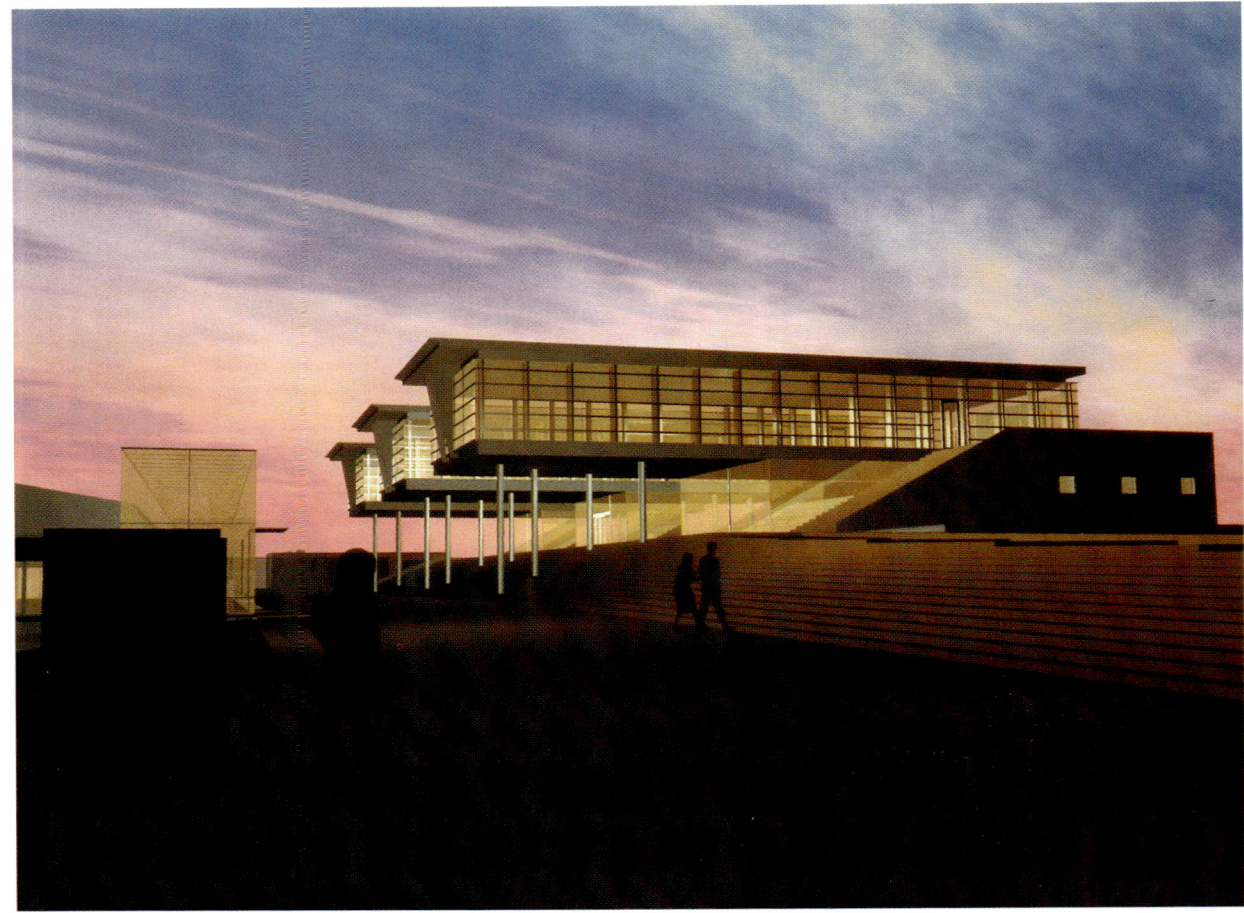

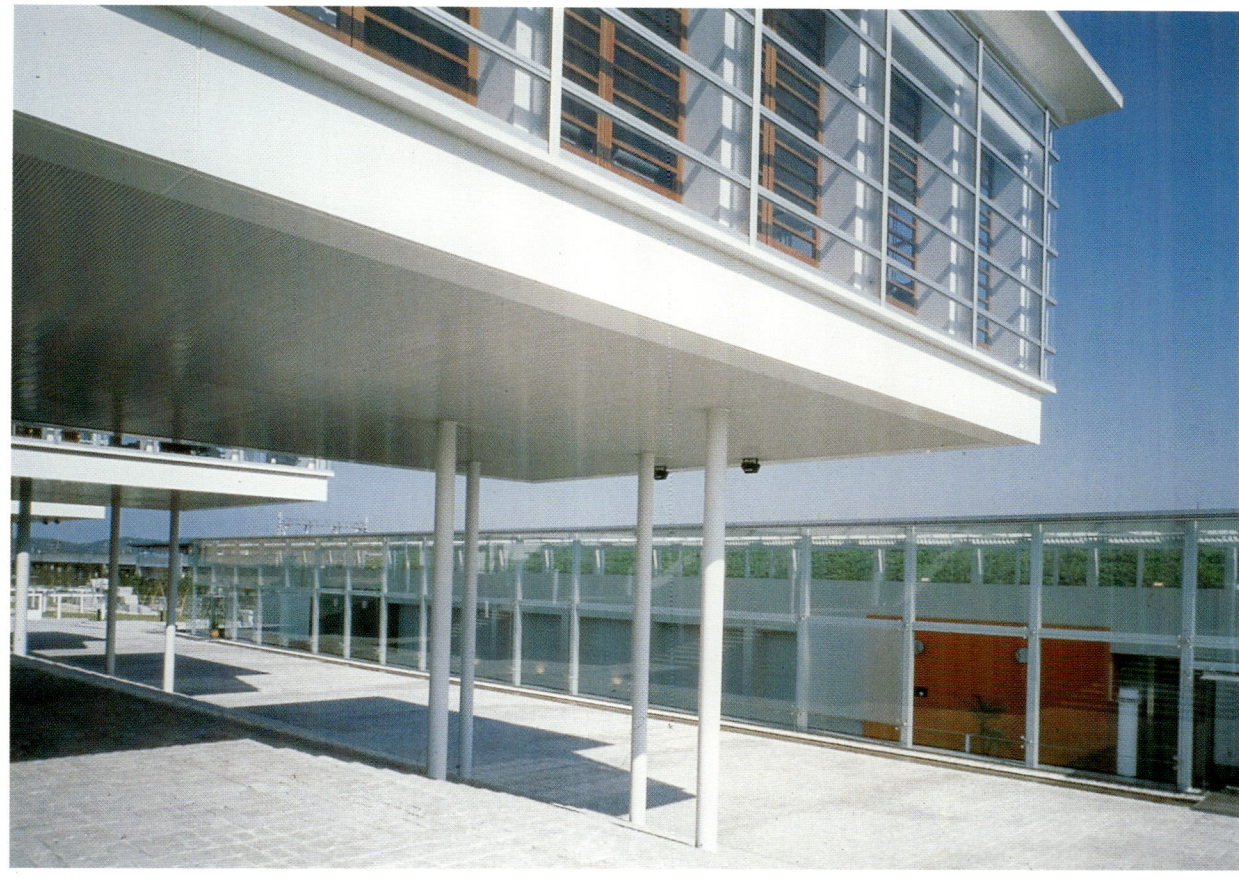

Two Cad rendering showing the layout of architectural structures.

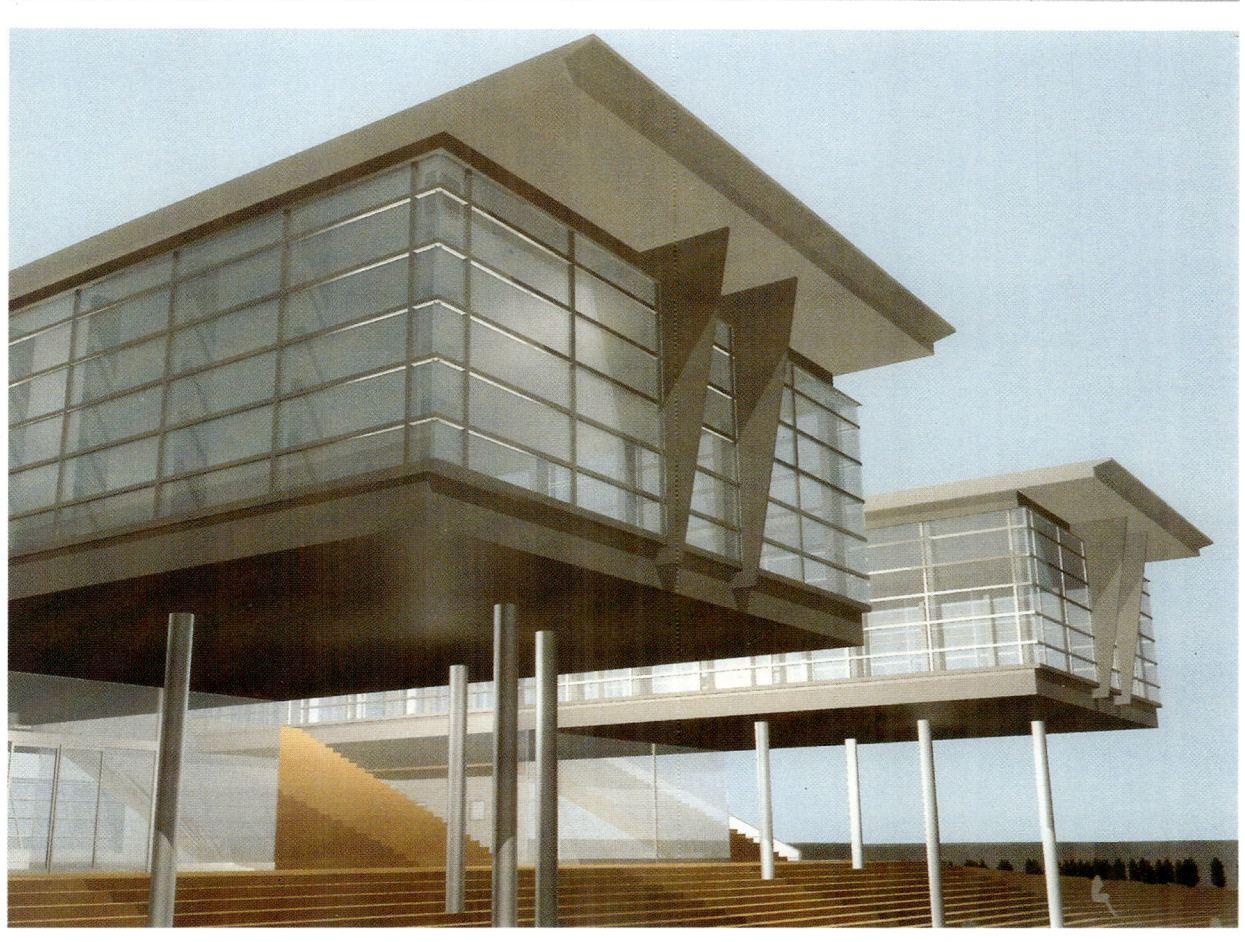

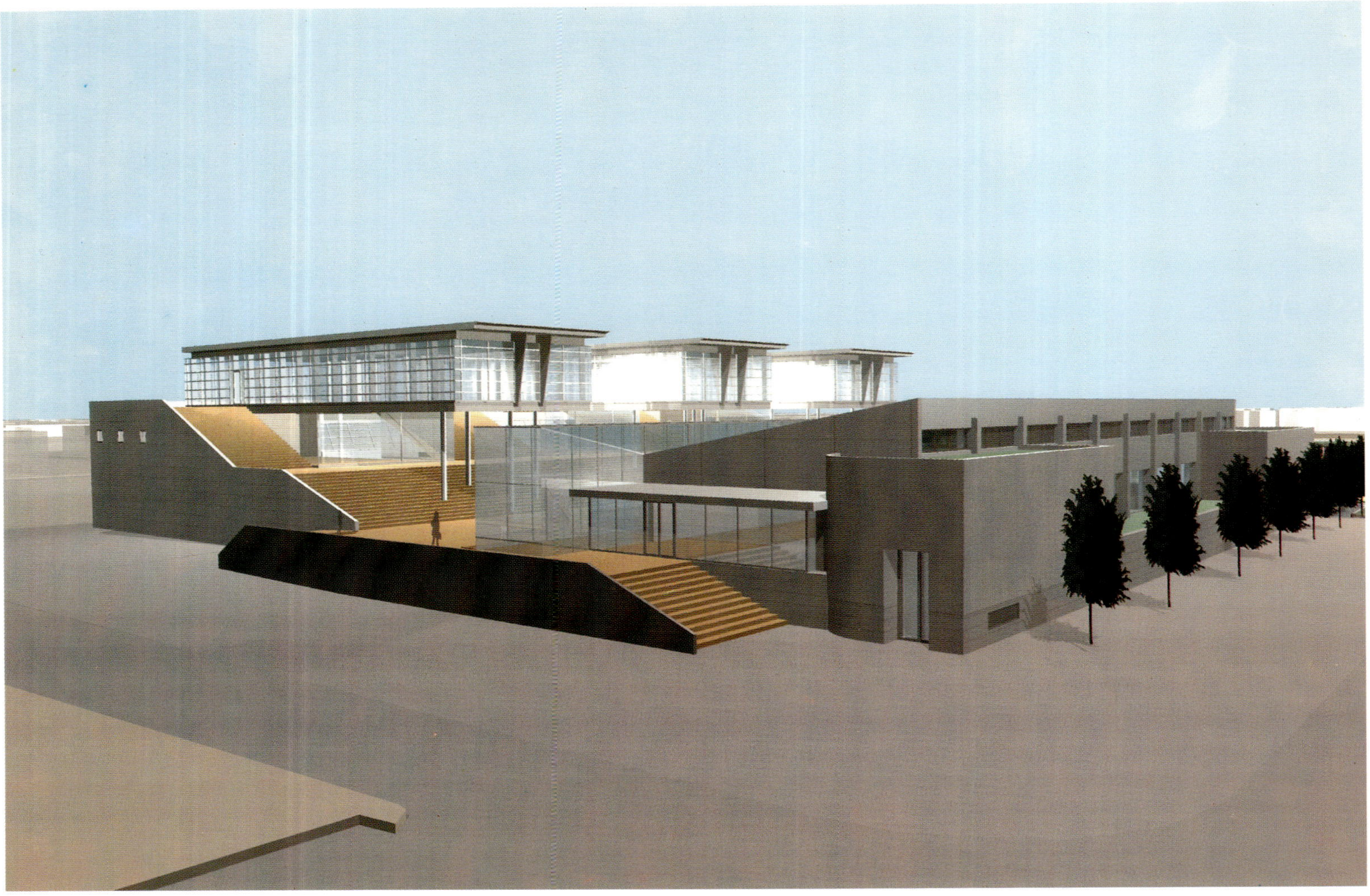

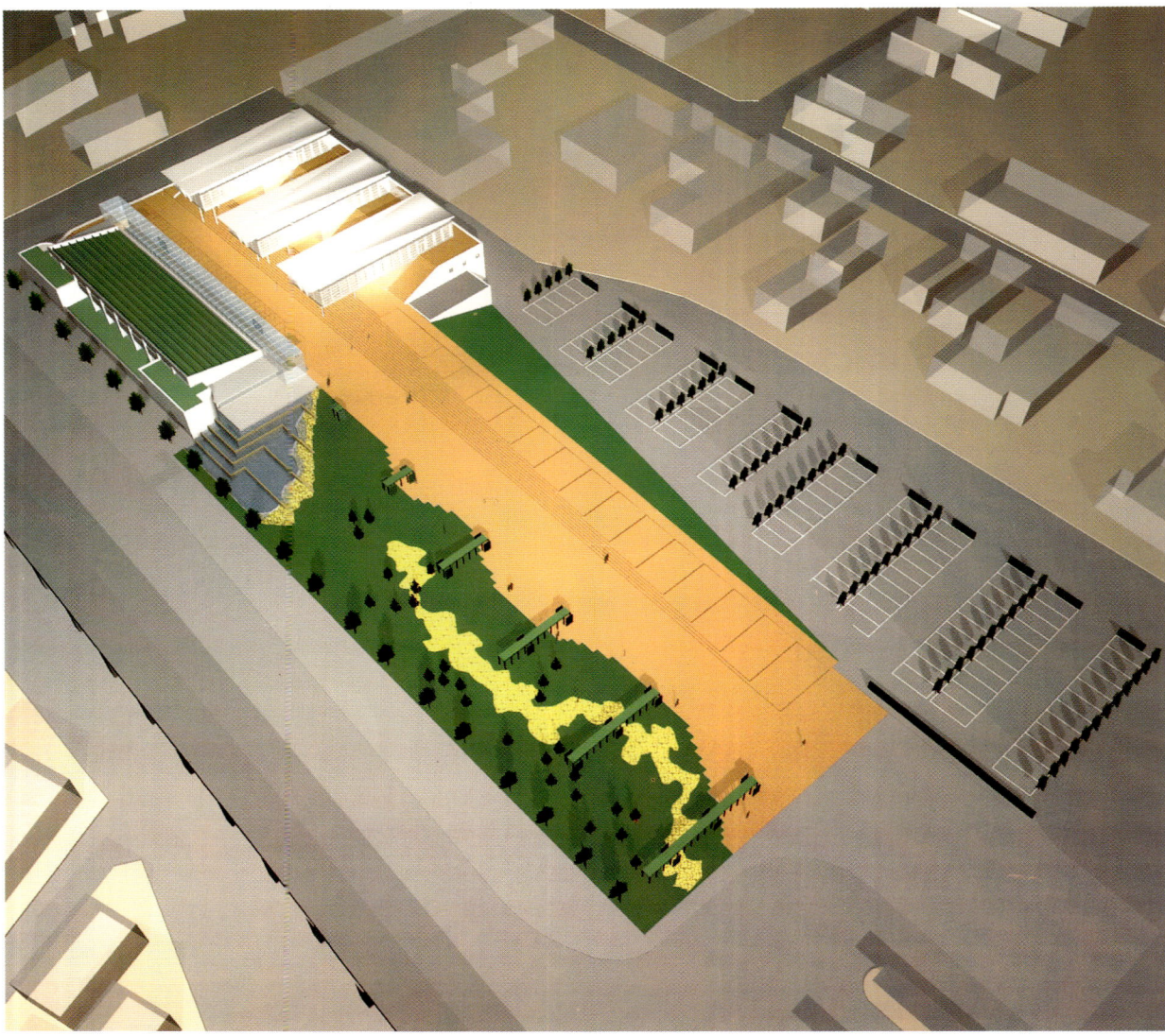

Other Cad renderings and, opposite, two internal views of one of the "boxes".

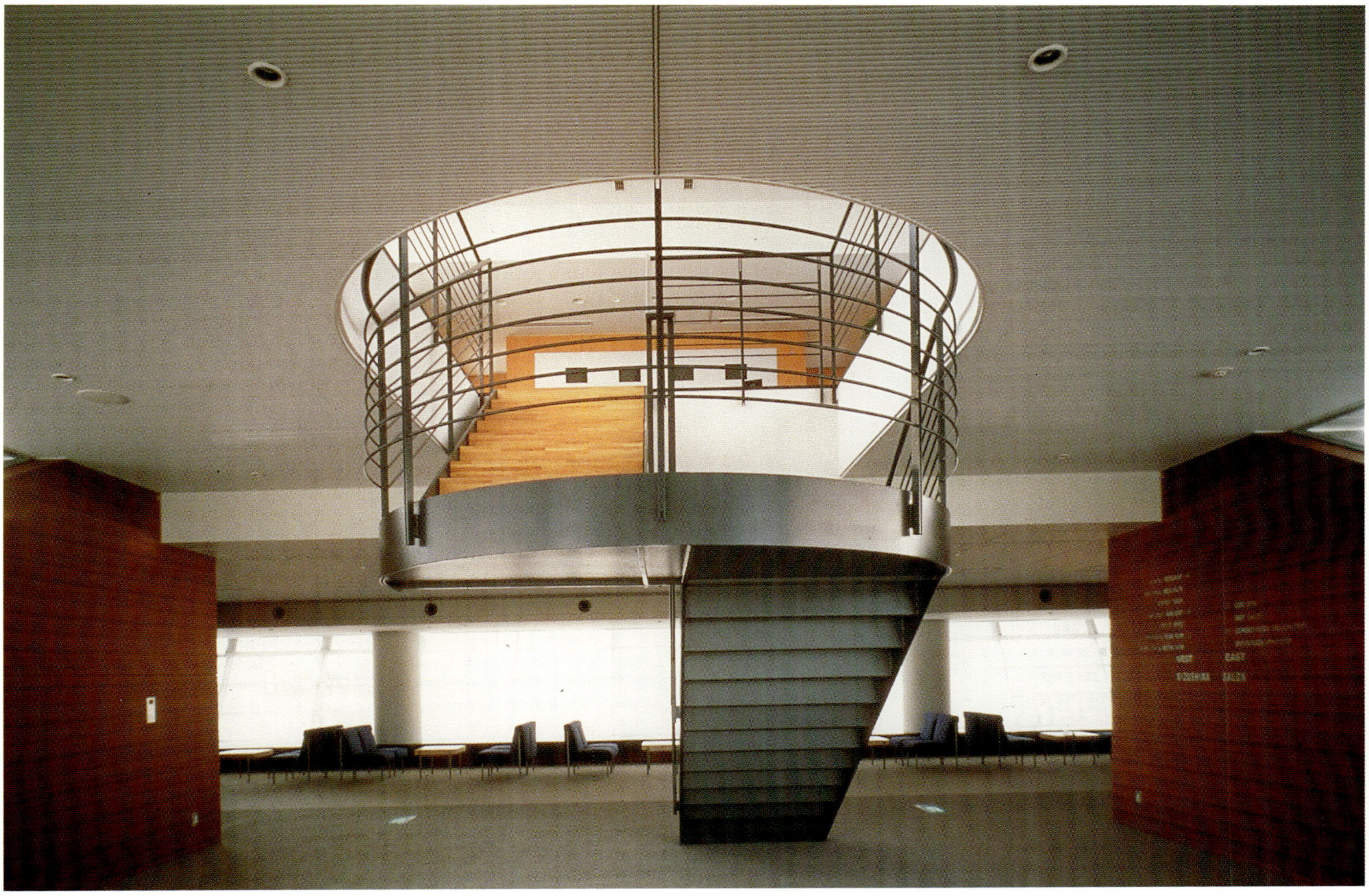

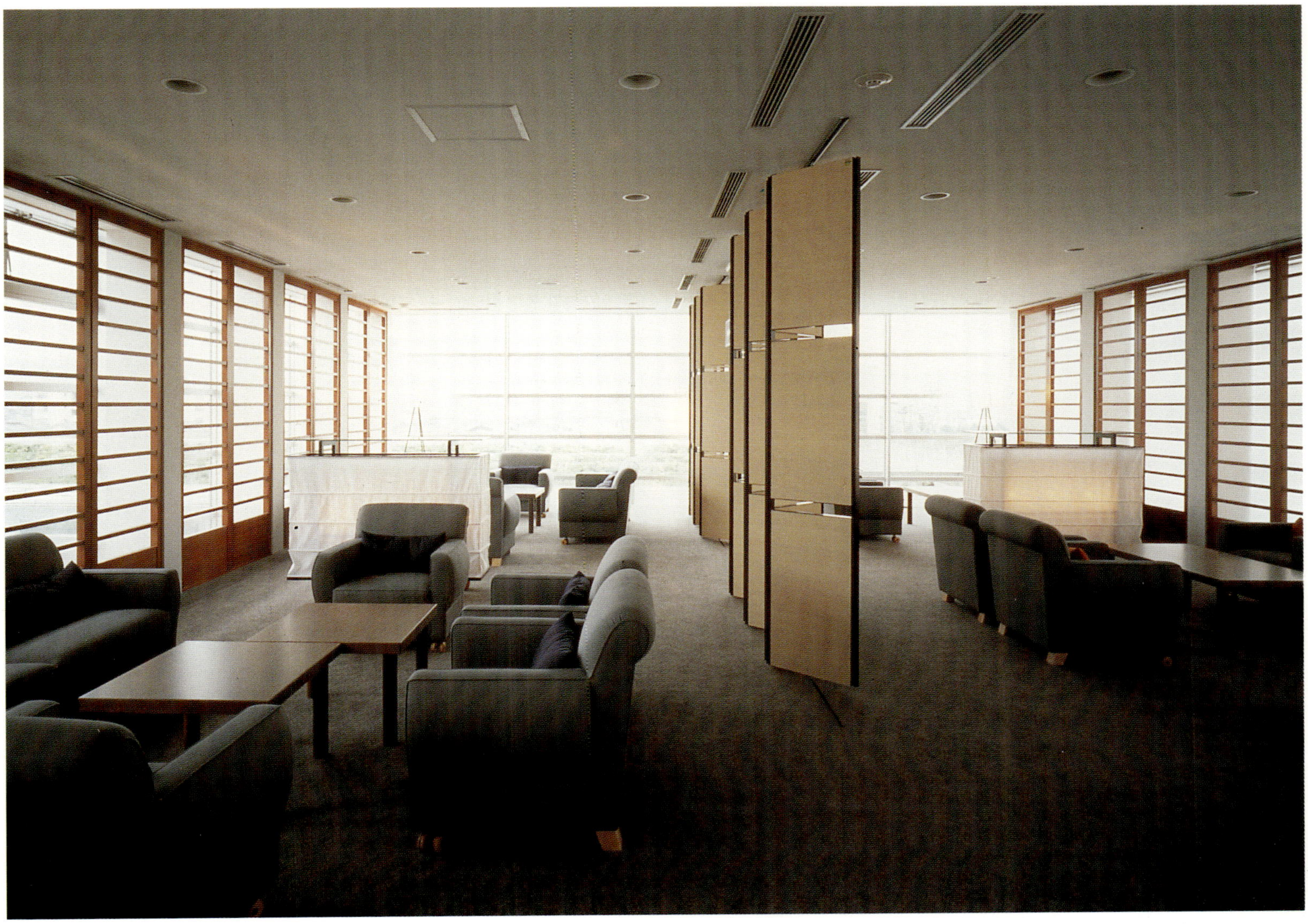

131

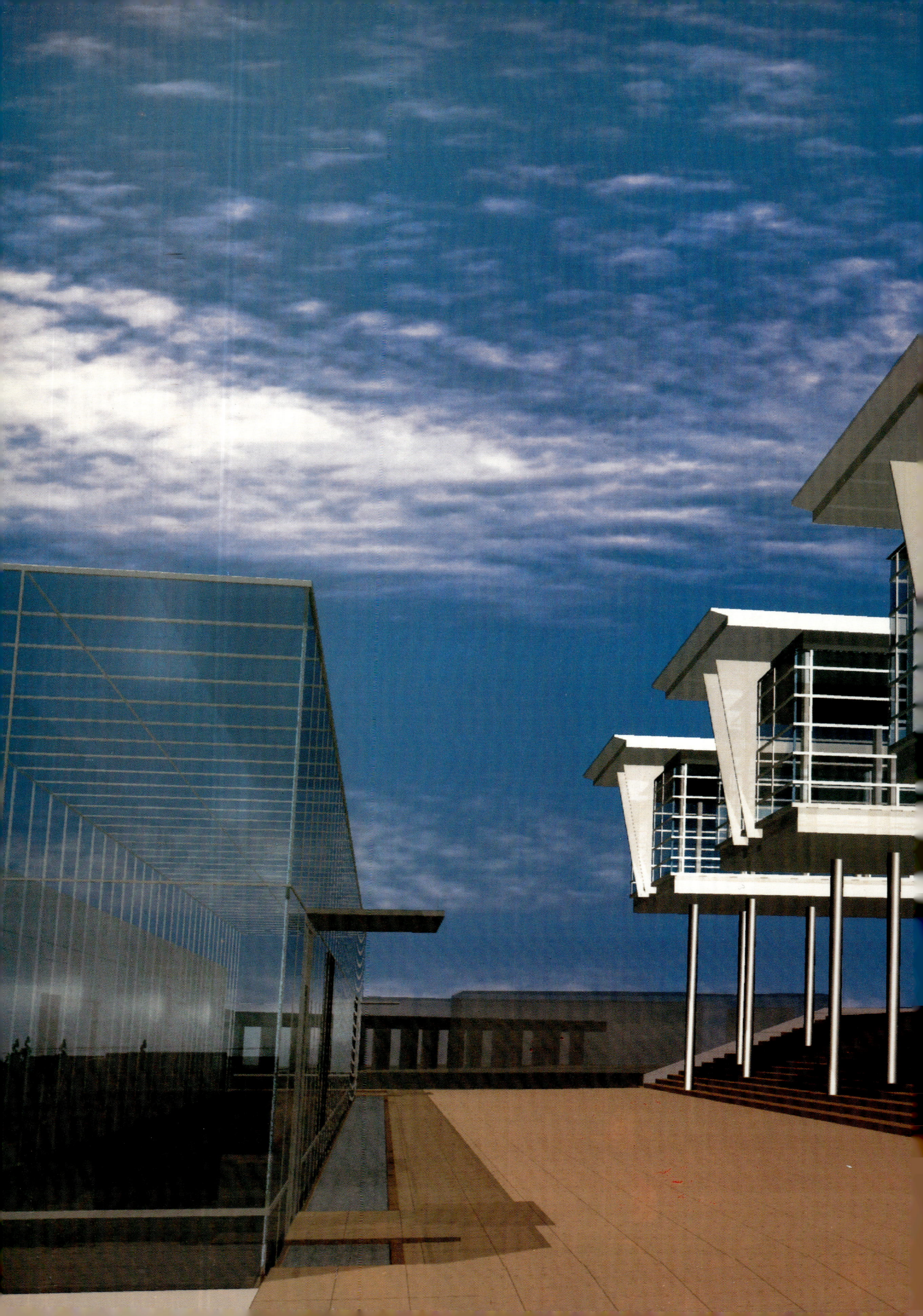

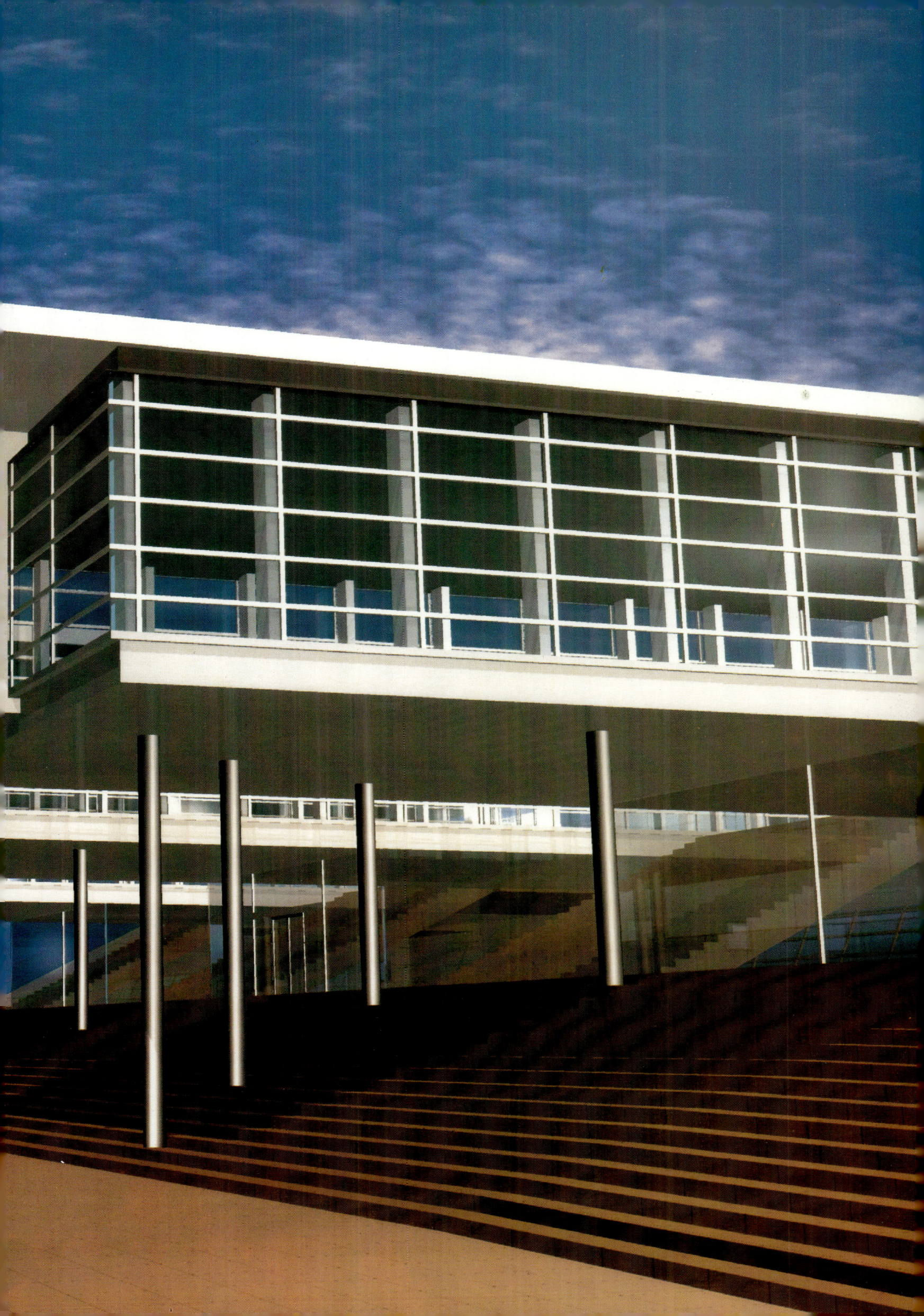

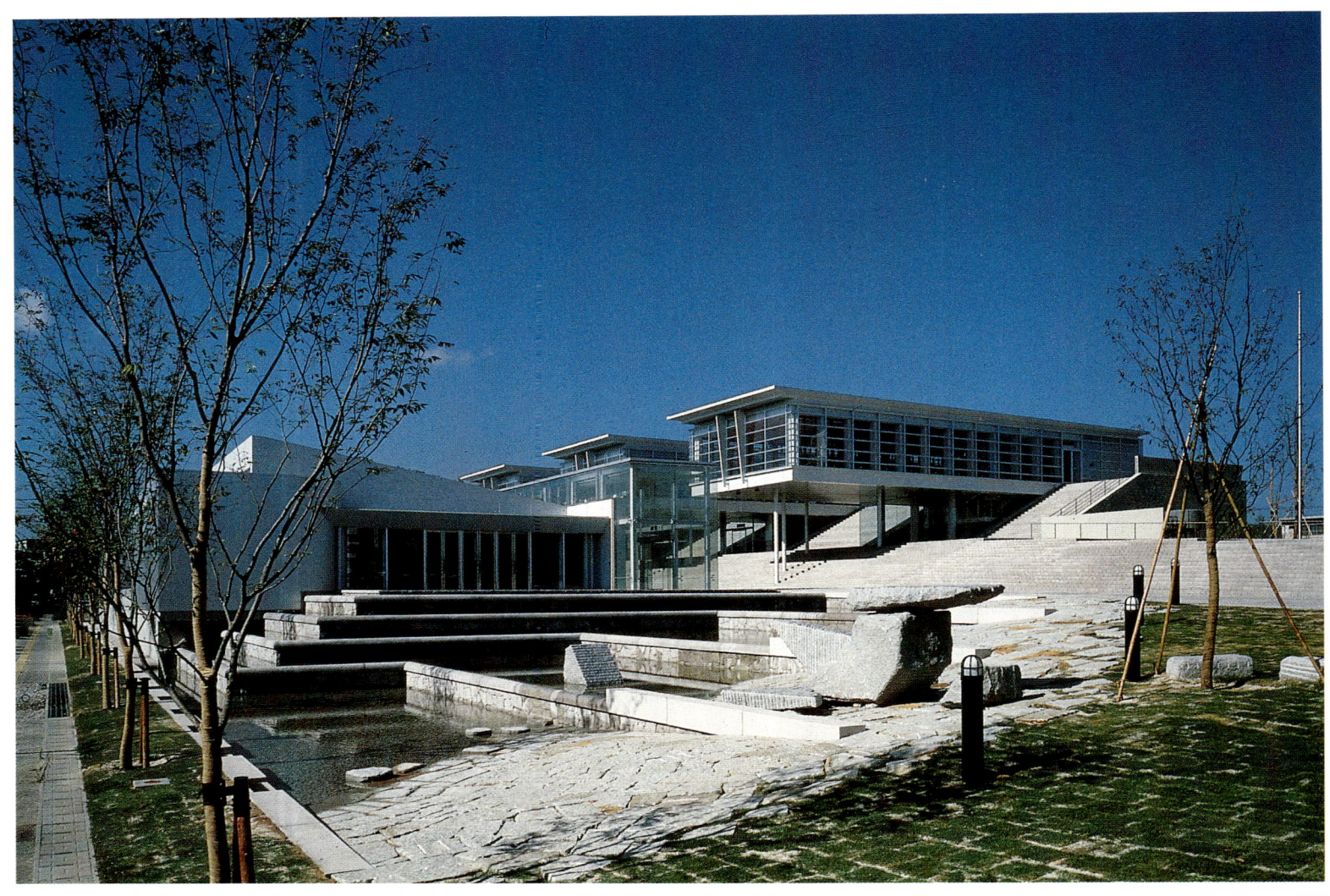

The stairway provides an open public space for people, and the framework of the facility acts as an approach to the buildings.

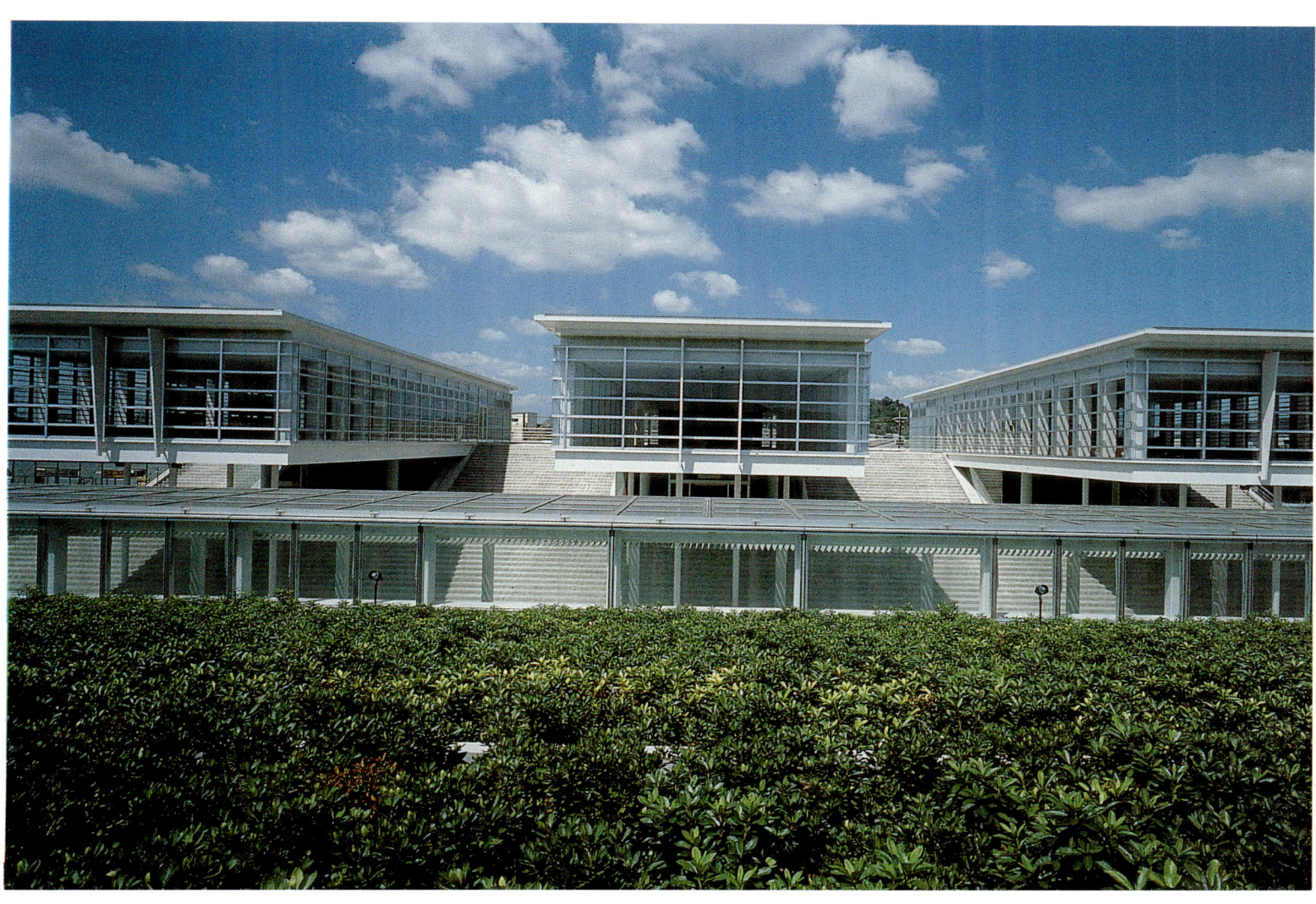

Front view of the three multi-purpose buildings forming the municipal centre for the arts.

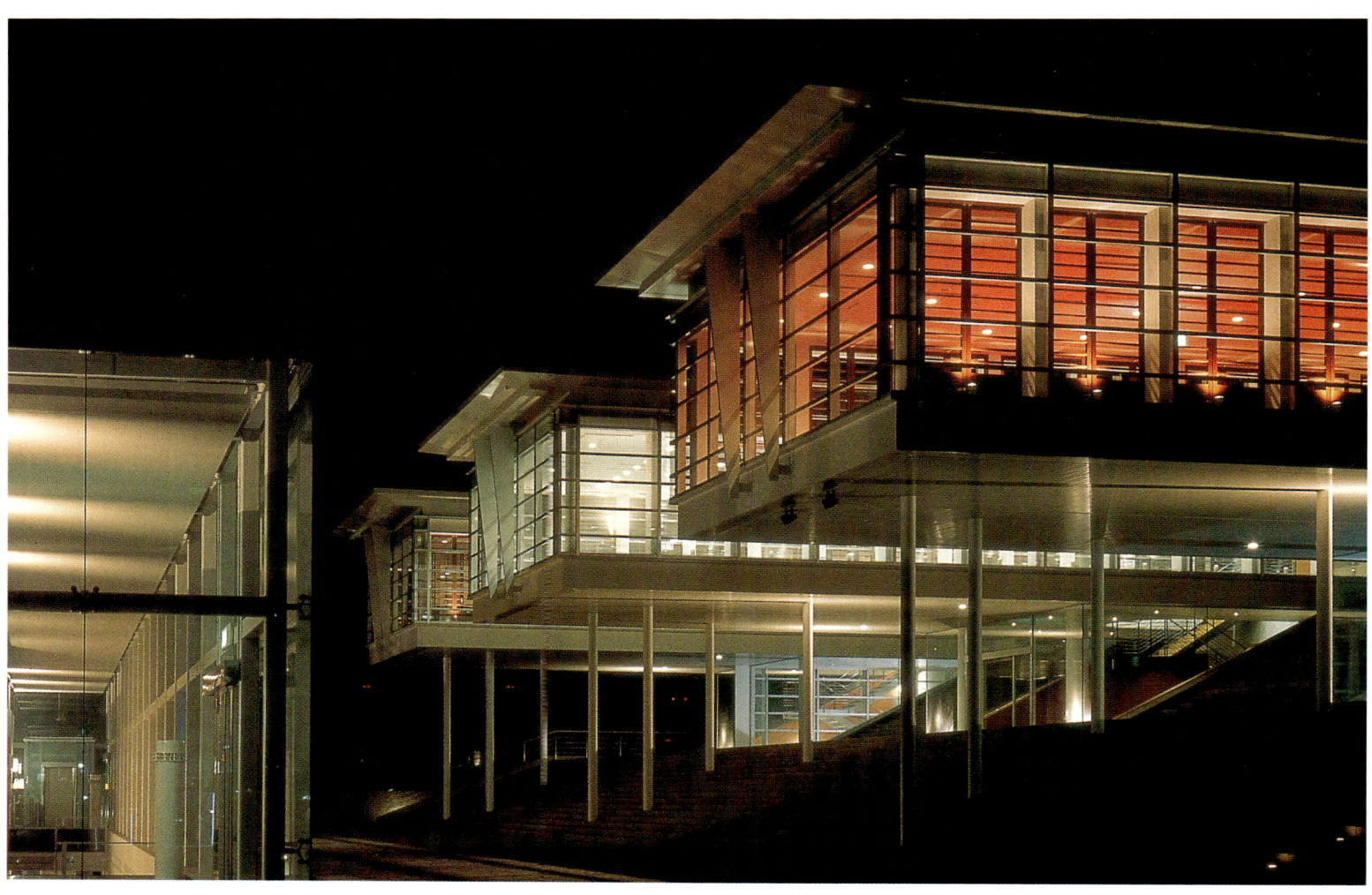

Nighttime view of the complex, which can also be used throughout most of the day thanks to all the activities it hosts.

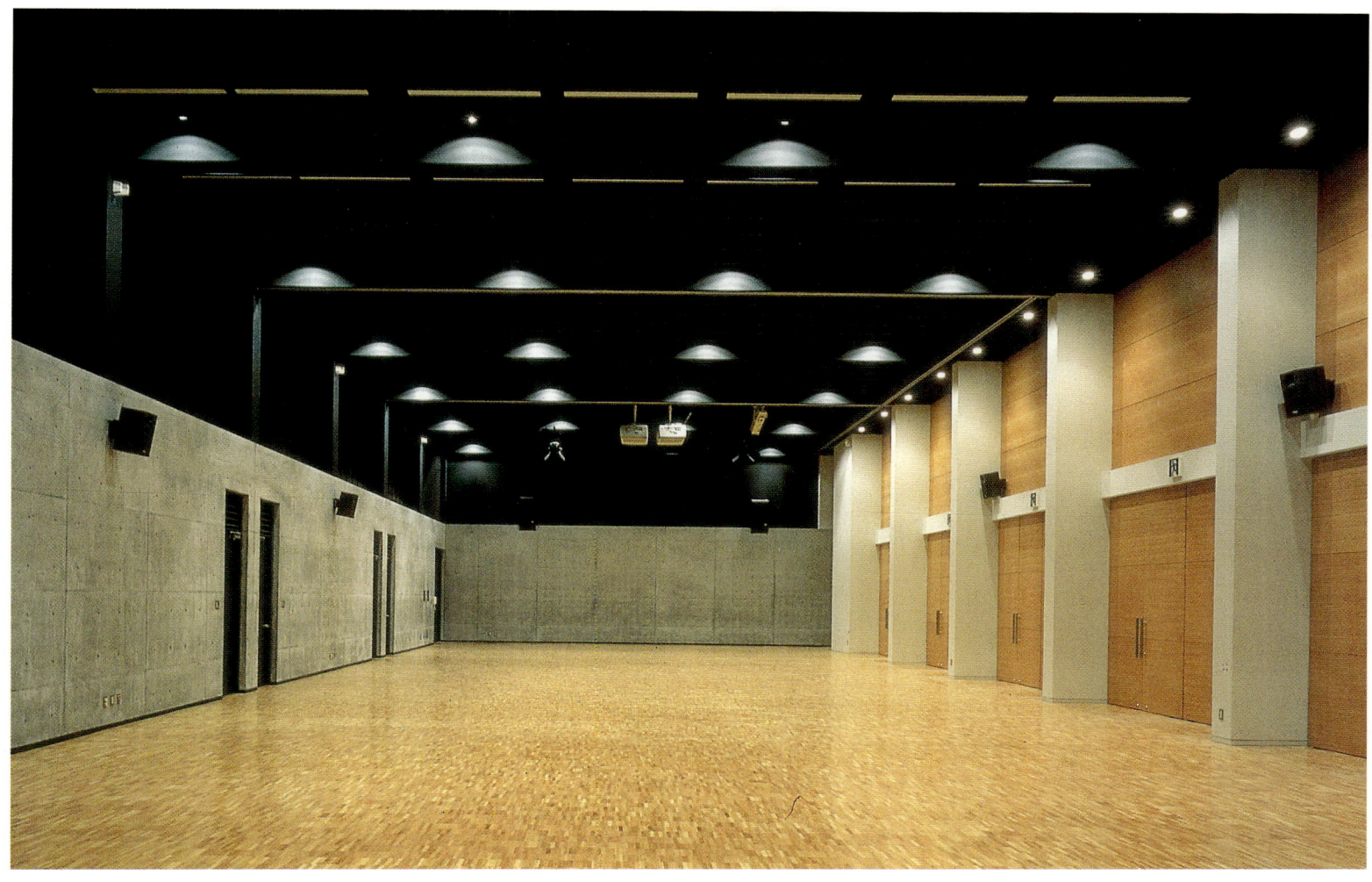

One of the inside halls used
for sports activities.

List of Works

M-House
Tokyo
1985-1986
Area: 300 sq.m.
Owner: Yaeko Mito
Photo: Shinkenchiku, Co., Ltd.

G-House
Tokyo
1985-1987
Area: 1,070 sq.m.
Owner: Kan Goto

Kamiosaki-House (co:Kukan Studio)
Tokyo
1986-1987
Area: 848 sq.m.
Owner: KC Corporation

S-House
Tokyo
1987-1989
Area: 80 sq.m
Owner: Endeavor Inc.
Photo: Shinkenchiku, Co., Ltd.

Ichikudo Building
Tokyo
1987-1989
Area: 2,930 sq.m.
Owner: Ichikudo Printing Office
Photo: Seihan Sato, SS Tokyo

Kasama Nichido Museum of Art
Ibaragi
1988-1989
Area: 1,655 sq.m.
Owner: Gallery Nichido
Photo: Shinkenchiku, Co., Ltd.,
Kouji Horiuchi, Isao Inbe

Australian Embassy, Tokyo (co:DCM)
Tokyo
1987-1990
Area: 22,740 sq.m.
Owner: Australian Government
Photo: Shinkenchiku, Co., Ltd.

Villa-N
Nagano
1990-1991
Area: 180 sq.m.
Owner: Makiko Nakanishi
Photo: Shinkenchiku, Co., Ltd.

Sirocco
Tokyo
1990-1992
Area: 397 sq.m.
Owner: Shibuya Foods, Co., Ltd.

Yamanashi Prefectural Nurshing Junior College
Yamanashi
1992-1994
Area: 6,800 sq.m.
Owner: Yamanashi Prefectural Government.

Tokyo Metropolitan Office, Niijima Branch
Niijima
1994-1995
Area: 928 sq.m.
Owner: Tokyo Metropolitan Government
Photo: Shigeru Kanedo, Koji Horiuchi

F-House
Saitama
1993-1995
Area: 487 sq.m.
Owner: Makoto Fukuhara
Photo: Shinkenchiku Co., Ltd.

Shiroishi N°2 Primary School (Co: Workshop)
Kurashiki, Miyagi
1993-1996
Area: 8,820 sq.m.
Owner: The City of Shiroishi
Photo: Shinkenchiku, Co., Ltd., Nikkei
Architecture, Katsuaki Furudate

Hinomaru Driving School
Tokyo
1993-1996
Area: 4,965 sq.m.
Owner: Hinomaru Sogyo Co. Ltd.
Photo: Harunori Noda (Gankosha),
Shinkenchiku, Co., Ltd.

Johnson Products Kakegawa New Factory
Shizuoka
1994-1996
Area: 10,906 sq.m.
Owner: Johnson Products Co., Ltd.

Mizushima Salon (co: Niwa Architect &
Associates) - Town Okayama Project
Okayama
1993-1996
Area: 5,230 sq.m.
Owner: Okayama Prefectural Government
Photo: Kouji Horiuchi, Shinkenchiku, Co., Ltd.